W9-ARN-831

The Social Work Practicum

A Guide and Workbook for Students

Fourth Edition

Cynthia L. Garthwait
The University of Montana

PEARSON

Boston • New York • San Francisco
Mexico City • Montreal • Toronto • London • Madrid • Munich • Paris
Hong Kong • Singapore • Tokyo • Cape Town • Sydney

Senior Series Editor: Patricia Quinlin
Editorial Assistant: Nakeesha Warner
Marketing Manager: Laura Lee Manley
Editorial-Production Service: Omegatype Typography, Inc.
Composition Buyer: Linda Cox
Manufacturing Buyer: Debbie Rossi
Electronic Composition: Omegatype Typography, Inc.
Cover Administrator: Elena Sidorova

For related titles and support materials, visit our online catalog at
www.ablongman.com.

Copyright © 2008, 2005, 2002, 1999 Pearson Education, Inc.

All rights reserved. No part of the material protected by this copyright notice
may be reproduced or utilized in any form or by any means, electronic or
mechanical, including photocopying, recording, or by any information storage
and retrieval system, without written permission from the copyright owner.

To obtain permission(s) to use material from this work, please submit a written
request to Allyn and Bacon, Permissions Department, 75 Arlington Street,
Boston, MA 02116 or fax your request to 617-848-7320.

Between the time website information is gathered and then published, it is not
unusual for some sites to have closed. Also, the transcription of URLs can result
in typographical errors. The publisher would appreciate notification where these
errors occur so that they may be corrected in subsequent editions.

ISBN-13: 978-0-205-50179-3   ISBN-10: 0-205-50179-6

Printed in the United States of America

10 9 8 7 6 5 4 3 2 1   10 09 08 07 06

To the social work practicum students who inspire and teach me daily
and to the social work field instructors and faculty supervisors who give
so generously of their time to the education and mentoring of future social workers

To my family,
Gary, Nathan, and Benjamin

Contents

Foreword

Linking academia and practice is a key educational challenge faced by all schools of social work. Focused on professional practice, social work educators find the task of linking the classroom to practice is best faced across the entire curriculum. To help students make the connection, contemporary social work courses have multiple discussions, class exercises, and role play situations accompanying lectures that emphasize application of theory, knowledge, and skills to practice situations. In spite of comprehensive approaches, students often find the linking of classroom learning and practice challenging.

Tools to assist students with this task are in constant demand. Organizing paradigms with which to link classroom instruction and practice learning within a generalist approach are also needed. This text offers such an organizing framework. It helps students make the necessary connections between the classroom and practice through a hands-on format designed to engage, to provoke thought, and to enhance learning by effectively breaking down the practice experience into its respective components of skills and knowledge in a manner that students can grasp.

Social work education is all about application. Within the practicum, students engage in environments where learning takes place by engaging with real clients with real problems within real agency settings. One key feature of the practicum is that students process their experiences with knowledgeable field instructors. Often, students also review these learning experiences with other students receiving group supervision or with university-based faculty either individually or in a seminar. It is in the combination of hands-on practice with quality supervision that learning is most effective. This text provides tools that can be used to optimize this integrative effort.

It is in practice that social work students revel. In acts of helping and in supportive supervisory relationships students find value and meaning. It is well known in social work education that students report practicum experiences and the accompanying positive supervisory relationships to be the most memorable and valued components of their school experience. It is also widely known that successfully helping the student establish links between classroom and field work makes practicum experiences most valuable. Perhaps not as well known is that facilitating this level of integration in student learning can be very challenging for the educator.

To be most successful, practicum students must stretch. In spite of the attraction to practice, integration of theory and practice is difficult for many students. Integration becomes especially challenging when students are faced with requirements to do so across a generalist curriculum within real agency settings. Self awareness, the ability to think in multiple dimensions, to handle stress, to communicate clearly, to collaborate effectively, to plan, to persuade, and to remain ethical in the face of real world problems is required of every student. All of these elements combined simultaneously can make for confused and overwhelmed students. Such integrative capabilities do not happen accidentally or at once, but are achieved through progressive learning, structured to assist the student to see the differing elements that impact each decision and action. Promoting such development is the task of the supervisor and teacher. Needed is an organizing paradigm that promotes classroom and field integration but also allows for the building of a progressive learning model. Faculty and field supervisors who successfully guide students in this process provide a gift to their charges who are thereby able to make full use of the life-long process of understanding how to connect theory and doing. It is in the learning of this process that beginning professionals find an avenue to effective social work practice.

In *The Social Work Practicum: A Guide and Workbook for Students*, Professor Garthwait provides an outstanding tool set to assist educators, supervisors, and students in meeting the challenge of integrating the classroom with practice. This text is abreast of current trends in the field. Important additions have been made in the areas of leadership and social justice, social work as planned change, and diversity. The text also provides an easy to use format that allows for progressive planning of practicum experiences.

Included are multiple hands on exercises that can be utilized by supervisors and faculty to assist students in thinking through practical applications of issues encountered previously only in the classroom or not at all. Dealing with and discussing issues such as ethics, client engagement, safety, communication, and professionalism within the context of specific practicum experiences makes the bridge between classroom and field much more meaningful.

Written by an experienced practitioner and educator and tested with hundreds of students, this text has proven to be a valuable integrative tool that makes clear the application of the classroom to individualized student practice experiences. It is useful as a tool for seminar and supervision. It can serve as a launching point for a comprehensive overview of social work practice and professional behavior. It can be used to augment classroom activities and serve as a foundation for a practicum seminar syllabus. Pages can be readily removed for combination with other materials in notebook format. Finally, this text can assist in preparing for exit exams, professional papers, and portfolios.

I consider it an honor to have been asked to write the foreword for such an important book. As a current social work educator and former practicum director with numerous years of experience engaging in direct practice, program development, administration, consultation, and research, I have always been most appreciative of professionals who can connect theory and practice. These are professionals who are effective across practice environments and who also understand their limitations more clearly than others. The ability to understand the empirical and theoretical roots of one's actions is requisite for effectiveness across a career. In this text I find a valuable tool to help beginning social workers make these connections. In practice I have seen students who use this text become able to clearly describe the connections expected of beginning professionals and who thereby engage in more effective practice and rapid learning.

David Schantz, Ph.D.
Dean, Faculty of Social Work
University of Regina

Preface

My career in social work spans thirty-three years. During those years I have served as an agency-based field instructor, a faculty liaison to practicum agencies, an instructor of practicum seminars, and as the coordinator of a university practicum program. I have directly taught, assisted, and guided hundreds of students during their practicum, both in baccalaureate and graduate social work programs.

Almost universally, the practicum is cited by students as the most useful and challenging learning experience during their social work education. My observations have been confirmed by numerous surveys of student opinion.

I have been privileged to share in the students' excitement as they developed and polished their skills, expanded their knowledge bases, and grew in self-confidence. I have also experienced pain and frustration watching students flounder or become angry or disillusioned either because their practicum setting failed to provide sufficient learning opportunities or because they could not make good use of the opportunities that did exist.

I am aware of the importance of the integrative experience of the practicum that assists students with blending theory and practice. Because some students easily integrate the two while others struggle to do so, this book is meant to serve as a tool to facilitate the process of weaving together academic concepts and real experiences in practicum.

Years of assisting students at this stage of their professional development has taught me the value of strategically designed assignments that encourage students to assess their own experiences in light of theoretical frameworks and to reflect on their learning.

This book grew out of those experiences and the search for a better way. It offers students, field instructors, and the leaders of practicum seminars a structure and a set of learning activities that facilitate learning in the practicum. At the same time, it allows for and encourages creativity and experimentation in learning. The student who makes thoughtful use of the Background and Context, Guidance and Direction, and Workbook Activity sections in this book will make significant progress toward developing the competencies required of beginning social workers.

An Overview of the Chapters

Chapter 1 serves to introduce the book and explain how it is to be used. In addition, it includes two workbook activities that focus on the prerequisites to and the process of learning. Chapters 2, 3, 4, and 5 are designed to assist you in clarifying expectations and formulating a written plan for learning during the practicum. By

reading these chapters and completing the workbook assignments, you will identify many of the desired learning outcomes and activities that can be written into
the school's practicum learning contract or learning agreement. Chapters 4 and 5
will be especially helpful in getting the practicum off to a good start and in clarifying the relationship between you and your field instructor. Chapter 6 focuses on
a topic of growing importance in the practicum—personal safety.

Chapters 7 through 16 focus on broad areas of practice competency. Most
schools ask their practicum students to formulate learning goals and objectives in
relation to these areas. Chapter 17 offers information and a perspective on the evaluation of student performance in the practicum. Chapter 18 addresses the issues
and concerns related to developing self-awareness and the choice of social work
as a career. Finally, Chapter 19 asks you to look beyond graduation and consider
several personal concerns, while also encouraging you to develop your leadership
skills and commit yourself to the pursuit of social justice.

CSWE Accreditation Considerations

The Council on Social Work Education's (CSWE) Commission on Accreditation requires programs of social work education to include certain content in their
curricula. Some of those content areas are listed below in the column on the left.
Chapters in this book that address these areas, at least to some degree, are listed
to the right of each.

Values and Ethics	Chapters 14, 15, 18
Diversity	Chapter 12
Social Welfare Policy and Services	Chapter 11
Social and Economic Justice	Chapters 14, 15, 19
Human Behavior and the Social Environment	Chapters 7, 8, 9, 10
Populations at Risk and Social and Economic Justice	Chapter 12
Social Work Practice	Chapters 13, 16
Research	Chapters 8, 10, 16

Acknowledgments

Many individuals helped shape my ideas and offered encouragement on the evolution of this manuscript. Although they cannot all be acknowledged by name, I
want to recognize and thank the many students who helped me, even though they
were not aware that they were teaching me. Their questions, criticisms, and practical suggestions have helped me to better understand the social work practicum
from the student's point of view.

A special thanks to friends and colleagues who offered encouragement, suggestions, and assistance: Tondy Baumgartner, Tim Conley, Janet Finn, Kerrie Ghe-
nie, Carol Hand, Kristina Gottsch, Charles Horejsi, Maxine Jacobson, Sue Polich,
David Schantz, John Spores, Ryan Tolleson Knee, Monica Trimble, and Charlie
Wellenstein. Acknowledgment also goes to the Allyn and Bacon staff.

I offer my heartfelt thanks to my colleague Charles Horejsi, whose enthusiasm for preparing competent and caring social workers led to our collaboration on
the first two editions of this text.

1

The Purpose of a Practicum

Congratulations to you as you embark on your social work practicum experience. You are to be congratulated for reaching this stage in your professional education and for being selected and approved for a practicum. The practicum offers a unique opportunity to apply what you have learned in the classroom, to expand your knowledge, and to develop your skills. It is time for you to move from the role of a student to the role of a social worker, which is exciting because you will soon be considered a professional.

Welcome to this guide and workbook. It is designed to provide direction and assistance during your exciting practicum journey.

Background and Context

A *practicum* is a mode of study emphasizing the practical application of theory or conceptual knowledge. Most types of professional education—whether in medicine, nursing, law, pharmacy, speech therapy, or social work—wisely employ some form of practicum, internship, or preceptorship to help the student learn how to apply knowledge and general principles to specific and very real situations, problems, and concerns.

Many social workers, agency supervisors, and social work educators use the terms *practicum, field work, field instruction, field education, field practicum,* and *internship* somewhat interchangeably. This book will use the term *practicum.*

The Council on Social Work Education's (CSWE) Handbook of Accreditation Standards and Procedures, Educational Policies, and Academic Standards (2001) states that:

> The field practicum is an integral component of the curriculum in social work education anchored in the mission, goals, and educational level of the program. It occurs in settings that reinforce students' identification with the purpose, values, and ethics of the profession; fosters the integration of empirical and practice-based knowledge; and promotes the development of professional competence. Field education is systematically designed, supervised, coordinated, and evaluated on the basis of criteria by which students demonstrate the achievement of program objectives. (10)

The social work practicum typically occurs within a social agency or a social welfare–related organization in which the student works under the direction and supervision of an experienced professional employed by that agency. That organizational context or setting may be termed a *practicum agency, field agency, practicum setting,* or a *field placement.* This book uses the term *practicum agency.*

Students of social work at both the BSW and MSW levels usually describe their practicum as the single most useful, significant, and powerful learning experience of their formal social work education. It is during their practicum that the concepts, principles, and theories discussed in the classroom come to life. During the practicum students work with real clients and have the opportunity to try out the skills and techniques they previously rehearsed in role plays and simulations. It is also during the practicum that students make considerable progress in developing self-awareness and come to a better understanding of their particular strengths and limitations and the influence of their personal values, attitudes, and prior life experiences on their social work practice. The practicum can and should be a time when classroom theory is integrated with social work practice and a time when students merge with the values and fundamental principles of their chosen profession.

For many students, the practicum is an outstanding experience, but for some, the practicum can fall short of expectations. Based on my experiences in the areas of practicum supervision and practicum coordination, I believe that the quality of every practicum experience can be enhanced if students are provided with guidance in identifying and making use of learning opportunities. Providing a structure that helps students to examine and analyze their settings in ways that build on prior classroom learning is of critical importance. Some of the most meaningful learning occurs as a result of having to deal with frustrations and unexpected events during the practicum.

How to Use This Book

This book is designed to provide you with guidance and structure during the social work practicum. If used in a thoughtful manner throughout the practicum, it will help you make the best of whatever your practicum setting has to offer. Needless to say, this will not happen without effort. It requires a real commitment and a willingness to invest time in the learning process.

The practicum is a unique learning opportunity. As you begin your journey through the practicum experience, always remember that when we are truly ready to learn, all people and all experiences become our teachers.

How the Chapters Are Structured

Although the chapters are numbered in the conventional manner, this is not to suggest that you are to necessarily move through the book sequentially, one chapter after another. Rather, it is expected that you will be gathering information to complete the workbook activities in several of the chapters at the same time. Moreover, it is expected that you will move back and forth between sections and will also revisit the same section several times as you gain experience in the practicum and begin to look at various questions and issues from a new perspective.

Each chapter begins with a section titled Goals for Learning. It lists possible goals or desired outcomes related to the knowledge, values, and skills that you can expect to learn and develop during the practicum.

The next major section, Background and Context, presents selected concepts and principles related to the topic addressed by the chapter. The box titled Food for Thought will contain several relevant quotations. The concepts and definitions presented in these two sections are not a substitute for a textbook or assigned readings, but rather should act as a review of key ideas that set the stage for what follows, stimulate creative thinking, and raise important questions.

In each of the sections labeled Guidance and Direction, you are offered general suggestions, guidance, and advice, and sometimes a few specific dos and don'ts intended to encourage and facilitate learning in relation to the chapter's objectives and its particular focus.

In most of the chapters, several pages have been cast into a workbook format and titled A Workbook Activity. You will be asked to seek answers to each of the questions and record the answers or related comments in the spaces provided. Several of the questions in each chapter are written in ways intended to encourage critical thinking. If you perform these tasks conscientiously, you will establish a detailed record of practicum learning.

A section titled Suggested Learning Activities lists several specific tasks and activities that provide additional opportunities and experiences for learning.

The sections labeled Additional Suggestions and Hints include a few additional ideas, words of encouragement, and specific cautions that may be important to you and the practicum experience.

Each chapter ends with a Selected Bibliography that lists several books or articles related to the topics addressed in the chapter. The sources listed should be fairly easy for you to locate in a college or agency library. Frequent reference will be made to the *Encyclopedia of Social Work* and to commonly used social work textbooks. Because the book *Techniques and Guidelines for Social Work Practice* by Sheafor and Horejsi (2006) is frequently used in social work practicum seminars, the list will usually include a reference to specific sections in that book.

Practicum-Related Strengths: A Workbook Activity

I wish to introduce you to the workbook format used in this book. This first workbook activity focuses your attention on the knowledge, skills, and experiences that you may bring to the practicum.

It is important for you to clearly identify your strengths and build on them. Building your skills and enhancing your strengths in a well-planned manner will gradually give you the confidence and ability to practice competently. Below is a list of strengths that are important to a successful practicum experience. Depending on the nature of the setting, some will be of more importance and relevance than others. This list can also be used to assess the appropriateness of a match between a student and a particular practicum setting.

Place a check mark by all items that apply to you. There are no right or wrong answers. However, there are good answers. A good answer is one that is honest and accurate. Therefore, acknowledge your strengths, because you will enhance them in the practicum. Identify the areas in which you lack experience, and begin to set goals for professional development in those areas. Some of these strengths are specific to the social work profession and others are more general strengths that will contribute to success in any new venture.

Important Strengths for a Successful Practicum

Attitudes and Values

_____ Empathetic, caring, and concerned for clients or consumers served by the practicum agency

_____ Personal values, beliefs, and perspectives are compatible with the agency's mission, goals, and philosophy

_____ Personal values, beliefs, and perspectives are compatible with the National Association of Social Workers (NASW) *Code of Ethics*

_____ Committed to achieving social justice

_____ Respectful of a broad range of diversity among clients and communities

Motivation and Desire to Learn

_____ Eager and open to new learning experiences

_____ Self-discipline and motivation to do what needs to be done, even when you may not feel like doing it

_____ Willingness to take on new responsibilities and perform tasks and activities within your range of abilities

_____ Open to building self-awareness

_____ Adequate time and energy to devote to the practicum

_____ A sense of "calling" to the social work profession

_____ Excitement about helping people improve the quality of their lives

Abilities and Skills

_____ Writing skills (selecting and organizing content, drafting reports, preparing letters, keeping professional records, and utilizing technological communication tools)

_____ Verbal communication skills (explaining, describing, and informing)

_____ Ability to listen (understand what others are saying and respectfully consider their views, perspectives, and opinions)

_____ Ability to quickly process information, understand new concepts, and learn new skills

_____ Ability to read rapidly, grasp ideas quickly, and pull meaning and information from the written word

_____ Ability to organize and plan work to be done and effectively manage and use available time

_____ Ability to meet deadlines and work under pressure

_____ Ability to follow through on planned actions and complete tasks and assignments

_____ Ability to make thoughtful and ethical decisions under stressful conditions

_____ Assertiveness and self-confidence in professional relationships and group discussion

_____ Committed to self-awareness and professional competence, including a desire to evaluate your own effectiveness

_____ Ability to build relationships with the agency's clients

_____ Thoughtful, organized, confident, and comfortable when meeting with a wide variety of people

_____ Thoughtful, organized, confident, and comfortable when working in groups

_____ Ability to identify a need and formulate a course of action to address that need

_____ Ability to solve problems creatively and effectively

Knowledge and Experience

_____ High level of self-awareness (an understanding of how your own values, beliefs, attitudes, family background, lifestyle, appearance, and life experiences might be perceived by others)

_____ Familiarity with communication methods and equipment used in the practicum agency (word processor, e-mail, computer software)

_____ Prior successful experience in adapting to change, new situations, and new work environments

_____ Prior successful employment or volunteer experience with services or programs similar to those provided by the practicum agency

___✓___ Prior successful employment or volunteer experience in working with types of consumers or clients served by the practicum agency

_____ Working knowledge of the state and federal laws, rules, regulations, and policies relevant to the practicum agency

___✓___ Knowledge of the assessment and planning tools, methods, and techniques used by the practicum agency

_____ Knowledge of the intervention methods and techniques used by the practicum agency

___✓___ Knowledge of the research and evaluation tools, methods, and techniques used by the practicum agency

_____ Understanding of the process of planned change

_____ Understanding of the generalist perspective in social work practice and other practice perspectives, theories, and models relevant to the practicum setting

1. What are the most significant strengths that you bring to the practicum experience based on the preceding checklist?

_____

_____

_____

_____

2. What other strengths do you bring to your practicum experience?

_____

_____

_____

_____

3. What can you do to secure learning experiences that will build on your strengths?

_____

_____

_____

_____

_____

4. In what areas do you hope to develop additional competence and skill during the practicum?

_____

_____

_____

_____

_____

_____

5. What are the most significant limitations that you bring to the practicum experience?

_____

_____

_____

6. What practicum-related learning experiences will help you to address or overcome your limitations?

_____

_____

_____

_____

_____

Additional notes and comments:

_____

_____

_____

_____

_____

_____

How Do We Learn? A Workbook Activity

The social work practicum is an opportunity to learn. Your experience will be enhanced if you are aware of how you learn. This workbook activity focuses on the learning process.

Learning is a type of change. Sometimes change can be exciting and exhilarating. Sometimes change is difficult and frustrating. We would like all of our learning experiences to be enjoyable and fun, but real and significant learning can also be scary and painful.

Basically, we learn when we take risks—when we begin to think in a different way, when we view the familiar from a different angle, or when we try out new behavior. Openness to this type of learning can bring unexpected insights and unanticipated growth. When we are willing to place ourselves in situations in which old habits of thought and behavior are stretched and challenged, we begin to learn.

The social work practicum, if it is effective, should push and pull you in new directions. This new learning will excite and inspire you. It will create some discomfort, but that is the price of learning. When the learning is about ourselves— our biases, prejudices, and emotional hang-ups—the experience can be especially challenging. However, this can free us from attitudes and behaviors that limit personal growth and effectiveness. Answer the following questions about your learning style and learning goals, and think ahead about how you can maximize your learning experience.

1. What learning experiences do you expect to be most effective in helping you acquire knowledge and develop social work practice skills?

   _____

   _____

   _____

2. As you begin your social work practicum, what are you most excited and enthusiastic about?

   _____

   _____

   _____

3. As you begin your social work practicum, what are your greatest fears or worries?

   _____

   _____

   _____

4. Given what you know about yourself and how you learn, what types of assistance, guidance, or structure would help you lower your defenses and be more open to learning in the areas that cause you some level of anxiety or worry?

_____

_____

_____

5. If you have a learning disability, what accommodations will you request in your practicum agency?

_____

_____

_____

Additional notes and comments:

_____

_____

_____

_____

Suggested Learning Activities

- Conduct a cursory examination of each chapter in this book. Note the topics addressed and how the content is organized.
- Pay special attention to the various Workbook Activities presented in the book and to the types of questions you will be asked as you work through this book during your practicum experience.

Additional Suggestions and Hints

- Keep this book with you while at your practicum agency and strive to answer all of the workbook questions. We suggest you write in pencil because you may wish to modify answers as you gain experience and new insights.
- Do not record in this workbook any information that might identify an agency client or violate rules of confidentiality.

Selected Bibliography

Alle-Corliss, Lupe, and Randy Alle-Corliss. *Advanced Practice in Human Service Agencies*. Boston: Brooks/Cole, 1999.

Barker, Robert. *The Social Work Dictionary*. 5th ed. Washington, DC: NASW Press, 2003.

Berg-Weger, Marla, and Julie Birkenmaier. *The Practicum Companion for Social Work: Integrating Class and Field Work*. Boston: Allyn and Bacon, 2000.

Chiaferi, Rosemary, and Michael Griffin. *Developing Fieldwork Skills*. Pacific Grove, CA: Brooks/Cole, 1997.

Cochrane, Susan F., and Marla Martin Hanley. *Learning through Field: A Developmental Approach*. Boston: Allyn and Bacon, 1999.

Commission on Accreditation. *Handbook of Accreditation Standards and Procedures, Educational Policies and Accreditation Standards*. 5th ed. Alexandria, VA: Council on Social Work Education, 2001.

Edwards, Richard L., ed. *Encyclopedia of Social Work*. 19th ed. Washington, DC: NASW Press, 1995. (See the article by Frumkin and Lloyd on social work education.)

Grobman, Linda May, ed. *The Field Placement Survival Guide: What You Need to Know to Get the Most from Your Social Work Practicum*. Harrisburg, PA: White Hat Communications, 2002.

Rogers, Gayla, Donald Collins, Constance Barlow, and Richard Grinnell. *Guide to the Social Work Practicum*. Itasca, IL: F. E. Peacock, 2000.

Rothman, Juliet. *The Self-Awareness Workbook for Social Workers*. Boston: Allyn and Bacon, 1999.

Rothman, Juliet. *Stepping Out into the Field: A Field Work Manual for Social Work Students*. Boston: Allyn and Bacon, 2000.

Royse, David, Surjit Singh Dhooper, and Elizabeth Rompf. *Field Instruction*. 2nd ed. White Plains, NY: Longman, 1996.

Schneck, Dean, Bart Grossman, and Urania Glassman. *Field Education in Social Work*. Dubuque, IA: Kendall and Hunt, 1991.

Sheafor, Bradford, and Charles Horejsi. *Techniques and Guidelines for Social Work Practice*. 7th ed. Boston: Allyn and Bacon, 2006.

Sweitzer, H. Frederick, and Mary A. King. *The Successful Internship: Transformation and Empowerment in Experiential Learning*. 2nd ed. Boston: Thomson Learning, 2003.

2 | School, Agency, and Student Expectations

GOALS FOR LEARNING

- To understand what you can and should expect of your school's practicum program and your practicum agency
- To understand what will be expected of you by your school program and your practicum agency

A key to making your social work practicum a quality learning experience is the clarification of expectations. What do you really expect? What does the agency expect of you? What does your college or university expect of you and your practicum agency? Identifying and clarifying expectations will ensure a smooth and positive practicum experience. Not doing so may lead to problems. The purpose of this chapter is to encourage and facilitate a clarification of expectations.

Background and Context

Standards issued by the CSWE's Commission on Accreditation (2003) require a minimum of 400 social work practicum hours at the baccalaureate level (BSW) and a minimum of 900 hours at the master's (MSW) level. Some programs of social work education require additional hours. It is important to note that schools may use slightly different terms to describe the personnel associated with a practicum program. In this book I use the term *field instructor* when referring to the agency-based person who is responsible for the day-to-day supervision of a practicum student. This person is usually an agency employee.

The faculty member who is responsible for organizing and guiding the practicum program is here termed the *practicum coordinator,* although other common terms are *director of field practicum* and *field coordinator.*

Most schools assign a faculty member to function as a liaison to individual practicum agencies and organizations. In this book I refer to this individual as the *faculty supervisor.* Other commonly used terms are *faculty liaison* and *school-based supervisor.* These individuals maintain regular contact with an agency's field instructor and with the student placed in that agency setting. They monitor the practicum and serve as troubleshooters when problems arise. These individuals are usually involved with the field instructor in the evaluation of the student's performance.

Programs of social work education typically use some type of *practicum seminar* to help students connect or integrate what they have learned in the classroom with their real-world experiences in their practicum setting. These seminars are usually under the direction of a faculty member who may or may not also be the student's faculty supervisor.

The specific objectives associated with a practicum can be found in the school's practicum or fieldwork manual, in official descriptions of the social work curriculum, and in other documents issued by the program of social work education. All parties to the practicum are expected to adhere to the National Association of Social Workers (NASW) *Code of Ethics.* Below are listed general expectations of all the parties that will be involved in your practicum. Please note that the expectations described by your school's practicum program may differ somewhat from the general expectations listed here.

The practicum coordinator is expected to:

- Assume responsibility for the overall management and coordination of the school's practicum program.
- Conduct an initial screening of students applying for a practicum and assess their readiness for this experience.
- Assign a faculty supervisor to work jointly with the agency-based field instructor and practicum student.
- Provide suggested learning goals to aid in the design of learning objectives and the selection of learning activities by the student and field instructor.
- Provide guidelines, evaluation tools, and protocols for the evaluation of the student.
- Provide orientation and training on the practicum program and practicum instruction to agency-based field instructors.
- Facilitate a resolution to problems that may arise.
- Monitor and evaluate the quality of practicum experiences provided by the various agencies and organizations used as practicum settings.

The social work student in a practicum setting is expected to:

- Meet with the field instructor on a regular basis (at least weekly).
- Prepare for all meetings with the field instructor and alert the field instructor to topics that need to be discussed during the upcoming meeting.
- Meet with the field instructor and the faculty supervisor jointly several times during each academic term.
- Meet with the faculty supervisor according to a schedule that is consistent with school policy and requirements.
- Be in attendance at the agency on days and at times agreed on by the student and field instructor and, if unable to attend, notify the field instructor prior to or at the start of the work day.
- Behave in a professional manner, including taking responsibility as an adult learner to understand and carry out assigned duties, meet all deadlines, and seek direction when needed.
- Carry out practicum assignments in a manner consistent with agency policy and procedures.
- Prepare records and reports in accord with agency policy, procedures, and format.
- Identify learning needs and prepare a learning agreement with specific learning objectives, learning activities, and evaluation criteria that are acceptable to the field instructor and the faculty supervisor.

- Provide proof of professional malpractice insurance, if required by school or agency.
- Bring to the attention of the faculty supervisor or practicum coordinator any practice or behavior within the agency that is clearly unethical.
- Complete and submit all practicum written documentation and reports required by the agency and school (e.g., time sheets, evaluations of student performance, student's evaluation of practicum experience).
- Discuss with the field instructor, faculty supervisor, or practicum coordinator any areas of significant disagreement, dissatisfaction, or confusion related to the practicum experience.
- Devote the required number of hours to the practicum.

The field instructor and/or practicum agency are expected to:

- Describe and explain what is expected of the student during his or her practicum within the agency.
- Provide the student with a thorough orientation to the agency and its purpose, structure, policies, procedures, and ethical standards.
- Provide regularly scheduled supervision to the practicum student.
- Provide the practicum student with suitable office space, equipment, and support staff.
- Include the student in regular staff meetings and staff training sessions.
- Assign duties and responsibilities that are appropriate to the student's learning needs and that are increasingly challenging.
- Assign duties and responsibilities that help the student develop a broad range of social work knowledge and skills at the micro, mezzo, and macro levels.
- Work in collaboration with the student to expand the student's opportunities to learn.
- Assign duties and responsibilities that help the student fulfill a broad range of social work roles.
- Participate in university-sponsored training for field instructors.
- Monitor the student's work and progress and regularly provide feedback and constructive criticism.
- Evaluate the student's performance in a fair, respectful, rigorous, and thorough manner.
- Meet regularly during each academic term with the student and the faculty supervisor to discuss the practicum and the student's progress.
- Complete all evaluation forms and reports required by the school.
- Model ethical practice and refrain from any inappropriate or unethical behavior toward the student (e.g., verbal abuse, sexual harassment, dual relationships).
- Reimburse the student for any out-of-pocket expenses incurred in agency-related work.

The school's faculty supervisor is expected to:

- Develop a plan in collaboration with the student and field instructor that will provide the student with an array of appropriate and challenging learning opportunities.
- Monitor the student's practicum experience and assist in evaluating the student's performance.
- Help the field instructor and other agency personnel learn about the school's expectations of students, the social work curriculum, and the school's goals for the practicum.

- Assist the student in identifying his or her learning needs, formulating learning objectives, and preparing a written learning agreement.
- Facilitate the student's learning by providing guidance and serving as a source of information.
- Meet regularly during each academic term with the student and the field instructor to discuss the practicum and the student's progress.
- Assist the student in integrating social work theory and the specific experiences of the practicum.

The practicum seminar will:

- Bring together students from various practicum settings to give them an opportunity to learn about different types of agency settings and to learn from each other's experiences.
- Arrange or structure learning activities that will help students integrate social work theory with practice (e.g., discussions, student presentations, outside speakers, summative papers, or professional portfolios).
- Provide a forum for student discussion and problem solving regarding practicum.

Your Responsibilities to Agency Clients

Given the fact that you are in the process of learning to become a social worker and you generally lack experience, you must be especially concerned about how this lack of skill and experience might affect the client and the quality of the services provided to the client. You have a special obligation to provide the field instructor with a complete and accurate description of your work with clients, including what has already happened and what you plan to do. You are expected to consult with your field instructor whenever faced with an unusual or especially complex decision or issue.

The clients served by a student social worker are to be made aware that they are being served or assisted by a student. Section 3.02(c) of the 1999 NASW *Code of Ethics* states that:

> Social workers who function as educators or field instructors for students should take reasonable steps to ensure that clients are routinely informed when services are being provided by students. (19)

Guidance and Direction

The practicum placements that are most beneficial are those in which there is a good match between the student's learning needs and the learning opportunities available within the practicum setting. In contrast, the source of most problems in the practicum is a mismatch between what the student needs to learn and what the setting has to offer. For this reason, the careful assessment of your abilities and needs prior to the selection of a practicum setting is of critical importance. This is not to imply that you need to know everything about your agency or possess the skills that social workers in the agency display. It is only to suggest that your practicum experience will be more satisfying if your learning needs and career goals match the learning experiences your practicum agency can offer.

Food for Thought

Life is a journey that we take only one time. As a social worker makes that one journey through life, it is important that he or she is truly comfortable with social work as a traveling companion. (Sheafor and Horejsi 2006, 18)

• • •

What one hears, one forgets.
What one sees, one remembers.
What one does, one understands.
    —*Chinese Proverb*

• • •

Are you ready to change your mind? If not, you are not ready to learn, for learning is the process of changing your mind. We can learn—change our minds—only when we can admit that we don't yet know it all.

• • •

The only person who is truly educated is one who has learned how to learn and continues to learn throughout his or her life.

Three major factors will determine the overall quality of your social work practicum experience:

1. Your motivation to learn
2. Your capacity to learn
3. Your opportunity to learn

In order for those who will be assisting you during the practicum to be truly helpful, they need information about your motivation. What do you really want and expect from the practicum? What are you willing to do to obtain the learning experiences you seek? What do you already know and what skills do you possess? Be sure to communicate your hopes and expectations to your field instructor, faculty supervisor, and practicum coordinator. Be honest and open in describing your expectations and motivation.

Similarly, in order for others to help you make the practicum a good learning experience, they need to know about your capacity to learn. They need to know both your special strengths and limitations. They need to know about your strengths so they can help you build on them. They need to know your limitations so they can help you find ways to work around them or enhance your knowledge and skills. Do not withhold important information. Do not assume that others already know about your strengths.

When your field instructor accurately understands your expectations, strengths, and limitations, he or she will be in a better position to select and arrange those learning opportunities, activities, and work assignments that will advance your learning. Remember that you will be learning in the context of human relationships with your field instructor and faculty supervisor, who will provide guidance, feedback, and encouragement.

We urge you to acknowledge and confront any special limitations that may affect your practicum learning. You can expect to have significant difficulties and challenges during the practicum if you:

- Have poor writing skills
- Have difficulty managing time, meeting deadlines, organizing work, and staying on task
- Are unusually shy and lack assertiveness
- Are unusually aggressive, dominating, or opinionated
- Are unable or unwilling to conform with agency policy and procedures
- Are unable to maintain an appropriate separation between your personal life and your professional responsibilities
- Disagree with the NASW *Code of Ethics*

In order to learn, you must have high expectations of yourself and place demands on yourself. You will need to set up a plan designed to facilitate learning. Chapter 3 will help you identify learning goals and objectives and formulate such a plan.

Clarifying Expectations: A Workbook Activity

1. You will be spending hundreds of hours in your practicum setting. What do you expect from this investment of your time? What do you expect to gain?

   _____

   _____

   _____

   _____

   _____

   _____

2. List the key things you are expecting of your field instructor.

   _____

   _____

   _____

   _____

3. List the key things you are expecting of your faculty supervisor.

   _____

   _____

   _____

   _____

4. List the key things you are expecting of the practicum coordinator.

   _____

   _____

   _____

   _____

5. List the key things you are expecting of the practicum seminar.

   _____

   _____

   _____

   _____

6. Knowing that what you are willing to invest in the practicum determines what you will get out of it, list the key things you expect of yourself during the practicum.

_____

_____

_____

_____

_____

7. In what specific areas, if any, are your expectations of the practicum at variance with what will be expected of you?

_____

_____

_____

_____

_____

_____

Additional notes and comments:

_____

_____

_____

_____

_____

Suggested Learning Activities

- Most schools make use of a signed contract or written agreement to clarify what the school expects of the agency and what the agency expects of the school. Read this document. (A sample school–agency agreement can be found in the Appendix.)
- Read your school's practicum manual. Pay special attention to descriptions of what is expected of the practicum student.
- Ask your field instructor if there is a job description for social work practicum students. If there is, read it carefully to determine what your agency expects of its students.
- Carefully examine the student evaluation form and specific criteria that will be used to evaluate your performance in the practicum. What do these documents tell you about what is expected of you? (See Chapter 17 for additional information on evaluation.)

Additional Suggestions and Hints

- Talk to former students who have completed a practicum in your agency. Ask them for advice and guidance on what to expect. Ask about any special problems they experienced. Ask them to identify any special learning opportunities and experiences available in your practicum setting.
- Listen carefully to other students in your practicum seminar. Are their concerns similar to or different from yours? Do various agencies have similar expectations of practicum students? What are they doing in their practicum settings that might work for you?

Selected Bibliography

Baird, Brian. *The Internship, Practicum, and Field Placement Handbook: A Guide for the Helping Professions.* 4th ed. Upper Saddle River, NJ: Prentice Hall, 2005.

Bogo, Marion, and Elaine Vayda. *The Practice of Field Instruction in Social Work.* 2nd ed. New York: Columbia University Press, 1998.

Council on Social Work Education. *Handbook of Accreditation Standards and Procedures, Educational Policies and Accreditation Standards.* 5th ed. Alexandria, VA: Council on Social Work Education, 2001.

National Association of Social Workers. *Code of Ethics.* Washington, DC: NASW Press, 1999.

Sheafor, Bradford, and Charles Horejsi. *Techniques and Guidelines for Social Work Practice.* 7th ed. Boston: Allyn and Bacon, 2006.

3

Planning to Learn

GOALS FOR LEARNING

- To become familiar with terms such as *learning goal, learning objective,* and *learning activity*
- To identify learning goals, objectives, and activities relevant to your social work practicum setting
- To write a learning contract outlining your proposed practicum experience in collaboration with your field instructor and faculty supervisor

Good learning experiences in practicum are usually the result of a well-planned learning agreement. You may also have some very good learning experiences that were unplanned, but, for the most part, a good practicum experience is usually one that has been well conceived and outlined.

As you begin your practicum, it is important to list your desired outcomes for learning and then identify and arrange activities and experiences that will help you reach those goals. A well-conceived learning plan will result in a challenging, exciting, and worthwhile learning experience. If you do not develop a plan based on your interests and needs, you may waste an invaluable learning opportunity and fail to maximize your practicum experience.

This chapter provides basic information, guidance, and a workbook activity that can assist you in developing a plan for learning. This plan will be extremely useful, but it is also important to recognize that not everything will go as planned. Unexpected experiences may also provide you with insightful and valuable learning.

Background and Context

A plan for learning during the practicum is like a road map, identifying destinations and possible routes for getting where you want to go. The development of this plan is important, but it is not a simple or easy task. However, it is always better to have a plan—even if it is a rather general one—than to have no plan at all.

A plan for learning will incorporate educational goals and anticipated outcomes from three sources: the school's curriculum, the field instructor, and the student. These goals will usually fall into three categories: knowledge, skills, and values.

Social work *knowledge* consists of terminology, facts, principles, concepts, and theories and perspectives. No doubt you have spent many hours learning about individuals and families, communities, and social policy. This knowledge will be used in the practicum as you apply it in real-life situations.

Social work *skills* are the behaviors of practice. They are the techniques and procedures used by social workers to bring about desired change in the social functioning of clients or in social systems within which clients interact. For the most part, skills are learned by watching and following the lead of skilled practitioners. You can learn about skills from a textbook, but you cannot acquire skills simply by reading about them. Your practicum experience will afford you the opportunity to learn and enhance your social work skills.

A *value* is a strong preference that affects one's choices, decisions, and actions and that is rooted in one's deepest beliefs and commitments. Values determine what a person considers important, worthwhile, right, or wrong. Social work values (e.g., service, social justice, integrity) can be learned or "caught" from others, but it is doubtful that they can be taught by others in a systematic and deliberate way. Typically, our values are picked up from observing someone who is respected and admired. (See Chapter 13 for a listing of core social work values.) Your practicum will undoubtedly be a time for you to more clearly understand what your values are, and you will also begin to see how your values may at times be in conflict with the values of others, including your clients.

It is possible to separate social work knowledge, skills, and values for purposes of discussion and analysis, but in the actual practice of social work, they are interwoven. For example, one's skill is a reflection of one's knowledge and values. Likewise, the possession of social work knowledge and values is of little use unless they are expressed in action.

Preparing a Plan for Learning

The most common approach to the formulation and writing of a plan for practicum learning is described next. It is called the *Goals, Objectives/Activities, and Monitoring/ Evaluation Criteria Approach.* I prefer this approach because it is the easiest for students and agency personnel to implement and it provides sufficient direction in most practicum settings.

The Goals, Objectives/Activities, and Monitoring/Evaluation Criteria Approach

In this approach, the written plan lists separately:

1. Learning goals that will provide an overall structure to your practicum
2. The specific objectives and activities that will help you progress toward each of those learning goals
3. Monitoring and evaluation criteria for determining whether the specified goals have been reached

A form for preparing a written learning plan using this approach can be found in the Appendix. This sample form, and the ideas behind it, can be modified to fit the requirements of a particular program of social work education. This form lists the school's general goals for the practicum in the left-hand column. The field instructor or student selects additional goals specific to the practicum setting and adds them to the form.

A *goal* is a rather broad and general statement of intended outcome. For example, a learning goal might be "to become familiar with the history of a social agency." Another would be "to develop the skills of interviewing." The following verbs often appear in goal statements:

to acquire	to comprehend	to learn
to analyze	to develop	to perceive
to appreciate	to discover	to synthesize
to become	to explore	to understand
to become familiar with	to know	to value

Once the goals have been specified, various learning activities are listed in the second column. A *learning objective* or *activity* is some specific task, activity, or assignment that will help you advance toward a learning goal.

A *learning objective* is a statement of desired outcome that is written in a way that allows measurement. An objective is a precisely worded, specific, and concrete statement of activities to be undertaken to reach a goal. It stipulates what the learner will do, and how and when he or she will do it.

Writing an objective can be a challenging task. Such writing requires the use of behavioral language. A behavior is an activity that can be observed. The use of completion dates and counting completed tasks and activities can often transform an unmeasurable goal into a measurable objective.

The words and phrases used in writing objectives are ones that describe specific actions and activities. For example:

to answer	to decide	to obtain
to arrange	to define	to participate in
to circulate	to demonstrate	to revise
to classify	to direct	to schedule
to collect	to discuss	to select
to compare	to explain	to summarize
to compile	to give examples	to supervise
to conduct	to list	to verify
to count	to locate	to write

When selecting and writing learning objectives, it is important to remain focused on outcomes that are truly important and relevant to the learning of social work practice. Although being able to measure progress is desirable, one must avoid becoming so preoccupied with trying to achieve measurability that the focus shifts to outcomes that are most easily measured rather than most important.

Finally, this sample form has a third column for statements that describe the *method and criteria for evaluating progress* toward the goal. Two common methods of documenting and evaluating progress are listing proposed dates for completing the task or assignment and stating that the work is to be reviewed and critiqued by the field instructor. Other forms of measurement could include direct observation of your work by your supervisor, review of your written documentation, or the use of video or audio taping. Whatever method of evaluation you use to measure your learning, remember that there may be facets of your learning that are hard to measure in behavioral terms, but that can be areas of significant professional growth for you.

The Generalist Perspective and the Plan for Learning

The curricula for BSW programs and the first year of MSW programs are built around the concept of generalist social work practice. Thus, the practicum experiences of many students are expected to reflect a generalist perspective.

The *generalist perspective* is a way of looking at and thinking about the process and activities of social work practice. It is a set of ideas and principles that guide the process of planned change at all levels of practice, in a wide variety of settings, and as you practice a number of social work roles. Keeping that definition in mind, we can better understand that the terms *generalist social work practice* and *generalist social worker* refer to a social work practitioner who:

- Has a broad range of knowledge and skills
- Draws on a variety of theories and models of practice
- Is able to conduct beginning level practice at the micro, mezzo, and macro levels
- Is capable of performing numerous social work roles
- Can move readily from one field of practice to another
- Can move readily from one level of practice to another and recognize how these levels are interrelated
- Can determine the most appropriate course of action based on client needs and resources

The alternative to generalist practice is social work that is characterized by specialization, either by type of client served, by method used, by level of intervention, or by the role assumed by the social worker. Some MSW programs prepare students for specializations for advanced practice, while other MSW programs prepare students for advanced generalist or integrated practice.

The client of a generalist social worker may be an individual, a couple, a family, a group, an organization, or a community. Thus, the generalist is prepared to work with various client systems. He or she may, for example:

- Work at the face-to-face, one-on-one level with a single person.
- Work with a whole family or household.
- Work with groups such as treatment or support groups.
- Work with committees or task groups.
- Work with an agency or a network of agencies.
- Work with legislators and policy makers.

The generalist is prepared to assume a variety of social work roles. These include, for example, the roles of advocate, case manager, counselor or therapist, group facilitator, broker of service, community organizer, program planner, policy analyst, and researcher.

A generalist social worker will examine and consider a wide range of factors that may contribute to a client's problems in social functioning. These may include conflicts among values and beliefs, broken relationships, distortions of thinking, lack of knowledge and information, destructive individual and family behavior, alienation and loneliness, oppression, injustice and racism, poverty and the lack of basic resources, misuse of power by those in authority, and misguided or unworkable social programs and policies. A generalist social worker also recognizes that a broad range of factors impacts groups and communities and leads to social problems such as poverty, violence, and addiction.

Food for Thought

If acknowledging what you do not know is a first step toward learning, being willing to take some risks and extend yourself is a key second step. Internships allow you to try new skills that you may have only read about before. To develop these skills, you have to test them and learn from both your successes and your mistakes. A concept that is useful to interns, and that will later be useful in treatment, is the idea of a "learning edge." This term refers to the point just beyond one's present level of knowledge or skill. It is not so far ahead that we are in danger of making mistakes that could be calamitous for ourselves or others, but it is beyond our habitual level of functioning and comfort. (Baird 2005, 12)

• • •

Teachers open the doors.
Students must enter by themselves.
—*Chinese Proverb*

• • •

The classroom remains the most radical space of possibility in the academy. (hooks 1994, 12)

• • •

Social workers need to be intermediaries, to open up the world to another, even as they gain a new or altered perspective from the same source. The energy of mutual discovery feeds on itself, recharges itself. Social work imagination makes it possible to perceive the incongruities, to discern the false dualism between the private and the public, to experience the beauty of social work against the bureaucratic assaults, and to see the past in the present and in the present, vestiges of what has gone before. (van Wormer 2006, 32)

The generalist fits or adapts his or her approach to the needs and circumstances of the client and the local community, rather than expecting the client or others to conform to the preferred methods of the professional or the agency. The generalist avoids selecting an intervention method or approach until after he or she and the client or client system have worked together to complete a careful assessment of the client's concern or problem and have considered various ways in which the client's problem or concern can be defined, conceptualized, and approached. Finally, the generalist is prepared to draw on and use a wide range of intervention techniques and procedures, and is not bound to a single theory or model.

Guidance and Direction

Develop a written plan that will guide your practicum experience. A plan that will truly enhance your learning experience will take time to prepare. As a first step in this planning process, find out what your school expects. Your school may call this plan a *learning contract* or a *learning agreement*. Most likely, your school has a preferred format for organizing the content of your plan.

A learning contract or agreement is negotiated between you, your field instructor, and your faculty supervisor. It outlines what you want and need to learn, and identifies the activities you will undertake in order to learn. Most learning agreements are working documents that are modified throughout the practicum as additional learning needs are identified and new learning opportunities arise.

Your plan should be exciting and ambitious. It should stretch and expand your knowledge and skills. It must also be realistic given your practicum setting, your abilities, your prior experience, and the time available to you.

Think of the learning contract as an opportunity for you to negotiate for and obtain the learning experience you want, as well as to develop specific skills. If you are proactive about your own learning, your practicum is much more likely to help you reach your learning goals.

Each of us has a unique approach to learning or a particular learning style. As you develop your plan, consider your preferred method of learning. For example, you may be inclined to jump into the middle of an activity or opportunity because you learn best by doing. Perhaps you learn best by first observing others and then later trying your hand at the activity. Maybe you need to first understand the theory or rationale behind an activity before you feel ready to take action. No one learning style is best or most effective in all situations. Examine your prior learning experiences and identify the methods and approaches that work best for you. You may want to use a learning styles inventory or assessment instrument to better understand your preferred method of learning. (See, for example, Kolb 1981.)

Give your field instructor as much information as possible about how you learn. That information may help him or her select assignments and responsibilities as well as determine your readiness for certain experiences. However, even if you and your field instructor could fully understand your learning style, that does not mean you should wait around for just the right opportunity to come along. Rather, I urge you to follow the ancient principle of *carpe diem,* which means "seize the day" or "seize the opportunity." Take full advantage of whatever opportunities exist, whenever they appear.

If you have a learning disability or a condition that, without accommodation, may in some way limit your learning or performance, be sure to share this information with your field instructor and faculty supervisor. Such conditions need to be considered in developing a plan for practicum learning. If you suspect you may have a learning disability, consult with a learning specialist who can assess the nature of the disability, recommend ways of compensating for the limitation, and guide you toward a program of remediation and accommodation. Your university may also have services available to students with disabilities, and may have professionals skilled in adapting practicum experiences to meet individual needs as well as advocating for reasonable accommodations in practicum settings.

Include in your plan experiences and activities that will help you to integrate theory and practice. Classroom learning should come alive during the practicum. Strive to identify the beliefs, values, and theories behind your decisions and your selection of an intervention. Seek exposure to practice and programs based on various beliefs about how, when, and why people and social systems are able to change.

If your practicum is to reflect generalist social work practice, construct your plan so it will allow you to:

- Learn a variety of skills, techniques, and approaches to intervention.
- Assume several different social work roles (case manager, counselor, broker, educator, advocate, community organizer).
- Learn the basics of practice at various levels of intervention (micro, mezzo, macro) and how the levels of intervention are interrelated.
- Learn skills that can be generalized to another agency setting.
- Observe and identify the knowledge base and practice theories used by social workers in your setting.
- Draw on a variety of theories and approaches tailored to meet individual client needs.

Even though your practicum learning experience will be specific to your practicum agency, remember that you are developing knowledge and skills that can be generalized to other social work settings. Secure a breadth of experience while also finding ways to go into depth in your particular area of interest. By doing so, you will prepare yourself for work in another setting while immersing yourself in practice issues about which you care deeply.

Describe your desired outcomes for learning in ways that permit the monitoring and the measurement of progress (see the Background and Context Section of this chapter). However, also recognize that many important outcomes such as developing a commitment to social work values, growing in self-awareness and self-confidence, and perfecting interviewing skills are inherently difficult to quantify and measure. Describe your desired outcomes as precisely as possible, but do not get hung up on measurability. It is better to describe outcomes in only general and imperfect ways than to not mention them at all. Consider how your attempts to measure your learning parallel your clients' attempts to demonstrate their growth. Your struggle to grow and to measure that growth will hopefully increase your sensitivity to your clients' hard work.

If your school requires you to complete a professional portfolio or paper as part of the practicum experience, build into your learning plan as many of the elements of the portfolio or paper as are possible and appropriate. Because a portfolio is usually focused on the demonstration of your knowledge and skills in a variety of areas, the practicum is an ideal opportunity to structure your learning and then to showcase the ways in which you integrated academic classroom learning with practicum activities.

Once you have completed your plan and it has been approved by your field instructor and faculty supervisor, follow it. Review it often. Modify it as needed, but resist the temptation to abandon a part of the plan simply because it calls for a learning opportunity that is difficult to arrange. Do everything possible to obtain the experiences you need to advance your learning. Become assertive in asking for meaningful learning experiences. If you need help to arrange these because of agency reluctance, ask your faculty supervisor to advocate on your behalf. In addition, be alert to learning experiences that become available to you unexpectedly during your practicum, and find ways to integrate these experiences into your learning plan.

As you formulate your learning plan, give careful thought to your personal plans for the next five years. For example, if you are a BSW student hoping to go on to graduate school, what can you do during the practicum to prepare yourself for graduate study or to increase your chances of being accepted into graduate school? If you expect to enter the job market immediately after graduation, what can you build into your plan that will prepare you for the job you seek? What specific licensing or certification may be required for you to practice social work in your state or to become certified in a specialty area? If you are an MSW student, what learning goals can you set for yourself that will adequately prepare you for advanced practice?

During your practicum you may learn some things that are surprising or even discouraging. For example, you will probably discover that not all clients are motivated, that some are difficult to like and respect, and that some will not make use of needed and available services. You will probably learn that client, agency, or social changes can be slow, that social problems are more complex than you realized, that you must be skillful in the art of politics, and that not all professionals are competent and ethical. Your faculty supervisor can help you gain perspective on such matters, so be sure to share these experiences and observations with him or her.

In addition to the formal learning plans you develop, consider using a personal journal. This exercise can help you in many ways. A journal can document your progress in learning, show your professional growth over time, allow you to express your doubts and questions, and offer you the chance to reflect on the very personal nature of your work. Many students report that journal keeping is very useful because it serves as a written record of growth that is encouraging and reinforcing.

Do not be surprised if much of what you actually learn during your practicum was not anticipated and could not have been written into your plan. Expect some surprises. Perhaps your agency's funding will be drastically cut, and you may end up working in a different unit or service area. Maybe your field instructor will take another job and you will have to adjust to a successor with a different supervisory style. Although such experiences can be stressful, they may prove to be valuable learning opportunities. They will certainly teach you to be flexible and open to new experiences. You can also gain invaluable perspective on how agencies and the social workers in them cope with change and stress, capitalize on funding or policy shifts, and turn problems into opportunities.

Planning to Learn: A Workbook Activity

Your responses below will help you identify desired outcomes and prepare a plan that can guide and enhance your practicum. Respond honestly and with as much precision as possible. List potential learning goals, objectives, or activities that will deepen your understanding of the following key components of social work practice.

1. The core values and mission of the social work profession

   _____

   _____

2. The major social work roles (e.g., broker, case manager, organizer, educator, facilitator, counselor, advocate)

   _____

   _____

3. The organizational context of your practicum (e.g., agency purpose, structure, history, function, funding, goals, staffing)

   _____

   _____

4. The social problems addressed by your agency

   _____

   _____

5. The skills needed for practice with individuals (assessment, planning, intervention, evaluation)

   _____

   _____

6. The skills needed for practice with families (assessment, planning, intervention, evaluation)

   _____

   _____

7. The skills needed for practice with groups and organizations (assessment, planning, intervention, evaluation)

   _____

   _____

8. The skills needed for practice with communities (assessment, planning, intervention, evaluation)

_____

_____

9. The skills needed for practice at the social policy level (analysis, advocacy, planning, organizing)

_____

_____

10. The legal and ethical dimensions of practice

_____

_____

11. The impact of human diversity on the clients served by your agency

_____

_____

12. What type of orientation or initial training do social workers in your agency receive soon after they are hired? Can you take advantage of this training?

_____

_____

13. How do you plan to learn about yourself (e.g., your strengths and gifts, your core values, your biases)?

_____

_____

14. How do you plan to remain open to constructive criticism?

_____

_____

Additional notes and comments:

_____

_____

_____

_____

_____

_____

Suggested Learning Activities

- Consult your school's practicum manual and various descriptions of the curriculum in search of specific learning goals and objectives for the practicum.
- Work with a group of other students to brainstorm a list of possible tasks, activities, and special projects that might be pursued within your practicum agency as a way of expanding learning opportunities and enhancing the practicum experience.
- If your practicum agency cannot provide the learning experience that you need, ask your field instructor to help you gain that experience by working a few hours each week in another agency.
- Read your school's practicum evaluation form or rating instrument to better understand what you are expected to learn during the practicum and how you are expected to demonstrate that you have acquired specific knowledge and skills and that you possess certain values and attitudes.
- If you have a specific career goal such as chemical dependency certification, school social work certification, social work licensing, or graduate school, identify the requirements for this goal and seek practicum experiences related to that goal.

Additional Suggestions and Hints

- You will be asked to perform tasks and take on responsibilities for which you feel unprepared. That may give rise to anxiety, fear, and embarrassment, which are understandable and normal reactions. You must be willing to take on tasks and responsibilities even when you do not feel ready. If you were to wait until you feel confident and certain that you would not make mistakes, you might not afford yourself opportunities to learn something new.
- If at any time you feel disappointed with your field experience, discuss this concern with your field instructor. Do not delay or avoid this discussion. Do not let your negative feelings build up inside. Be very specific in describing what you had expected from the practicum. If your discussions with your field instructor do not result in an improved practicum experience, consult with your faculty liaison or the school's coordinator of the practicum.

Selected Bibliography

Austin, Michael, Diane Brannon, and Peter Pecora. *Managing Staff Development Programs in Human Service Agencies.* Chicago: Nelson-Hall, 1984.

Baird, Brian. *The Internship, Practicum, and Field Placement Handbook: A Guide for the Helping Professions.* 4th ed. Upper Saddle River, NJ: Prentice Hall, 2005.

Bertcher, Harvey. *Staff Development in Human Service Organizations.* Englewood Cliffs, NJ: Prentice Hall, 1988.

hooks, bell. *Teaching to Transgress: Education as the Practice of Freedom.* New York: Routledge, 1994.

Kolb, David. *Learning-Style Inventory.* Boston: McBer and Company Training Resources Group, 1981.

Kolb, David. *Experiential Learning: Experience as the Source of Learning and Development.* Upper Saddle River, NJ: Prentice Hall, 1984.

Sheafor, Bradford, and Charles Horejsi. *Techniques and Guidelines for Social Work Practice.* 6th ed. Boston: Allyn and Bacon, 2003.

van Wormer, Katherine. *Introduction to Social Welfare and Social Work: The U.S. in Global Perspective.* Belmont, CA: Thomson Brooks/Cole, 2006.

4 | Getting Started

GOALS FOR LEARNING

- To become familiar with the professional staff and other personnel within your agency
- To become familiar with the various units, departments, and divisions within your agency
- To become familiar with the basic routines and procedures of your agency
- To prepare yourself for a positive entry into your agency

Previous chapters have asked you to learn about what will be expected of you in the practicum and what you can expect of the practicum. They have underscored the importance of formulating learning goals and identifying activities that can facilitate your learning and help you reach those desired outcomes. This chapter focuses on questions and concerns that are common during the first days and weeks of the practicum.

Beginning a practicum is similar to starting a new job. It is a time of excitement and confusion. Because there are so many new people to meet and so much to learn, the first few weeks can feel overwhelming. Entering an unfamiliar organization is something like entering an unfamiliar culture. You will be aware that you are encountering a new set of norms, rules, and customs, but you will be unsure what they are until you have been oriented or have become familiar with what is expected of you. You will probably feel some anxiety about your knowledge and skills, and you will wonder if you will be able to perform competently. However, within a matter of weeks you will be familiar with the setting and much more comfortable.

Background and Context

The success of the practicum experience is based on a number of factors, most of which are under the control of you and your field instructor. These factors include clear learning objectives, a thorough orientation to your agency, and mutual agreement on the variety of cases, activities, and projects that will be assigned to you. It is at this entry point in your practicum that plans will be made to provide you with a broad range of learning opportunities, and you will be intimately involved in selecting learning activities.

First experiences are pattern setting. If the first days and weeks of contact with a new student are positive for the field instructor and other agency staff, the field instructor will likely conclude that the student can be trusted and given responsibilities. If, on the other hand, these first contacts give the field instructor cause to doubt whether the student is capable and responsible, he or she may hesitate to assign meaningful work to the student.

In order to get the practicum off to a good start, you must anticipate how you might be perceived by the field instructor and what he or she might be thinking and feeling about your presence in the agency. Among the field instructor's thoughts might be the following:

- I'm glad that we have a practicum student because we're understaffed and have too much work to do. The student can do some of my work.
- I look forward to having a student. Practicum students usually have a lot of enthusiasm, and they tend to look at the work of this agency from a fresh perspective.
- I hope this student works out. I remember one student who did not do well in this agency because she was too insecure and immature.
- I wonder if I can find the time necessary to properly supervise this student. I hope the student catches on quickly, because I am too busy to baby-sit.
- I worry about students overstepping the bounds of their assignments and responsibilities. I dislike having to clean up messes made by others.
- I don't think this student has much experience in the real world. I hope he is ready for a taste of harsh reality.
- I like having students here because their questions encourage me to think critically about what I do and why.

Some of the challenges encountered in a practicum are related to the need for a social work student to shift from the university's focus on education to the agency's focus on training. The faculty within a social work education program emphasize the learning of general knowledge, theory, and broad principles that can be applied in many practice settings. By contrast, agency administrators and supervisors are concerned mostly with training that emphasizes the learning of policies, procedures, and skills specific to their agency. Education encourages discussion, debate, and the consideration of alternative ways of assessing and responding to a problem or situation. By contrast, training is designed to teach what the agency has established as the standard or correct responses to given situations. Because these responses reflect the agency's purpose, policy, and procedures, they are to be followed by the student rather then challenged and debated. Hopefully the student will integrate the broad knowledge obtained from the academic world with the specific training provided within the agency.

All social agencies have what is often called an *office culture*. This term refers to the general ways of operating that are based in history, agency values, theoretical underpinnings of services provided, morale, policies and procedures, and staff interaction. Hopefully the office culture is positive and optimistic, as this will allow you to see an organization at its best and learn how a healthy and functional agency operates.

All organizations, including human services agencies, have a political dimension. For example, an agency's managers must make difficult and unpopular decisions, and thus must use their power and authority to accomplish the agency's goals. Some conflict and power struggles are inevitable in organizational life, and these will soon become apparent to you. You need to be aware that aligning yourself with one side or another in these conflicts can undermine the success of your practicum.

The term *office politics* refers to the undercurrent of power struggles created by factors such as conflict between various factions within an organization, personal ambition, jockeying for greater power, and efforts to lobby on behalf of a certain opinion. The larger the organization, the more complex its internal politics. Even though office politics are normal and difficult to avoid, if you become caught up in these power struggles and conflicts, learning opportunities may be closed and some agency staff may withdraw their support.

As a general rule, the larger and more political an organization, the more active the office grapevine. Rumors, gossip, and speculations are common within organizations having many bureaucratic layers, and are especially frequent during times of uncertainty, conflict, and rapid change. Participating in agency gossip can be another major pitfall for you.

Guidance and Direction

First impressions have a powerful impact on personal and professional relationships. It is vital that you make a favorable first impression on your field instructor and the other staff members in your practicum agency. Make a deliberate effort to get the practicum off to a good start.

As suggested previously, there are a number of reasons why a field instructor will feel confident about assigning challenging responsibilities to a student. To give these assignments, the field instructor must trust the student and believe that

Food for Thought

All social workers, by virtue of their professional education and status, and regardless of their personal histories, occupy a privileged social position. Social workers are members of the elite, managerial class, with professional credentials that grant them authority to make important decisions about others. As advocates of people who often lack such membership and its concomitant authority and privileges, social workers have a responsibility to critically examine the impact of this difference upon their ability to build effective relationships with their clients, the basis of all good practice. (Lieberman 2004, 1)

• • •

Among possible teaching tools are: process records; use of critical incidents; case notes; psychosocial summaries; case conferences; role playing; simulations; direct observation of supervisor by supervisee or supervisee by supervisor followed by feedback, discussion, and exchange of views; sitting in on interviews or observation through one-way mirrors; co-leadership; construction of alternative scenarios; observations of other staff members; written and/or verbal self-reports, logs, journals; skill practice with helper, person being helped, and observer; brainstorming; transferring a case or project; modeling through live experiences, videotapes or audiotapes; paper and pencil tasks such as checklists, profiles, and personal insight tests; drawing, moving, pantomime, and other nonverbal actions; role reversal and letting the supervisee teach the supervisor or other unit members. (Dolgoff 2005, 112–113)

• • •

[O]ngoing learning within organizations is inevitable. Workers *will* learn every day. They learn from co-workers, supervisors, subordinates, clients, clerical staff, and any one else with whom they have contact. The issue . . . is *What* do they learn, and is what they learn desirable for promoting effective and efficient client services? Sometimes it is, and sometimes it most definitely is not. . . . If [an agency] manager fails to provide for formal learning, other learning will take place to fill the void. But it could just be learning that should never be allowed to occur. (Weinbach 2003, 127–128)

he or she is capable of doing the work and is not likely to make significant mistakes. Very often, the field instructor makes this decision on the basis of patterns he or she sees in the student's ordinary behavior (i.e., on the basis of the little things he or she notices about the student). Thus, you should strive to display behaviors that can assure your field instructor that you can and will perform in a responsible manner. For example:

- Demonstrate your enthusiasm for learning and applying your knowledge in the agency.
- Inform your field instructor of your prior work and volunteer experiences to help him or her better understand your abilities.
- Demonstrate initiative and a willingness to take on responsibilities and assignments.
- Take all assignments seriously, no matter how trivial and unimportant they may seem.
- Keep your field instructor informed about what you are doing, why you are doing it, and what you plan to do next.
- Consult with your field instructor immediately if you encounter an unusual or unanticipated problem or difficulty, especially one that has legal ramifications or one that might create a public relations problem for the agency.
- Be a good listener and be attentive to your field instructor and to other staff members during supervisory conferences and staff meetings.
- Demonstrate the ability to accept and use constructive criticism of your work, skills, and attitudes.
- Prepare all letters, reports, and client records with great care, according to the agency's prescribed format, and in a timely manner.
- Meet all deadlines. Be on time for all scheduled appointments and meetings. Remain on the job for all the hours you are expected to be in the practicum agency.
- If you must make a change in your work schedule, or if you discover that you will not be able to keep an appointment, contact your field instructor immediately and work out an alternative plan.
- Be well prepared for all meetings with your field instructor and for agency staff meetings.
- Demonstrate that you have read agency manuals and other materials and are therefore familiar with your agency's mission, programs, policies, and procedures.
- Ask questions that reveal a desire to learn and to understand the work of the agency and its policies and procedures, but avoid asking in a manner that appears to challenge or criticize the agency.
- Do your best to understand a new assignment or responsibility the first time it is explained to you. If you are unclear on something, ask for clarification rather than pretending you understand.
- Keep your desk and work space neat and organized.
- Pay attention to your personal grooming, and dress appropriately for the practicum.
- Do not engage in gossip, spread rumors concerning other agencies or professionals, or criticize other students, agency staff, clients, or other agencies in the community.
- Be extremely careful to protect your clients' rights to privacy and the confidentiality of agency records.
- Volunteer to take on tasks that are not attractive to regular agency staff.
- Make friendly overtures to others in the agency. Demonstrate a capacity to build relationships and get along with a variety of different people.

As you enter your agency, recognize that there are both formal and informal aspects to the structure and function of your setting. There are the official policies and procedures, the formal organizational chart, and the chain of command, all of which serve to describe the work of your agency, show who is responsible for what, and provide written guidelines for employees. There are also the informal workings of the agency, and they may differ greatly from what is documented in organizational charts or policy manuals. You may discover that official titles and actual job descriptions do not match, that those with official power may not be the ones to whom others look for guidance, and that exceptions may be made to official policies under certain circumstances.

As you encounter office politics, make very thoughtful decisions concerning how you can respond in ways that will protect your practicum experience and avoid offending others. Although it is difficult to offer guidance on how to handle office politics because every situation is different, here are some general guidelines for you to consider:

- Use the first several weeks and months in the practicum to carefully observe how staff members maneuver and use their power and influence.
- Be cognizant of and sensitive to the official lines of authority and to the power relationships inherent in the chain of command as described by the agency's organizational chart. Follow the chain of command. To disregard those established power relationships will cause confusion and may put your practicum in jeopardy.
- Do not jump to conclusions concerning who is most valued and respected within the agency and who has the most power and influence. Power relationships are often more subtle and complex than they appear at first. Consequently, your first impressions may be erroneous.
- Cultivate relationships with those in the agency who command the respect of most fellow professionals and the support staff and who are respected and valued by their administrative superiors. Longtime office staff are often very powerful in an organization.
- Do not align yourself with someone in the agency who has a reputation for being a complainer, a loose cannon, a troublemaker, a back stabber, or who has little loyalty to the agency.

Deciding how to respond to office gossip and rumors is also difficult for a practicum student. In general, there are two types of office gossip and rumors: people gossip and professional banter. *People gossip* has to do with purely personal matters about other staff members (e.g., who is dating whom, who is getting a divorce, who is deeply in debt). *Professional banter* focuses on matters related to the work of the agency (e.g., who is getting promoted, who is getting hired, what is being said by top administrators, what new policies are being discussed).

Here is some general guidance on dealing with the gossip and rumors you may hear in your practicum agency:

- Avoid becoming a party to people gossip. It is not relevant to your work as a practicum student. Engaging in gossip may cause others to view you as unprofessional and untrustworthy.
- In some situations, you may have no choice but to passively listen to someone engaging in people gossip. Say nothing that would further encourage their gossip. Never repeat what you have heard.
- Pay attention to professional banter. It may reveal important information about the informal structure of your agency, but do not assume that what you are hearing is necessarily true. Often this banter is inaccurate or only partially true.

Do not base a decision on rumor. If it is an important matter, get accurate information before making a decision.

Every organization has many unwritten rules. It is likely that no one will think to tell you about them until after you ask about or have broken one. For example, you might be breaking a rule if you bring food or drink to a staff meeting, or you might be breaking a rule if a certain report is submitted late even though it is permissible to be a little late on other types of reports. The best way to learn about these informal rules and procedures is to observe the work of others in the agency and ask why things are done a certain way.

Remember that there is no such thing as a stupid question. Your field instructor expects you to ask many questions, especially in the beginning, but he or she also expects you to remember the answers that you are given. Thus, record the answers so you do not ask the same questions over and over. Your field instructor expects that you will make some mistakes, but he or she expects you to learn from each mistake and not make it a second time.

Also remember that your actions and your behavior always speak louder and more clearly than do your words. In the professional world, you will be judged primarily on the basis of your performance. Judgments about your potential will likely be based on your past and current performance, so take your practicum as seriously as you would a professional social work position.

Basic Information about Your Practicum: A Workbook Activity

The following questions are designed to assist you in securing the information and orientation needed to get your practicum experience off to a good start. Some can be answered by your field instructor; others will need to be answered by the practicum coordinator of your school.

1. Who are the social workers who will supervise your work during the practicum?

    Name   Phone Number   E-Mail Address

    _____

    _____

    _____

2. Who is the faculty member who will serve as your faculty supervisor and primary contact to your practicum agency?

    Name   Phone Number   E-Mail Address

    _____

3. Who are you to contact if you encounter unusual or unexpected problems related to supervision, learning opportunities, or learning activities within your practicum?

    Name   Phone Number   E-Mail Address

    _____

    _____

4. What are the names and numbers of other practicum students in your agency?

    Name   Phone Number   E-Mail Address

    _____

    _____

    _____

    _____

5. How many hours each week are you to be at your practicum agency?

    _____

6. How are you to document the number of hours you devote to your practicum? To whom is this documentation to be submitted? How often are you to report?

    _____

    _____

7. On what days each week and at what times each day are you to be at your practicum agency?

_____

8. What regularly scheduled agency meetings are you expected to attend?

_____

_____

9. What are you to do if you are sick or for some other good reason cannot be at the practicum agency when scheduled and expected to be there? Who do you contact? Who will fill in for you when you are absent? How much notice are you required to give?

_____

_____

10. How are you expected to dress when at the agency? Is there a dress code? What types of clothing, jewelry, or attire are considered inappropriate?

_____

_____

11. How do the regular staff members want to be addressed? Do they prefer to be called Ms., Mrs., Mr., or Dr.? Is it appropriate to use first names?

_____

_____

12. What term is used to refer to the people who make use of your agency's programs and services (e.g., clients, consumers, members, patients, customers, recipients)? How are they to be addressed (e.g., Mr., Mrs., or Ms.)? Is the use of first names permitted?

_____

_____

_____

13. Are you expected to sign an agreement to protect the confidentiality of your clients?

_____

14. Do you need to obtain an agency staff identification card, name badge, keys, cell phone, or security code? If so, how is this to be done?

_____

_____

_____

15. Is there a specific support staff person assigned to work with you? If yes, what is his or her name?

_____

16. Are you permitted to send out a letter from the agency without prior approval or a countersignature? If not, who must approve or countersign your letters and reports?

_____

17. Are there personal safety concerns that you need to understand and keep in mind while in this agency, neighborhood, and community? (See Chapter 6 on Personal Safety.) What policies and procedures are in place to ensure your safety and that of the staff?

_____

_____

_____

_____

18. Are you permitted to make personal phone calls, use the Internet, or send and receive personal e-mail while in your practicum agency? What rules apply?

_____

_____

_____

Additional notes and comments:

_____

_____

_____

_____

_____

_____

Suggested Learning Activities

- Locate and read agency manuals and websites that describe agency policy and procedures.
- Request opportunities to be introduced to agency staff. Write down their names and job titles so you will learn their names quickly.
- Attend any staff meetings open to you to observe employee interaction.

Additional Suggestions and Hints

- Maintain an up-to-date appointment book or PDA in which you enter the times and dates of all staff meetings, appointments, and other obligations.
- Carry a notebook in which you can record important information and instructions.
- Walk around the agency building. Locate potentially critical features such as emergency exits, fire alarms, and fire extinguishers.

Selected Bibliography

Dolgoff, Ralph. *An Introduction to Supervisory Practice in Human Services.* Boston: Allyn and Bacon, 2005.

Healy, Karen. *Social Work Theories in Context: Creating Frameworks for Practice.* New York: Palgrave Macmillan, 2005.

Rothman, Juliet. *Stepping Out into the Field: A Field Work Manual for Social Work Students.* Boston: Allyn and Bacon, 2000.

Walsh, Joseph. *Theories for Direct Social Work Practice.* Belmont, CA: Thomson Brooks/Cole, 2006.

Weinbach, Robert. *The Social Worker as Manager: A Practical Guide to Success.* 4th ed. Boston: Allyn and Bacon, 2003.

5

Learning from Supervision

GOALS FOR LEARNING

- To understand the nature and purpose of practicum supervision
- To understand the types of supervision, including individual, group, and peer supervision
- To use supervision for practicum learning and professional growth
- To understand the levels of supervision provided within your practicum agency
- To identify styles of supervision

The quality of your practicum is closely tied to the nature and quality of the teacher–student relationship you develop with your field instructor. Learning from a skilled and caring supervisor can enrich a practicum experience and provide a positive model of staff interaction.

Every supervisor or field instructor, like every student and every client, has both strengths and limitations. You will need to identify your field instructor's strengths and plan your practicum to take advantage of them.

Background and Context

In order to understand practicum supervision and how to make good use of it, it is necessary to examine the purpose and functions of supervision within an organization. Although the word *supervision* has its roots in a Latin word that means "to look over" or "to watch over," modern supervisory practice places less emphasis on the supervisor being an overseer of work and more emphasis on the supervisor being a skilled master of the work to be done, a leader, a mentor, and a teacher.

There are few jobs more challenging than that of a supervisor in a human services agency. It is a job that takes sensitivity, skill, common sense, commitment, good humor, and intelligence. Supervisors are mediators between the line-level social workers and the higher-level agency administrators. They frequently represent the agency in its interactions with other agencies and the community. In addition, they are often faced with the challenging tasks of responding to the concerns and complaints of clients who are dissatisfied with the agency's programs or with the performance of a social worker or other staff member.

Although being a supervisor can be demanding, it can also be a satisfying job, especially for those who understand and appreciate the teaching aspect of supervision. Watching a new social worker or social work student learn and develop on the job can be a rewarding and inspiring experience. That is one reason why many busy agency supervisors volunteer to serve as field instructors to social work students. Hopefully your field instructor is highly motivated to teach you about social work practice.

Kadushin (2002) identifies three components of agency-based supervisory practice: the administrative function, the supportive function, and the educational function. The *administrative function* includes such responsibilities as recruiting, selecting, and orienting new staff; assigning and coordinating work; monitoring and evaluating staff performance; facilitating communication up and down within the organization; advocating for staff; serving as a buffer between staff and administration; representing the agency to the public; and encouraging needed agency change.

The *educational function* is concerned with providing informal training and arranging for formal in-service staff training. Basically, the supervisor is responsible for ensuring that the staff receives all of the initial training needed to perform well in their positions. In addition, the supervisor is responsible for recognizing training needs and providing ongoing in-service training.

The *supportive function* has to do with sustaining staff morale, cultivating a sense of teamwork, building commitment to the agency's goals and mission, encouraging workers by providing support, and dealing with work-related problems of conflict and frustration. This aspect of supervision is extremely important in human services agencies in which stress and burnout can be common problems. The supervisor must strive to create a work environment that is conducive to the provision of quality services to clients, while also supporting staff who may at times feel stressed and unappreciated.

A field instructor, even when not officially an agency supervisor of other social workers, will be concerned with these three functions as they relate to practicum students. He or she will pay attention to whether you are performing the work of the agency in an appropriate manner and in keeping with agency policy and procedure. He or she will be sensitive to your fears and insecurities, and to the fact that you have personal responsibilities in addition to those related to the practicum. He or she will want to do everything possible to facilitate your learning but, in the final analysis, his or her primary obligation must be to the agency's clients or consumers and to the agency that serves those clients.

You may receive the following types of supervision. Each type of supervision is able to meet a certain need or situation, and it is recommended that you expose yourself whenever possible to as many forms of supervision as you can.

- *Individual supervision*—regularly scheduled, one-to-one meetings between the field instructor and the student (e.g., one hour per week)
- *Group supervision*—regularly scheduled meetings between the field instructor and a small group of students
- *Peer supervision*—regularly scheduled meetings attended by a small group of social workers who assume responsibility for providing guidance and suggestions to each other and to the agency's practicum students
- *Formal case presentations*—regularly scheduled meetings at which one or more social workers (including students) describe their work on a specific case and invite advice and guidance on how it should be handled
- *Ad hoc supervision*—brief and unscheduled meetings with a field instructor to discuss a specific question or issue
- *Virtual supervision*—computer, e-mail, or web supervision

A social worker who assumes the role of field instructor or field supervisor has special ethical obligations. Supervisors assume responsibility for the quality of work done by those they supervise. According to Section 3.01 of the NASW *Code of Ethics* (1999, 19), social workers who provide supervision:

- Should have the necessary knowledge and skill to supervise . . . appropriately and should do so only within their areas of knowledge and competence
- Are responsible for setting clear, appropriate, and culturally sensitive boundaries
- Should not engage in dual or multiple relationships with a supervisee in which there is a risk of exploitation of or potential harm to the supervisee
- Should evaluate the supervisee's performance in a manner that is fair and respectful

Certain behaviors or patterns may prompt the school's faculty supervisor or practicum coordinator to reevaluate the suitability and appropriateness of using a particular field instructor as a supervisor for students. This may include:

- The field instructor is not readily available to the student or often misses scheduled appointments with the student.
- The field instructor shows little interest in teaching and helping the student learn social work knowledge and skills.
- The field instructor's behavior or practice is discovered to be unethical or incompetent.

Food for Thought

If practitioners are to treat their clients with the deepest possible integrity, they must have a place to go where they can carefully and honestly examine their own behavior. That place, ideally, is the supervisory relationship. (Kaiser 1997, 7)

• • •

Supervisors are apt to forget the steps they followed to deepen their own insights into the content. Ideas that have become obvious to them in their current practice may not be simple or obvious to their staffs. . . . Unless supervisors work at it, they can forget how they had to construct, element by element, their understanding of a complex construct such as contracting. They believe they can hand over the years of learning and are surprised to discover that a student or staff member is having great difficulty constructing even a simple version of the idea. . . . [Because they] have discovered some of the short-cuts, and are aware of some of the pitfalls, supervisors can guide their staff members and make their journey more certain and quicker, but they cannot take the journey for them. (Shulman 1993, 159)

• • •

The supervisor can be an active participant in the formulation or reformulation of agency policy. Having learned from the direct-service workers about client and community needs, having learned about the deficiencies and shortcomings of agency policy when workers have attempted to implement it, the supervisor should do more than act as a passive channel for upward communication of such information. The supervisor has the responsibility of using his or her knowledge of the situation to formulate suggested changes in agency policy and procedure. The supervisor is in a strategic position to act as a change agent. Standing between administration and the workers, he or she can actively influence administration to make changes and influence workers to accept them. (Kadushin and Harkness 2002, 75)

• • •

The supervisor should not apologize for corrective feedback. This discounts its importance and attenuates its impact. The supervisee needs feedback to help overcome performance deficiencies so that he or she can do better work. Feedback helps make learning explicit and conscious. The supervisor has the perspective, the objectivity, and the knowledge of what good performance is supposed to look like—a *super vision,* so to speak. (Kadushin and Harkness 2002, 160)

• • •

Vicarious liability may be charged when . . . errors of commission or omission were those of the supervisee. In addition to mistreatment of clients or patients by a practitioner, some claims may implicate supervisors. These claims are made under the legal doctrine of *respondeat superior,* that is "let the master respond." This doctrine means a supervisor is responsible for the actions of a supervisee that were conducted during the course of employment, training, or field instruction. (Dolgoff 2005, 84)

If your supervisior exhibits any of these behaviors or attitudes, consult with your faculty supervisor or practicum coordinator to determine a course of action in order to ensure the quality of supervision available to you.

Supervisors have a variety of styles or preferred ways of doing their jobs, all of which will affect the student's experiences in the agency. No one style or approach is necessarily more right or better than others. Different styles are more or less effective depending on the nature of the work to be done and the level of training and experience of those being supervised. The following examples illustrate the variety of approaches to supervision to which the student will generally need to adapt:

- Some supervisors focus mostly on the tasks necessary to get the job done, whereas others also focus on the interactions or processes required to get it done.
- Some prefer to make decisions alone, whereas others prefer to involve many people in making decisions.
- Some make decisions quickly, whereas others take more time to do so.
- Some strive to obtain and retain authority and power, whereas others easily share power and try to empower others.
- Some are reluctant to share information with others unless they have a need to know, whereas others are eager to share information with staff and students.
- Some prefer routines and clear procedures, so they will not be caught unprepared, whereas others prefer to keep things flexible and fluid and function well on an ad hoc basis.
- Some want decisions and agreements in writing, whereas others are comfortable with verbal agreements.
- Some pay great attention to the details of the work, whereas others prefer to deal with only the "big picture" and leave details to others.
- Some closely monitor the work of others, assuming that things can and will go wrong, whereas others assume everything is fine unless someone says there is a problem.
- Some are task oriented and work at a fast pace, whereas others are more relaxed, laid back, and work at a slower pace.
- Some do not see the personal needs, concerns, and problems of colleagues and those they supervise as their responsibility, whereas others pay close attention to such matters.
- Some are quick to delegate work to others, whereas others are hesitant and cautious about making new work assignments.
- Some emphasize organizing, planning, and directing the work assigned to those they supervise, whereas others assume that they will know what to do and can figure out how to do the work.

Guidance and Direction

Learning to use supervision is of central importance to the success of a practicum. Because social work is challenging and sometimes stressful, and also because your work directly affects clients' lives, you will need guidance, direction, support, and feedback from your field instructor.

Strive to use supervision in a purposeful and responsible manner. Having a regularly scheduled supervisory meeting time each week will help you avoid the difficulties of constantly having to arrange a suitable meeting time. Prepare for each meeting. Do not expect your field instructor to do all of the talking. Bring questions, observations, and requests for input and feedback to the meeting. Use this time to examine your performance and explore new ideas.

Your field instructor will have expectations of you and it will be important for you to understand these expectations. In general, you will be expected to exhibit:

- Dependability and follow-through on assigned work
- Attention to detail and proper procedures
- Initiative in work-related assignments
- A cooperative attitude toward the field instructor and other staff
- Willingness to learn from whatever tasks are assigned
- Ability to assume assignments of increasing complexity and challenge
- Openness to supervision, including asking for, and learning from, constructive criticism
- Willingness to seek help when needed

Expect your field instructor to ask some very pointed questions in order to learn about and monitor your work in the agency. Supervisors ask these questions in order to be of support to you. They will help you analyze your performance, understand why an intervention was successful or not, and develop your critical thinking skills. Possible supervisory questions about an intervention in which you have been involved may include the following:

- What specific problem or issue were you attempting to address?
- What information did you gather?
- What assessment tools did you use?
- What meaning did you assign to this information?
- What were your goals and objectives?
- What were your client's goals and objectives?
- What were you trying to accomplish?
- Why did you choose that specific intervention?
- What ethical and legal concerns affected your decision?
- Was the intervention successful? If not, what are the ramifications for the client and agency?
- How do you know the intervention was or was not successful?
- What other interventions might have worked better?
- What needs to be done next?
- What did you learn from this experience?
- What would you do differently next time?
- What did you learn about yourself?

The job of a supervisor is to give instruction and feedback, and you will increase your chances of success if you seek and are open to this input about yourself and your work. You may be anxious because your field instructor will be evaluating your performance. However, that is his or her responsibility. He or she has been asked by your school to guide your learning and offer constructive criticism in order that you might learn about yourself and develop your knowledge and skills.

Your field instructor should evaluate your performance in an ongoing and continuous manner. You should receive feedback and constructive criticism during all phases of your practicum so that you can continue to grow professionally. If this is not happening, discuss the matter with your field instructor and ask for an ongoing critique of your performance.

Your field instructor is responsible for conducting a comprehensive evaluation of your learning and performance at the end of the academic term, and this will likely translate into a final grade in your practicum. You can expect that this evaluation will be based on:

- Direct observation of your work by your field instructor or other social workers in the agency
- Your verbal descriptions of what you are doing and learning
- Your written documentation, reports, and case notes
- Feedback received from clients regarding your work
- Observations and input from social workers in the community who have worked with you

As you begin your practicum and take on new responsibilities, you may be afraid of making a serious mistake or in some way hurting your clients. Such worries are to be expected. In fact, your field instructor will become concerned if you do not have these concerns, because that could mean that you are overconfident or that you do not understand the seriousness of your situation. Do not hesitate to express your fears. Your field instructor can to help you with these issues.

Supervision is an interactional process that parallels in many ways the social worker–client relationship and the helping process (Shulman 1993). In order to help you improve your performance, your field instructor will employ many of the helping skills and techniques that you and other social workers use in working with clients. However, supervision is not counseling or therapy. If the supervision you receive feels too much like therapy, consult with your faculty supervisor. If you need counseling for personal issues or issues related to your practicum, seek counseling from a professional other than your field instructor.

Field instructors use a variety of techniques to help students examine and process their experiences and deepen their learning. For example, your field instructor may use didactic instruction (lecture or presentation), role play and behavioral rehearsal, demonstration or modeling, and case consultation. View them as valuable learning opportunities, although you may feel threatened or put on the spot by these teaching techniques.

You will move through several stages during your practicum experience. I identify three stages: orientation, exploration and skill building, and beginning competency. Your field instructor will provide specific types of help at each stage.

When you begin your practicum, you are in what is called an *orientation stage*. At this stage, you may feel anxious, overwhelmed, unsure, and incompetent. It is your field instructor's job to provide orientation and training so that you know what the agency is all about and what is expected of you. He or she will offer guidance, provide encouragement, help you select learning activities that build skills, and help you develop confidence so you are willing to take on additional tasks and responsibilities.

After becoming familiar and comfortable with your practicum setting and what is expected, you enter the *exploration and skill building stage*. During this stage, you will gain knowledge, skills, and confidence as you participate in various interventions and projects and take on added responsibilities. You will feel less anxious than when you first began the practicum and although you will still make mistakes, you can analyze them and learn from them. Your field instructor will help you to build on prior experiences and to become comfortable taking risks and working with more difficult and challenging situations. He or she will help you learn general principles of practice, as well as the theory underlying interventions. You will be able to function more independently at this stage.

As the end of the practicum approaches, you will enter the *beginning competency stage.* At this stage, you will have developed a variety of skills and acquired considerable knowledge about your agency, its clients, and its specific programs and approaches. You will have identified your strengths, your limitations, and your interests. Your field instructor will reinforce your successes, encourage you to refine your skills, and expect you to work with an even wider variety of clients and projects. Hopefully you will need less supervision and will be gaining knowledge and skills that can be generalized to other similar client situations and other agency settings. You will be encouraged to examine how the work of the agency addresses community needs and fits into the social welfare system.

Some students begin the practicum with the hope that their field instructor will become a true mentor. When this happens, it is a great experience for a practicum student. Mentors can be role models and can inspire students to achieve higher levels of competence. However, this may not happen. When seeking a mentor, you may need to look to persons outside your practicum agency.

Conflicts may arise in the supervisory relationship. For example, you may feel that your field instructor does not devote enough time to you and your learning needs. Or you may feel that your field instructor is either too controlling or not structured enough. The two of you may have very different personalities. Perhaps you and your field instructor differ in terms of gender, race, ethnic background, or age and these differences affect your relationship. Whatever the conflict, talk about it. Do not avoid the problem. You will be expected to find ways to deal with these issues. If the problem cannot be worked out with your field instructor, consult with your faculty supervisor.

Rothman (2000, 167–168) stresses the importance of optimizing your relationship with your field instructor when problems arise and describes a variety of approaches often used by practicum students. *Confronting* your supervisor directly helps clarify the problem so you can work to resolve it effectively. *Circumventing* your supervisor may be necessary if your relationship with your supervisor is only a formal one or if he or she does not have time to supervise you. *Denying* the conflict and choosing to accept your supervisor's perspective on the problem may be necessary and even helpful at times. *Adapting* to your supervisor's style, perspective, and policies may help you learn to work flexibly with others very different from you. *Avoiding* the problem by not discussing it will limit the amount of guidance you receive from your supervisor. *Withdrawing* from the conflict may be necessary if you cannot resolve the problem, and you may choose to leave your practicum site.

I caution you on developing a dual relationship with your field instructor. He or she is to be a supervisor, not a friend or a counselor. Although there can be an element of friendship between students and supervisors, this can be problematic when supervisors need to provide feedback and students need to be able to accept it. If personal problems arise during your practicum, do not ask or expect your field instructor to provide counseling. If you need such services, arrange to receive them in another way.

The sexual harassment of a student by a field instructor is a very serious matter that should be immediately reported to your faculty supervisor or practicum coordinator. An allegation of sexual harassment is a messy and complex legal concern. Should this problem arise in your practicum, immediately seek consultation on how to proceed.

If you observe that your field instructor violates the NASW *Code of Ethics,* consult with your school's practicum coordinator or your faculty supervisor.

Using Supervision for Learning: A Workbook Activity

1. Is your field instructor also a supervisor of other social workers or agency staff?

   _____

   If yes, whom does he or she supervise?

   _____

   _____

2. Who supervises your field instructor?

   _____

3. Has your field instructor previously supervised practicum students?

   _____

   If yes, about how many students?

   _____

4. Has your field instructor received special training on staff supervision?

   _____

   If yes, what was the nature of this training?

   _____

   _____

5. Has your field instructor attended training on practicum supervision and instruction provided by your school's practicum program?

   _____

   If yes, what was the nature of this training?

   _____

   _____

6. In what areas do you want and welcome feedback from your field instructor regarding your performance?

   _____

   _____

7. In what areas of performance are you overly sensitive or fearful about receiving feedback from your field instructor?

_____

_____

_____

8. What might these feelings be telling you?

_____

_____

_____

9. Are you afraid of anything related to your practicum? What is a positive way of dealing with these fears?

_____

_____

_____

_____

10. It has been said that people often avoid the experiences they need most in order to learn and grow personally. Are you avoiding any practicum-related experiences? Why?

_____

_____

_____

_____

11. What specific types of knowledge and skills can you learn from your field instructor? Is your field instructor known to possess some special knowledge and skills? Has your field instructor had uncommon practice experiences or special training?

_____

_____

_____

12. Who else besides your field instructor could meet your learning needs in those areas of knowledge and skill (e.g., other professionals in your agency, faculty, other students)?

    _____

    _____

    _____

13. What teaching techniques does your field instructor use (lecture, presentation, demonstration, case consultation, role playing, or direct observation)?

    _____

    _____

    _____

14. How can you make sure any personal issues, problems, or biases do not negatively affect your work or your clients?

    _____

    _____

    _____

    _____

15. Which of the following learning experiences can you make use of to enhance your practicum?

    _____ Discussing the pros and cons of possible decisions and actions with your supervisor *before* you have met with your client

    _____ Discussing the pros and cons of possible decisions and actions with your supervisor *after* you have met with your client

    _____ Discussing how your decisions and actions fit with a particular conceptual framework, theory, model, or perspective

    _____ Using role play and simulations to rehearse the techniques, skills, or approaches you want to learn

    _____ Observing others performing the skill or technique you wish to learn

    _____ Brainstorming various ways in which a situation might be handled

    _____ Watching a video or listening to an audiotape of an experienced worker's session with a client

    _____ Reading and discussing an article related to the skills you wish to learn

    _____ Reviewing and discussing the case notes and the written record of others' work with their clients

16. How can you work with your field instructor in order to have as many of these learning experiences as possible?

_____

_____

Additional notes and comments:

_____

_____

_____

_____

_____

_____

Suggested Learning Activities

- Attend any group or peer supervisory sessions offered in your agency in order to learn about the various modes of providing and receiving supervision.
- Present a case you are working on at a peer supervisory session, asking for input from other social workers besides your field instructor.
- If appropriate and feasible, work with a variety of social workers, supervisors, and managers in your agency so that you can observe differing supervisory styles.
- Ask your field instructor how your agency provides support to its employees, such as through an employee assistance program or continuing education.
- Read your university practicum manual so you understand what is expected of both your faculty supervisor and your field instructor.

Additional Suggestions and Hints

- In Sheafor and Horejsi (2006), read the sections entitled "Giving and Receiving Supervision" (605–609) and "Developing Self Awareness" (584–588).

Selected Bibliography

Baird, Brian N. *The Internship, Practicum, and Field Placement Handbook: A Guide for the Helping Professions.* 2nd ed. Upper Saddle River, NJ: Prentice Hall, 1998.

Cohen, Robert. *Clinical Supervision: What to Do and How to Do It.* Pacific Grove, CA: Brooks/Cole, 2004.

Dolgoff, Ralph. *An Introduction to Supervisory Practice in Human Services.* Boston: Allyn and Bacon, 2005.

Ellison, Martha L. "Critical Field Instructor Behaviors: Student and Field Instructor Views." *Arete, Journal of the College of Social Work at the University of South Carolina* 18.2 (Winter 1994): 12–21.

Hayes, Robert. *Clinical Supervision in the Helping Professions: A Practical Guide.* Pacific Grove, CA: Brooks/Cole, 2003.

Houston-Vega, Mary Kay, Elane Nuehring, and Elisabeth Daguio. *Prudent Practice: A Guide for Managing Malpractice Risk.* Washington, DC: NASW Press, 1997.

Kadushin, Alfred. *Supervision in Social Work.* New York: Columbia University Press, 2002.

Kadushin, Alfred, and Daniel Harkness. *Supervision in Social Work.* 4th ed. New York: Columbia University Press, 2002.

Kaiser, Tamara. *Supervisory Relationship: Exploring the Human Element.* Boston: Brooks/Cole, 1997.

National Association of Social Workers. *Code of Ethics.* Washington, DC: NASW Press, 1999.

Rothman, Juliet Cassuto. *Stepping Out into the Field: A Field Work Manual for Social Work Students.* Boston: Allyn and Bacon, 2000.

Sheafor, Bradford, and Charles Horejsi, *Techniques and Guidelines in Social Work Practice.* 7th ed. Boston: Allyn and Bacon, 2006.

Shulman, Lawrence. *Interactional Social Work Practice: Toward an Empirical Theory.* Itasca, IL: F. E. Peacock, 1991.

Shulman, Lawrence. *Interactional Supervision.* Washington, DC: NASW Press, 1993.

Tropman, John. *Supervision and Management in Nonprofits and Human Services: How Not to Become the Administrator You Always Hated.* Peosta, IA: Eddie Bowers Publishing, 2006.

Weinbach, Robert. *The Social Worker as Manager: A Practical Guide to Success.* Boston: Allyn and Bacon, 2003.

6

Personal Safety

GOALS FOR LEARNING

- To identify the sources and types of danger most often encountered in social work practice
- To become familiar with agency policies and procedures that can reduce risk and protect staff and clients
- To become familiar with precautions and preventive actions that can reduce the risk of being harmed
- To become familiar with steps and actions that can de-escalate an already dangerous situation and protect a social worker in such a situation

Although social workers see themselves as helpers and expect most clients to be cooperative, at times they find themselves in situations in which they must deal with clients who are angry, volatile, and threatening. Accounts of violence toward social workers are increasing, due to client frustration with human service systems; cutbacks in services; increased levels of crime, drug use, and violence in society; and antiauthority or antigovernment attitudes.

Exposure to job-related danger can lead to worker anxiety, low morale, burnout, family stress, and high staff turnover. Social work practicum students must be cognizant of the dangers they face. They will need to exercise certain precautions so as to reduce risks to their own safety. Moreover, they must know what steps to take when they encounter a dangerous situation.

Background and Context

Broadly speaking, the potential sources of harm to a social worker include the following:

- Clients who are angry and feel mistreated by the agency and its staff.
- Persons who are not clients, but who are acquainted with or related to clients and are aware that the clients feel mistreated by the agency and its staff.
- Clients who present a special threat because of high-risk factors such as alcohol or drug use, a pattern of violent behavior, antiauthority attitudes, or unstable mental condition.
- Persons with criminal intent and inclination who are found in neighborhoods near the agency or in areas where the social worker travels and works. These individuals are not clients, nor do they have a relationship with the workers' clients.

- Biohazardous and toxic materials that may be encountered in hospitals and other health care facilities and during visits to clients in their homes.

Certain practice settings present more risk to social workers than others. Such settings include child protective agencies, programs in correctional settings, forensic units of psychiatric hospitals, shelters for the homeless, and residential facilities for youth who are especially aggressive and impulsive. These settings are inherently dangerous because some of those served have tendencies toward the use of violence. However, any practice setting can be threatening, because client–worker interactions often involve emotionally charged Situations and concerns. Even clients with no previous history of violence or high-risk behaviors can, under certain circumstances, pose a threat to social workers.

Individuals with mental illnesses are not inherently more dangerous than persons who do not suffer from such impairments. However, a small percentage of those with certain symptoms are a potential threat. Included in this group are persons who experience visual or auditory hallucinations that may lead them to harm others. It may also include those who hold bizarre, fanatical, or paranoid beliefs or delusions, and who as a result feel especially threatened by social workers. Clients with extreme antigovernment or antiauthority beliefs may see social workers as threats and may feel justified in resorting to violence.

Certain social work practices and interventions have a greater likelihood of placing the worker at risk. Such activities include the initial investigation of child abuse allegations, the involuntary removal of a child from a parent's home, providing protection to a victim of domestic violence, outreach to youth involved

Food for Thought

Daily interaction with those who are asked to reveal their private lives, discuss sensitive family matters, and even have their children removed from their custody, produces the potential for violence, running the gamut from verbal abuse to physical assault. Agencies which ignore worker safety issues, or accept them as a normal part of the job, imperil both their staff and the families they serve. Staff who ignore their own gut feeling about personal risk and fail to take defensive precautions are not dealing realistically with danger. (Farestad 1997, 2)

• • •

Human services workers are at risk for a number of reasons. When serving clients with high levels of frustration, coupled with desperate needs, hopelessness, and an inability to cope with the problems in their lives, risk is ever present. A client's perception that you are unable or unwilling to help them could make you a target for a tremendous unleashing of anger, frustration, and violence. Home visits, child protective issues, and transporting clients are all powder-keg scenarios that need only a small spark to set off a chain reaction that could put your life or safety in imminent danger.

Even office visits can be high risk without a safety net, [that includes] . . . policies and procedures that address risk management, proper office layout, escape routes, and personal safety training. One major

potential obstacle in assessing danger is the strong commitment toward helping others. This desire may lead to overlooking or dismissing the danger signs and failing to recognize that some people do not want to be helped. . . . With no weapon, no power of arrest, no bulletproof vest, and generally no backup, . . . [social workers] go into battle armed with only a genuine concern for their fellow human beings and a mission. (Harman and Davis 1997, 15)

• • •

Owing to the nature of their practicum placements, most students enter practicum agencies with limited background and skills to deal with difficult circumstances and have virtually no training in dealing with violence. . . . Without experience and training, students may be unable to manage or contain potentially dangerous situations with clients. . . . Although students may experience violence within their practicum sites, the occurrences may go unreported. Because students are evaluated on their performance in their field practicum, they may be unlikely to report their experiences for fear of receiving a negative grade. (Tully, Kropf, and Price 1993, 191–192)

• • •

Violence is the language of the unheard.
—*Martin Luther King, Jr.*

in gangs, treatment of aggressive youth, intervention with drug- and alcohol-involved clients, the transporting of clients who do not wish to be moved, the behavioral management of persons with certain forms of brain injury or mental retardation, and the monitoring of clients in correctional settings. In these situations, social work actions can be perceived as threatening or coercive, sometimes resulting in heightened emotion and defensiveness on the part of clients, and an inclination to use violence.

In their work with clients who are potentially dangerous, social workers face the difficult challenge of remaining humane, open, and accepting of clients while also being alert to the possibility of attack. It is important not to expect every client to be a threat, but to recognize a client who might be.

Social workers who routinely or frequently face verbal abuse from clients may become complacent. They may come to view verbal threats as part of their job, mistakenly assuming that the clients are bluffing and consequently fail to take reasonable precautions. Some social workers mistakenly believe that because they have been trained in basic helping skills, they will be able to talk their way out of a dangerous situation. These overly confident workers tend to minimize risk, erroneously conclude that they do not need special training in how to respond in truly dangerous situations, and put themselves at risk.

Practicum students in hospitals or other health care settings should be alert to the existence of biological or chemical hazards and receive instruction on how to protect themselves against infectious diseases and how to avoid or properly handle biohazardous materials such as used tissues, clothing, bed sheets, or pillows that have been stained with body fluids. In some instances, students will need to wear a mask and gloves when interviewing a patient. In some cases this will be done to protect themselves from disease and in other cases to protect a vulnerable patient.

Practicum students may also be exposed to client threats over the telephone or via e-mail. You will need to be trained in agency responses to such threats in order to protect yourself, your coworkers, and your clients.

Guidance and Direction

Most dangerous interpersonal situations are the result of tensions that have grown and intensified over time. It is vital to understand the phases of escalation, the client's needs and feelings during each phase, and what actions or interventions by the social worker might reduce the tension and level of risk. It is preferable to intervene as early as possible in order to prevent escalation and eventual loss of control by the angry client. Irwin (1997, 8–10) describes four stages of crisis management and suggests approaches to use at each stage to reduce the likelihood of violence. Consider these principles and employ these approaches should you feel threatened by the behavior of a client or another person. Discuss them with your supervisor in order to anticipate potentially dangerous situations and how your supervisor recommends dealing with clients at each of the following stages:

Stage 1: Initial Tension and Frustration

At this stage, the individuals who may become violent are anxious and experiencing high levels of emotion, especially anger, but are still rational and in control of their behavior. They are not yet acting on their feelings, so they will respond best to an approach that helps them vent emotions, reflect on the situation, and devise a solution on their own. The worker's use of active listening will help these individuals express and examine their feelings and usually reduce the level of tension. The use of basic listening skills also helps the worker build rapport and assess the severity of the crisis and the danger it presents.

Stage 2: Verbal Attack

During this second stage, the individuals are feeling threatened and vulnerable. They become very defensive and go on the offensive with verbal attacks. Irrational thoughts and strong feelings begin to override their self-control. They may direct their anger toward the worker, using verbal abuse and intimidation. Verbal communication with them becomes more difficult and further escalation is likely. Effective threat-reducing approaches by the worker include the display of calm body language, using a non-threatening tone of voice, reflecting clients' feelings and behaviors, and setting limits on what behavior is allowable. The worker should calmly validate the feelings being expressed and provide clear guidelines, choices, and alternatives if possible.

Stage 3: Loss of Control

Individuals at this stage have lost control over their behavior. They have physically struck, or are very close to, striking others. They pose a real danger. Workers need to immediately assess the level of danger and their ability to provide control. They should be preparing to escape, if necessary. Because most clients will fear their own loss of control, workers are more likely to gain control of the situation if they can empathize with the clients' fear about doing something they will regret. Workers must remain calm and continue to build rapport, while shifting focus to the threatening behavior. The out-of-control person must be controlled, either by the worker or by legal authorities.

Stage 4: Recovery after the Outburst

At this stage, the crisis has peaked and imminent danger has passed. Individuals struggle to regain their composure and, having fallen apart, need help in putting themselves back together. To help them recover, workers should allow them to further vent their anger, explain their feelings, and come to some closure regarding the incident. Allowing people to stabilize themselves decreases the risk of reescalation. At this stage, people may gain insight, allow mutual problem solving with the worker, and plan ways to prevent another such incident in the future.

Dealing with the Potentially Violent Client

- Remember that past behavior is the best single predictor of future behavior. Before meeting with a client that you do not know and who may be dangerous, consult agency records or the local police in search of information that may help you assess the risk.
- Remove all potential weapons from your office when dealing with a potentially dangerous client, including scissors, staplers, paperweights, and other small but heavy objects.
- Leave your office door partly open during an interview with a potentially dangerous client.
- Notify others if you are planning to meet a potentially dangerous client in your office and arrange for a way to signal for help. Arrange your office so that you are closest to the door. Place a desk or other barrier between you and the dangerous client.
- Avoid meeting with clients when you are alone in the office. If you must have the meeting, turn lights on in other offices and lead clients to believe that others will be coming into the office.

- When meeting with an angry client, provide him or her with as much privacy as is possible without compromising your safety.
- Make use of all safety procedures and devices available such as call devices or code systems to alert coworkers that you need help.
- Be very cautious when dealing with a person who is under the influence of alcohol or drugs, even when you know the person fairly well. A person under the influence of chemicals should be viewed as inherently unpredictable.
- Be cautious when around persons who may be involved in illegal activities such as manufacturing or selling drugs and may, therefore, feel threatened by your presence or by what you have seen. They may be willing to harm you in order to protect themselves from discovery by police.
- Remember that worker attitudes play a role in either controlling or provoking threatening behavior. Maintain a positive, nonjudgmental attitude toward clients.
- Recognize that both increased structure and decreased stimuli may help clients remain calm and gain self-control.
- Remember that clients use threats and violence when other forms of communication fail them, so utilize skills that facilitate communication and help clients express themselves in words.
- Address the person by name. Do not argue with or criticize an angry person. Avoid doing anything that might be perceived as ridiculing or embarrassing the person.
- Trust your instincts. Assume that you have a built-in unconscious mechanism that can recognize danger more quickly than your rational thought processes. If you feel afraid, assume that you are in danger, even if you cannot clearly identify why you feel this way.
- Remember that an attack by a client is almost always the reaction of someone who is afraid and feeling threatened. Thus, strive to speak and act in ways that lessen the client's need to be afraid of you. Demonstrate empathy and that you understand the reason behind their anger and fear.
- Avoid standing above others. If possible and safe, take a sitting position. Standing is more authoritarian and threatening than sitting.
- Attacks by clients are most likely when they feel trapped or controlled, either psychologically or physically. To the extent possible, give clients options and choices. Your location in a room should be one that allows the client to escape without having to come close to you.
- Be alert to signs of an imminent attack such as rapid breathing, teeth grinding, dilated pupils, flaring nostrils, choppy speech, clenched fists, and threatening movements of the body.
- Allow angry persons to vent their feelings. Most angry persons will begin to calm down after two or three minutes of venting or name calling. While this is going on, it is usually best to listen respectfully and allow them to express their feelings. However, some people are stimulated by their own words and grow even more angry because of what they are saying. If that occurs, the level of risk is increasing.
- Do not touch an angry person, especially if they may be under the influence of a drug. Do not move into their personal space. Remain at least four feet away from the person.
- An angry or dangerous person is more likely to attack someone who appears weak, insecure, and unsure. Therefore, present yourself as calm, composed, and self-confident, but not haughty.
- If an individual threatens you with a gun or other weapon, assure him or her that you intend no harm and slowly back away. Do not attempt to disarm the person. Leave that to the police, who have special training.

Handling the Potential Dangers of a Home Visit

- Do not enter a situation that could be dangerous without first consulting with others and formulating a plan to reduce risk. Do not hesitate to seek the assistance of other workers or the police.
- When visiting clients in their homes, keep your agency informed of your plans and itinerary and check in by phone on a prearranged schedule. When away from the office, carry a means of calling for help (e.g., cellular phone, push-button emergency signals, or radio).
- Assign two staff members for potentially dangerous home visits whenever possible.
- Do not enter a home or apartment building until you have taken a few minutes to determine its level of danger. Listen for sounds of violence or out-of-control behavior. Consider whether other people are nearby and if they would respond to a call for help. Identify possible escape routes.
- Be aware that guns are most often kept in a bedroom and that kitchens contains knives and other potential weapons. Leave immediately if a threatening person appears to be moving toward a weapon.
- Be aware that clients who leave a room could return with a weapon.
- Do not sit in an overstuffed chair or couch from which you cannot quickly get to your feet. Select a hard and movable chair. If necessary, it can be used as a shield.
- Park your car in a way that allows for a quick escape if necessary.
- Keep your vehicle in good running order and full of gasoline so that you will not find yourself stranded in a dangerous or isolated area.
- Educate yourself about drugs and illegal drug labs so that you can recognize the dangers inherent in entering a drug lab.
- Know as much as you can about the people living in the home you are visiting in order to anticipate negative attitudes toward authorities, previous history of violence, or previous experiences with social service agencies.
- If you are being followed, go immediately to a police or fire station or to a public place. Do not go to your home if you believe someone is following you or watching your movements.
- If you are likely to encounter dangerous situations while at work (or while walking to work), wear shoes and clothing that permit running. Avoid wearing long earrings or jewelry that could easily be grabbed and twisted to inflict pain and prevent your escape.
- Consider carrying a defensive device such as mace or pepper spray, and learn to use it prior to making the home visit.

Handling an Intense Argument between Two or More People

- When two or more individuals are in a heated argument and you need to intervene, begin by gaining their attention. Anything short of physical force may be used. A shrill whistle, a loud clap, a loud voice, a silly request (e.g., "I need a glass of water"), or other attention-getting devices may be used for this purpose.
- Ask those in conflict to sit down. If they will not sit, remain standing also.
- Separate the disputants as necessary without compromising your own safety. Bring them back together only after they have quieted down and gained self-control.
- If possible, always intervene in a crisis situation with a partner.
- Do not physically intervene if those in conflict are threatening each other with weapons or if they are engaged in a high level of physical violence.

Agency Procedure and the Dangerous Client

- The agency's record-keeping system should use color codes or other markings that identify individuals or households that have a history of violence.
- The agency should maintain a log of all threats of violence so staff can identify those individuals and situations that present a special risk.
- The agency should institute security measures within the building. This might include the installation of a call-for-help button in each office space and establishing telephone code words that are requests for police assistance.
- The agency should develop policy and protocols on how staff are to respond to dangerous situations, such as bomb threats or hostage taking. These procedures should be rehearsed regularly.
- The agency should develop a protocol about when and how to use police assistance, including a written agreement with local law enforcement officials.
- The agency should keep waiting rooms and offices clean and strive to create a pleasant and inviting physical environment. Rooms that are dirty, unpleasant, or unkempt convey disrespect to clients and tend to generate hostility.
- The agency should post in waiting rooms and in other prominent places a statement explaining that alcohol, drugs, and weapons are not allowed in the building and that threats and violence or the possession of a weapon will prompt an immediate call to the police.
- The agency should make sure that the exterior of the agency's building and its parking lot are well lighted.
- The agency should provide training on personal safety and related agency procedures to staff and students and repeat or update this training on a regular basis.
- The agency should designate a specific office or room for meetings with potentially violent clients. This room should be one that is easily observed by others nearby.
- The agency should file criminal charges against those who harm or threaten physical injury to either the worker or the worker's family.
- When a worker is harmed, the agency should respond with appropriate counseling and emotional support to lessen the effects on the worker and the worker's family.

Reducing the Risk of Harm: A Workbook Activity

1. What training is provided in your agency to help workers prevent and deal with threatening or violent clients or situations?

   _____

   _____

   _____

2. What kinds of high-risk clients or situations are you likely to encounter in your practicum? How will you prepare yourself to deal with them?

   _____

   _____

   _____

3. What agency policies and procedures are in place to ensure personal safety and reduce risk to agency employees and clients?

   _____

   _____

   _____

4. Have any employees in your practicum agency been threatened or harmed by clients or consumers? If yes, describe the circumstances that gave rise to the incident.

   _____

   _____

   _____

5. What precautions, if any, might have prevented the above incidents or reduced their seriousness?

   _____

   _____

   _____

6. Do agency workers carry defensive devices such as mace or pepper spray? What are the pros and cons of doing so?

_____

_____

_____

7. Given the area served by your agency, what specific locations or neighborhoods are known to be especially dangerous?

_____

_____

_____

8. Does your agency have an incident reporting system for documenting threats and violence toward workers?

_____

_____

_____

9. Does your agency have a formal, written agreement with the police detailing when they are to be called for assistance?

_____

_____

_____

10. Are there any clients or situations that frighten you? If so, how can you deal with your fears?

_____

_____

_____

11. If your practicum is in a hospital or health care setting, what precautions are you to take in order to protect yourself and your vulnerable clients from infectious diseases or biohazards?

_____

_____

_____

12. What services does your agency provide to workers who are threatened, injured, or traumatized by threats or violence (e.g., counseling, critical incident stress debriefing, or support groups)?

_____

_____

_____

Additional notes and comments:

_____

_____

_____

_____

_____

_____

Suggested Learning Activities

- Invite a local police officer to offer guidance on how to reduce risk in and around your agency.
- Interview experienced social workers and get their advice on how to reduce personal risk.
- Role-play situations that illustrate each of the four stages of crisis management described in this chapter.
- Educate yourself on the specific safety issues faced by your agency (e.g., methamphetamine abuse, use of restraining orders).

Additional Suggestions and Hints

- In Sheafor and Horejsi (2006), read the section entitled "The Dangerous Client" (230–233).

Selected Bibliography

Farestad, Karen. "Worker Safety: Agencies Should Recognize the Issue." *Protecting Children* 13.1 (1997): 2.

Harman, Patricia, and Molly Davis. "Personal Safety for Human Service Professionals: A Law Enforcement Perspective." *Protecting Children* 13.1 (1997): 15–17.

Horejsi, Charles, Cindy Garthwait, and Jim Rolando. "A Survey of Threats and Violence Directed against Child Protection Workers in a Rural State." *Child Welfare* (March, 1994): 173–179.

Irwin, Diane. "Safety Training for Human Services Professionals." *Protecting Children* 13.1 (1997): 8–10.

Rey, Lucy. "What Social Workers Need to Know about Client Violence." *Families in Society* 77 (January, 1996): 33–39.

Sheafor, Bradford, and Charles Horejsi. *Techniques and Guidelines for Social Work Practice*. 7th ed. Boston: Allyn and Bacon, 2006.

Tully, Carol, Nancy Kropf, and Janet Price. "Is the Field a Hard Hat Area? A Study of Violence in Field Placements." *Journal of Social Work Education* 29.2 (Spring, 1993): 191–199.

Weinger, Susan. *Security Risk: Preventing Client Violence against Social Workers*. Washington DC: NASW Press, 2001.

7

Communication

GOALS FOR LEARNING

- To identify the communication systems used by your agency
- To become aware of skills and guidelines for effective verbal and written communication
- To identify common sources and occasions of miscommunication and misunderstanding
- To identify barriers to effective communication

Communication is at the heart of social work practice. A social worker must be able to communicate with clients or consumers, other social workers, members of other professions (such as physicians, teachers, lawyers, and judges), agency supervisors and administrators, leaders and decision makers (such as elected officials), and with a cross section of the people who make up the community served by the agency. The social worker must be able to communicate in a one-on-one situation, within the context of a small group, and sometimes before a large audience. Moreover, the worker must be able to use several modes of communication effectively, including the written word, the spoken word, and nonverbal communication. A social worker must also be able to use a variety of communication tools effectively, including a telephone, a computer, and e-mail.

Students are often surprised at how much time social workers must devote to reading and writing. Because of the demands of written documentation, effective writing skills will help to reduce unnecessary time spent documenting your written work. Written communication may take the form of a letter, memo, case record, the minutes of a committee meeting, a lengthy formal report, or a grant proposal. The extensive use of written communication in social work requires that the worker be able to write well and read rapidly.

Effective and skilled communication is central to success in any social work setting. A variety of problems can result from insufficient, inaccurate, or somehow distorted and misunderstood communication. Even during the practicum, many of the problems that frustrate the student are fundamentally problems in the communication between the student and the field instructor or between the student and the practicum coordinator. This chapter is designed to assist students in developing essential communication skills for use in the practicum agency.

Background and Context

Communication can be defined as the process by which a person, group, or organization transmits information to another person, group, or organization. Both the sender and the receiver of information, whether on the personal or organizational level, must be skilled in both sending and receiving in order for communication to be successful.

Interpersonal communication refers to communication that involves talking, listening, and responding in ways that place an emphasis on the personal dimensions of those involved. It usually takes place in a face-to-face exchange but may occur on the telephone or in highly personalized correspondence or e-mail. Providing direct services to clients requires frequent and fairly intense interpersonal communication.

The term *organizational communication* refers to the somewhat impersonal exchange of messages and information between the various levels, departments, and divisions of an organization, and also between the organization and various individuals and groups outside the organization. As compared to other types of communication, the communication within an organization tends to be more formal and more often in written form. Moreover, the nature and flow of information within an organization is strongly influenced by lines of authority and the chain of command.

Downward communication consists of messages, directions, and instructions from those higher in the chain of command to subordinates at lower levels in the organization. The term *upward communication* refers to communication from a subordinate to those higher in the chain of command, such as when a supervisor sends a message to the agency's executive director. As a general rule, upward communication occurs less often than downward communication. This can be a source of problems within an organization because those persons lower on the chain of command often feel that they are not heard and that their communication is not valued. *Horizontal communication* refers to the exchange of messages among persons or units at the same level within the organization.

A wide variety of communication networks exists within social service agencies. Mainly, they differ in the degree to which they are centralized. In a highly centralized network, all messages must flow through some central office or person who can then control what information moves up or down. A decentralized network is characterized by an exchange of information between people and organizational levels without first passing through a particular channel or central point. As a general rule, centralized networks are faster and more accurate if the information has to do with relatively simple tasks. Decentralized networks are faster and more accurate if the communication is about complex tasks and unique activities. This type of communication network may also be more informal and feel more personal to those within an organization.

A common problem within organizations is *information overload*. This refers to frustration and miscommunication caused by an overwhelming volume of messages, instructions, and reports. A centralized communication network and highly bureaucratic organizations are especially vulnerable to information overload because so many messages must pass through all levels as they move up and down the organization.

Modern communication technology (e-mail, fax machines, cellular phones) has solved some problems caused by slow communication, but it has created others. It has probably added to the problem of information overload because it is now very easy to send a message and copies of it to many more people. E-mail encourages the use of written communication over face-to-face communication, thus eliminating the opportunity to observe nonverbal communication in order to accurately interpret a message.

Professions and organizations develop and communicate by the use of a specialized language, or jargon, as a way to simplify communication. However, this has the effect of making many of their messages unintelligible to outsiders, including students and clients. Practicum students will need to learn agency-specific terminology, acronyms, and jargon quickly in order to understand what is said and written on a daily basis.

The goal of communication is for the receiver to accurately understand the message being sent by the sender. That sounds like a simple process, but as everyone knows, communication is complex and many factors can prevent or disrupt the process. Sheafor and Horejsi (2006, 135–136) observe that communication problems develop whenever:

- We speak for others rather than let them speak for themselves.
- We do not take the time or make the effort to really listen.
- We allow prejudices, stereotypes, and presumptions to color how we interpret what others are saying.
- We keep things to ourselves because we fear others will disapprove of what we believe and feel.
- We make no attempt to communicate because we assume others already know, or should know, how we feel and what we think.
- We discourage or suppress communication by ordering, threatening, preaching, patronizing, judging, blaming, or humoring.
- We allow negative feelings about ourselves to keep us silent, fearing that we have nothing worthwhile to say and that no one will want to hear what we think or feel.

These impediments to communication can occur at the organizational level as well as at the interpersonal level. Practicum students may erroneously assume that because they are trained to use interviewing and counseling skills, they will be able to easily communicate at the organizational level. However, organizational communication has its own set of unique challenges and requires as much practice and special skill as does communication with clients.

The existence of trust between the sender and the receiver is a critical prerequisite to effective communication. To a large degree, it determines how the receiver will respond to the sender's message. There are three major barriers to the development of trust: insincerity (e.g., when managers ask for feedback from staff but do not value or listen to their opinions), time pressures (e.g., when the push to accomplish a task precludes a supervisor from hearing what the workers are saying), and defensiveness (e.g., when the manager's ego is threatened by an open discussion of agency operations).

A variety of factors can become barriers to effective communication. For example, in verbal communication the sender may speak too fast or too slow, or the receiver is distracted and does not listen. The sender may write or speak without first planning his or her message. The sender may use words that the receiver does not understand or words that mean different things to different people without clarifying how he or she defines the words.

Defensiveness and fear are also major barriers to communication. When people are in an environment in which they feel safe, accepted, and supported, they concentrate more on the content and meaning of the message, rather than spending time protecting themselves or searching for the sender's hidden agenda. Behaviors that tend to lower defenses include messages that give facts without value judgments, are spontaneous and genuine, offer mutual trust and respect, and display a willingness to consider different points of view.

Food for Thought

Communication in normal social interaction is a means by which individuals express feelings and develop relationships. In organizational life, such communication is stripped of its emotional significance. Communication becomes one-way and top-down. Language becomes a matter of technical jargon, a secretive way of maintaining control and organizational channels. Meaning is transformed into the context of organizational understandings and not human communication.

Social workers, however, prize the importance of two-way communication and are trained in the use of active listening, perception checking, paraphrasing, and giving feedback. Social workers who value interpersonal communication skills, such as the ability to express feelings and emotions, attending, genuineness, respect, and mutuality, often become confused when those skills are ignored in organizational communication. In many cases, mutuality in communication is actually precluded and is seen as dysfunctional. One-way communication is expected by those at the very top of organizations. (Brueggemann 1997, 298)

• • •

Supervisors are apt to forget the steps they followed to deepen their own insights into . . . content. Ideas that have become obvious to them in their current practice may not be simple or obvious to their staffs. . . . Unless supervisors work at it, they can forget how they had to construct, element by element, their understanding of a complex construct such as contracting. They believe they can hand over the years of learning and are surprised to discover that a student or staff member is having great difficulty constructing even a simple version of the idea. As learners who themselves have ventured into this subject area, have discovered some of the shortcuts, and are aware of some of the pitfalls, supervisors can

guide their staff members and make their journey more certain and quicker, but they cannot take the journey for them. (Shulman 1993, 159)

• • •

There are several problems with paper. One is that there is so much of it around that most of us are . . . wasting lots of time dealing with it. . . . Another problem with paper is that from time to time you have to write on it. And whenever you do, you put a little bit of yourself down on the paper to be examined and judged by someone else. Solely on the basis of what you set down on paper, someone may decide whether you . . . have exercised your professional judgment wisely.

There is something fleeting about a judgment or opinion that is expressed orally; it is less available for scrutiny than is the written word and it will probably be less far reaching in its impact. But ideas can be transformed by writing. Once put down on paper, mere suggestions or daily routines become rules and policies. And one person's (perhaps ill-informed) opinion becomes the last word on the subject.

So . . . you cannot afford to be a poor writer. If the words you put down on paper are not clear to your reader, they can take on a life of their own that is contrary to your intent. Or they can die on the spot, when you want them to come alive and make the reader take action. (Kantz and Mercer 1991, 221)

• • •

As a clinician, you cannot afford to be careless or haphazard about what you say or write. You must be aware of all the subtleties of language and learn to say what you mean. This is especially true of written reports, because once a report is written others may read it without you being present to explain, clarify, or correct mistakes. (Baird 2005, 106).

Effective communication is impacted by physical environmental factors. Examples include background noise, too much distance between sender and receiver, physical crowding that interferes with privacy, rooms with poor acoustics, uncomfortable room temperatures, and uncomfortable chairs that make paying attention difficult.

Dress, grooming, and image have a significant impact on communication—a fact well known to business people and public figures. Agencies may establish a dress code as a way of improving communication with certain people and groups in the community in order to avoid creating a barrier to communication based on social workers' dress and appearance.

Many sociopsychological factors can become barriers to communication. Examples include the sender's or the receiver's moods, emotional state, level of stress, defensiveness, and lack of trust. One's expectations have a great deal to do with communication. In general, we hear what we hope to hear and pay most attention to positions and information with which we agree. We also have a difficult time accepting criticism or negative feedback. Finally, previous ineffective communication between social workers, coworkers, or clients can color subsequent communications.

Communication is also influenced by such factors as one's life experiences, culture and ethnicity, familiarity with the language being used, social class, religious beliefs, and education. The symbols we use in language do not have universal meanings—they are influenced by our background, experiences, and the cultural content of the exchanges between sender and receiver. (See Chapter 12 on diversity for additional information on cross-cultural communication.)

Guidance and Direction

Good communication skills, both verbal and written, are of central importance in social work practice. Do your best to learn communication skills now because you will need them throughout your career. You will learn to appreciate the challenge of developing these skills and develop methods by which you can monitor the effectiveness of your communication.

Carefully observe the patterns and processes of communication in your agency. For example, when you attend a staff meeting or committee meeting, consider the following questions:

- Who selects topics for discussion and develops the agenda?
- Who initiates communication and who introduces new topics for discussion?
- Who are the active communicators? Who are the quiet ones?
- Who speaks to whom? Who interrupts whom?
- Who decides when discussion of a topic has ended?
- Is there a certain hierarchy that affects the direction of the messages?
- Are the meetings formal or informal? Are the meetings structured by an agenda and the use of *Robert's Rules of Order* or are they unstructured and free-wheeling?
- What matters are appropriate for discussion? Are the topics related only to work or do people also share personal information and talk about their families and leisure-time activities?
- Which staff members work hard at listening and understanding others? Which ones seem quick to assume they know what others are trying to say without really listening?

In nearly every organization you will have the opportunity to observe effective and ineffective, functional and dysfunctional communication. Take note of which styles and methods work and which do not. Consider why communication may be especially difficult and flawed at times. Knowing some of the pitfalls of communication may keep you from making these same mistakes. Major pitfalls to communication include the following:

- People who are busy and hurried sometimes forget or neglect to communicate with those who are in need of a certain message or information.
- People take shortcuts in communication to save time.
- People make erroneous assumptions about how much other people know and do not know.
- Communication often must go through several levels within an agency, and the meaning or clarity of the message can change at each level.
- Personal communication styles vary, and people may not be able to adapt to or appreciate other styles.
- People do not see the need to share information, and those who need it may not receive it.

- The message itself is confusing or flawed in logic and content.
- People do not feel empowered or listened to, so they withdraw and avoid communication with others.
- Differences in culture, gender, age, or socioeconomic status can impact effective communication in subtle ways that may increase the chances of misunderstanding between parties.

Sheafor and Horejsi (2006, 140) offer the following suggestions as ways to improve your listening skills:

- Stop talking. You cannot listen when you are talking.
- Put the message sender at ease. Do what you can to lessen his or her anxiety. Remove distractions (e.g., close the door).
- Demonstrate, verbally and nonverbally, that you want to listen. Really pay attention.
- Be patient with the message sender. Do not interrupt.
- Ask questions if it will help you understand or help the sender clarify his or her message.
- Control your emotions. Do not criticize or argue, for that will erect a barrier to further communication.

When sending a message, follow these rules:

- Use clear, simple language. Speak distinctly and not too fast.
- Pay attention to your body language, making sure it is congruent with your message. Maintain appropriate eye contact and utilize gestures.
- Do not overwhelm or overload the receiver with information. Break up a lengthy or complex message into several parts so it can be more easily followed and understood.
- Ask for comments, questions, or feedback so you will know whether you are being understood. (Sheafor and Horejsi 2006, 140)

Depending on your practicum assignments, you will probably be surprised at the amount of documentation required in agency practice. You will learn to write memos, letters, case notes, assessments, treatment plans, reports, and perhaps public relations material and grant proposals. At various times your writing will be used to document important events or actions, provide information to the general public, persuade someone to take some action, provide a base for legal action, or report to a funding source. First and foremost, all such written materials must be clear, accurate, and as concise as possible. Follow these guidelines in your written communication:

- Be sure you understand who your audience is, what they need to know, and how they want the information presented.
- Organize your material before starting to write, and recognize that you may need to make several revisions.
- Use language that is professional, but do not overuse jargon.
- Avoid slang and language that could be seen as judgmental, derogatory, or that could be interpreted in more than one way.
- Use direct, clear language rather than tentative, insipid words.
- Anticipate the reader's questions and answer them.
- Adhere to the KISS principle (Keep It Short and Simple).
- Use the format required by your agency.
- Make copies of all written communication that is sent out of the office, including correspondence, reports, and grant proposals.
- Make any modifications suggested by your supervisor.

Agencies differ somewhat in their standards and expectations. Therefore, it is important to ask your field instructor for specific directions on how to prepare work-related written materials. Also, ask your field instructor for feedback regarding the quality of your writing. Doing so will demonstrate your openness to learning and willingness to receive constructive criticism. It will also help you to better understand your strengths and limitations and help you avoid patterns of ineffective communication.

Because they want to meet agency expectations for good written documentation, students often wonder how much detail is required. A good guideline to follow regarding documentation about clients is to include enough detail to bring the client to life for anyone reading it, but not to overwhelm the reader with unnecessary and extraneous information. When writing about programs or client systems, remember to be clear, convincing, and attuned to the needs, requirements, or motives of those who may be the readers.

Because computer systems are used to record a wide variety of very personal information about clients, be very aware of confidentiality of client records, and learn to anticipate potential breaches in confidentiality that could occur when sharing information between agencies. Learn what can be shared and what cannot. Learn how to use release of information documents that demonstrate clients' permission and approval to share information with other professionals or agencies that need this information. Remember that even though clients waive some of their rights to confidentiality in order to be eligible for third-party payments for services, this does not mean that they understand the degree to which their confidentiality may be compromised. Informed consent means that clients understand the impact of what they are signing or agreeing to, and it is often the social worker's responsibility to advocate for clients so that they truly do understand and agree.

Be cautious with the use of computerized client database information, faxes, voice mail, and e-mail, so that client confidentiality is always guarded. Be aware of the possibilities that each of these forms of communication can be very helpful to social workers and managed care organizations, but potentially very harmful to clients if confidentiality is compromised.

Finally, learn to communicate via e-mail, voice mail, and fax. Pay attention to the advantages and disadvantages of each method, and know that they provide convenience and accessibility, but do not substitute for face-to-face communication. Do not use them as replacements for speaking directly with people if that would be more appropriate or effective.

Developing Communication Skills: A Workbook Activity

1. What are the major forms of written communication expected of social workers in your agency (e.g., assessments, treatment plans, reports, memos, letters, grant proposals)?

    _____

    _____

    _____

2. Do social workers in your agency receive special training in the use of written communication (e.g., use of medical terminology, report writing, grant proposal writing, correspondence)?

    _____

    Can you participate in such training?

    _____

3. Does your agency have specific policies regarding written communication (e.g., deadlines for completion, suggested or required formats, and supervisory review of documentation)?

    _____

    If yes, list those of special relevance to your work assignments.

    _____

    _____

    _____

4. Do the above mentioned policies contribute to more effective organizational communication?

    _____

    Why or why not?

    _____

    _____

5. What do social workers in your agency identify as the most common types of communication problems within the agency?

    _____

    _____

    _____

6. What do they see as the causes of these communication problems?

_____

_____

_____

7. What are the effects of these communication problems on agency operations and clients?

_____

_____

_____

8. What types of communication styles, patterns, and problems have you observed in the following situations?

   Case conferences

_____

_____

   Meetings with agency administrators

_____

_____

   Meetings with board members or funding sources

_____

_____

   Meetings between you and your supervisor

_____

_____

9. How do your agency's chain of command and organizational chart affect communication patterns and the flow of information? Is communication between management and staff mostly one way and from the top down, or does it flow easily both ways?

_____

_____

_____

_____

10. In your agency, how are the patterns and the effectiveness of communication affected by the following factors?

Titles and positions of message senders and receivers

_____

_____

_____

Level of professional experience of message senders and receivers

_____

_____

_____

Gender of message senders and receivers

_____

_____

_____

Racial, cultural, or ethnic background of message senders and receivers

_____

_____

_____

11. How might your cultural background, life experiences, gender, and special training enhance or limit your ability to communicate with agency clients or agency staff?

_____

_____

_____

_____

12. What steps can you take to enhance your verbal communication skills?

_____

_____

_____

13. What steps can you take to enhance your writing skills?

_____

_____

_____

Additional notes and comments:

_____

_____

_____

_____

_____

_____

Suggested Learning Activities

- Ask your field instructor to show you examples of both well-written and poorly written letters, memos, reports, and case records. Examine these materials and observe how writing style, organization, and choice of words affect their quality. Compare your written work to these examples.
- Rewrite a report you have written (three to five pages in length), using only half the space. Pay attention to eliminating unnecessary words. Shorten your sentences. Eliminate all repetition of content.
- Seek opportunities to make a speech or presentation before either agency staff members or a community group.
- Schedule time with your field instructor to focus exclusively on the quality of your oral and written communication and identify specific steps you can take to improve your skills in communication.

Additional Suggestions and Hints

- In Sheafor and Horejsi (2006), read the sections entitled "Report Writing" (182–184), "Letter Writing" (184–185) "Effective Telephone Communication" (185–187), and "Using Information Technology" (187–190).

Selected Bibliography

Brueggemann, William. *The Practice of Macro Social Work*. Chicago: Nelson-Hall, 1997.

Edwards, Richard L., John A. Yankey, and Mary A. Altpeter. *Skills for Efffective Management of Nonprofit Organizations*. Washington DC: NASW Press, 1998.

Evans, William J., Daniel H. Honemann, Henry M. Robert, and Thomas J. Balch. *Robert's Rules of Order Newly Revised in Brief*. Boulder, CO: Perseus Books, 2004.

Sheafor, Bradford, and Charles Horejsi. *Techniques and Guidelines for Social Work Practice*. 7th ed. Boston: Allyn and Bacon, 2006.

Shulman, Lawrence. *Interactional Supervision*. Washington DC: NASW Press, 1993.

8

The Agency Context of Practice

GOALS FOR LEARNING

- To understand your agency's mission, goals, and objectives
- To understand your agency's organization and administrative structure
- To understand your agency's sources of funding and operating budget
- To analyze how your agency's history, structure, and administrative procedures may affect its ability to provide effective services and programs
- To become aware of community perceptions of your agency
- To identify ways in which your agency relates to and interacts with other agencies within the overall social welfare system
- To identify changes in your agency that could improve services to its clients

The daily activities and decisions of a social worker are heavily influenced by the nature and purpose of the organization that employs him or her. Throughout its history, social work has been an agency-based profession. A majority of social workers are employed by agencies, and they provide their services within an organizational context. Given this reality, a practicum student must strive to examine and understand his or her practicum agency's mission, goals, structure, funding sources, and level of effectiveness.

Background and Context

The word *agency* refers to an organization that is authorized or sanctioned to act in the place of others. An agency performs activities that some larger group or organization desires and is willing to fund. This larger entity might be a community, a church, or a governmental body.

Most social workers are employed by human services agencies that fall into two broad categories: private nonprofit agencies and public agencies. Others are employed by private, for-profit organizations such as hospitals or drug treatment facilities. In addition, some social workers create private practice organizations.

Public agencies are created by a legislative body made up of elected officials (e.g., a state legislature, the U.S. Congress, or county commissioners). Such agencies are funded by tax dollars and possibly by fees charged for service. The purpose and goals of public agencies are described in legal codes and government regulations. Elected officials are ultimately responsible for the operation of public agencies and staff members of public agencies are considered government employees.

Private nonprofit agencies (also called *voluntary agencies*) are created by a legal process known as incorporation, which has the effect of creating a legal entity known as a *nonprofit corporation*. These corporations are given nonprofit status under section 501(c)3 of the Internal Revenue Service guidelines for charitable and nonprofit organizations. This type of agency is governed by a board of directors that represents the interests of the community or the group that wants the agency to exist and supports its work. The basic responsibilities of a *board of directors* (or *board of trustees*) are to establish the agency's mission and direction, set policies for its operation, set and approve budgets, ensure adequate funds for the agency, maintain a communication link with the wider community, and hire and regularly evaluate the executive director.

The basic responsibilities of an agency's *executive director* are to implement policy set by the governing board, hire staff and regularly evaluate their performance, make programmatic decisions, and direct and monitor day-to-day operations.

Some private nonprofit agencies are called *sectarian agencies,* which means that they are affiliated with or operated by religious organizations (e.g., Jewish Community Services or Catholic Social Services). The term *membership agency* is used to describe an agency (e.g., YMCA) that derives some of its budget from membership fees and in which members are involved in setting policy.

In contrast to a public agency or a private nonprofit agency, a *for-profit agency* is a business corporation that sells a set of services and is designed and operated to yield a profit for investors and stockholders. Increasingly, not-for-profit hospitals, treatment centers, and nursing homes are being purchased by large corporations and operated as for-profit organizations.

Many social workers are employed in *host settings* in which the organization's primary mission or purpose is something other than the delivery of social services. Examples include schools and hospitals where the primary missions are the provision of educational and medical services. In these host settings, the social worker must work with many other professionals (e.g., doctors, nurses, physical therapists, teachers, or school psychologists) and may be under the supervision of someone who has only a limited understanding of social work and possibly holds professional values somewhat different from those of a social worker.

Private nonprofit agencies are funded by private contributions, by grants and contracts, and sometimes by fees charged for the services they provide. Some conduct their own fund-raising activities and some receive funds from the local United Way organization. Private agencies may receive tax dollars indirectly through contracts with public agencies.

Both public and private agencies may establish *advisory boards* that provide advice and guidance to the executive director or to the board of directors. As suggested by the name, an advisory board does not have the authority to make final decisions or set policy. It simply serves in an advisory capacity. An advisory board often has members who are agency clients; this is intended to solicit client input and perspective on agency policies and services.

A typical social agency is designed and structured to provide one or more *social programs*. A social program is an organized and planned activity designed to accomplish one of the following:

- Remediation of an existing problem (i.e., address a problem such as child abuse, unemployment, or delinquency)
- Enhancement of social functioning (i.e., improve functioning when no significant problem exists, such as programs of marriage enrichment)
- Prevention of a social problem (i.e., prevent a problem from developing, such as reducing teen pregnancy)

According to Morales and Sheafor (2004), there are three categories of social programs:

> *Social provisions* involve giving tangible goods (e.g., money, food, clothing, and housing) to persons in need. *Social services* include intangible services (e.g., counseling, therapy, and learning experiences) intended to help people resolve and/or prevent problems. Finally, *social action* programs are concerned with changing aspects of the social environment to make it more responsive to people's needs and wants. (18–19)

Social programs may use one or more broad strategies to achieve their purposes:

- *Socialization*—assisting and encouraging people to understand, learn, and abide by the fundamental norms of society
- *Social integration*—encouraging and helping people to interact more effectively with other individuals and with the various social systems or resources they need in order to function effectively and cope with special problems
- *Social control*—monitoring and placing restrictions on those who exhibit behavior that is self-destructive or dangerous to others
- *Social change*—expanding the number and types of life-enhancing opportunities available to people, taking actions that will improve the environment in which people must function, and taking action necessary to reduce or eliminate negative and destructive forces in their social environment

Social agencies and the staff who work in them vary in terms of their attitudes toward their clients. The theories and models that underlie the services provided will often result in differing views of the desired relationship between social workers and clients. Some may view their clients essentially as objects to be manipulated or processed, others tend to view clients as recipients of services, and still others view clients as partners, experts, and resources to the helping process. Such varying attitudes bring forth different behaviors from the professionals. For example:

> *Clients as objects:* Professionals are the experts and know what should be done; clients are expected and encouraged to do what the professionals decide is best for them.
>
> *Clients as recipients:* Professionals possess and control the services needed by the clients; the clients are expected to use the services given to them in a cooperative and appreciative manner.
>
> *Clients as resources:* Professionals presume that the clients are in the best position to know what they need and what will and will not work. They actively solicit the clients' ideas on the problems they face and on possible solutions. The clients' thoughts and decisions are respected.

An agency's budget describes anticipated income and expenses for a given period of time, usually one or two years. The common categories of expense include: salaries, employee benefits, payroll taxes, consultation fees, staff training, malpractice insurance, supplies and equipment, telephone, printing and copying, rent, property insurance, staff travel, and membership dues. Once a budget has been set or approved, the agency administrator has only limited authority to shift funds from one category to another.

It is important to understand that the donations, grants, and legislative allocations received by an agency typically have many "strings attached." In other words, the money is given or allocated to the agency for a specified purpose and cannot be spent for another purpose. In addition, the agency's acceptance of money from a certain source (e.g., United Way or a federal agency) may require that it adhere to certain rules, regulations, accounting, and auditing procedures that add administrative costs. When much of an agency's money is earmarked for very specific purposes, the agency has limited capacity to modify its programs and little flexibility in responding to emergencies or unanticipated expenses.

Many human services agencies are quite bureaucratic, especially public agencies. Bureaucracies are characterized by:

- A clear chain of command in communication and assigned authority.
- An organizational structure consisting of a vertical hierarchy with numerous units (e.g., divisions and departments), each of which has a designated leader (e.g., an administrator or supervisor) who is responsible for that unit's operation and who has authority over those working in the unit.
- A set of written rules, policies, and guidelines that outline the procedures to be followed in performing the work of the unit.
- A division of labor giving each employee a specific job to perform. The nature of this job is outlined in a written job description. Everyone in the organization knows (or can find out) what the other employees are to be doing in their jobs.
- Supervision of each employee's work.
- An emphasis on formal communication, written documentation, and record keeping.
- A higher level of job security than that which exists in a business or in nonprofit organizations.

Some agencies have developed less bureaucratic structures in an effort to be more responsive to clients and to their ever-changing environments. They often use feminist, partnership, and empowerment principles; seek to involve their clients in the work of the agency; promote shared power and decision making at all levels; develop flexible guidelines and approaches; and strive to individualize and customize their interventions and services. As a general rule, these agencies are more flexible and provide a less stressful environment for the social workers employed by them. Agencies that operate on these principles often are private, smaller organizations that do not need to be bureaucratic in order to be efficient or to provide equal services to all clients.

All organizations, including businesses, universities, hospitals, and human services agencies, develop policies and procedures as ways of dealing with recurring situations, problems, and questions. These are written into a document usually called a *policy manual*. In a social agency, this document may be called the *agency manual*. Basically, it is a compilation of statements intended to guide the day-to-day activities of social workers and other staff employed by the agency. The content of the manual will reflect the mission and goals of the agency and, usually, certain social policies (see discussion of social policies in Chapter 11).

The content of an agency's manual is shaped, directly and indirectly, by many external forces. They include:

- Federal laws, rules, and regulations that could impact agency function
- State laws, rules, and regulations that could impact agency function
- Court decisions and legal opinions relevant to the work of the agency
- Accrediting bodies (e.g., Joint Commission on the Accreditation of Health Care Organizations) that require adherence to standards and requirements
- Formal interagency agreements that specify the ways in which collaborative work will be done

Food for Thought

Study your agency. Learn about its history, mission, goals, structure, culture, funding sources, budget, and decision-making processes. Strive to understand the special challenges your agency faces and the external economic, political, and community forces that push and pull it in one direction or another. Having such knowledge is a form of power that can be used to address various organizational problems, and it will help you to place your specific work and assignments within a wider context. (Sheafor and Horejsi 2006, 596)

• • •

Beyond formal and informal policies and procedures, discriminatory barriers are embedded in the "deep structure" of organizations. (Gardella and Haynes 2004, 48)

• • •

We live in an era in which organizational life is characterized by shifting priorities, changing patterns in the allocation of resources, and competing demands. As nonprofit managers we often must function in an environment of heightened demands for our services, higher expectations for accountability, and increased competition for funding, all the while being buffeted by change. Indeed, it seems the only constant in management today is change. (Edwards, Yankey, and Altpeter 1998, 5)

• • •

It doesn't take much time or effort to identify the primary culture of an organization. Nevertheless, culture is not easily influenced. It is not particularly permeable to either internal or external influences. It possesses all the properties of a norm—that is, it has a codified set of expectations, and it uses sanctions to enforce the culture and to resist change. While it isn't exactly the same dynamic, organizations fear and resist the unknown just as individuals do. They will often fight to maintain the status quo. (Meenaghan, Gibbons, and McNutt 2005, 33–34)

- Purchase of service contracts
- Requirements established by local fund-raising organizations that support the agency (e.g., the United Way)
- Requirements of managed care organizations
- Contracts with employee unions

An agency manual must be constantly updated in response to changes in policies and procedures developed over time, changes in legislation, court orders that give new interpretations to existing laws, and to new governmental rules and regulations.

In addition to a manual of policies and procedures, most agencies have developed an *employee handbook*. It typically contains information on the organization's mission, purpose, and chain of command, but focuses mostly on personnel policies (i.e., performance evaluations, advancement and promotion, salary, benefits, and vacations) and on behaviors by employees that are considered inappropriate or unethical within the organization.

As you enter into the life and activities of an organization, you must be alert to the fact that all organizations have both a formal and an informal structure. The *formal* or *official structure* of an agency is described by organizational charts, policy manuals, and documents that explain the structure and function of various organizational units and the official chain of command. The term *informal structure* refers to various networks of employees and unofficial channels of communication based mostly on friendships and personal relationships. This informal structure is sometimes cynically described by staff as "the way the agency really works." It becomes apparent only after working in the agency for an extended period of time.

Rae and Nicholas-Wolosuk (2003, 13) remind us that there is a difference between *organizational climate* and *organizational culture*. Positive organizational climate attributes include mutual respect, teamwork, and effective communication, all of which contribute to a good working environment and ultimately to high quality services to clients. Organizational culture refers to the values and norms that motivate and drive the organization, that are generally internalized by the social workers employed there, and that guide the way services are provided.

Guidance and Direction

Because your practicum agency will be a learning laboratory, expect to learn a great deal. It will be a laboratory in which you will develop professional social work skills, observe other social workers providing services, and learn how agencies are organized and structured to address social needs and problems. Although every agency is different, you will begin to understand how organizations are administered and managed, learn about the common problems of organizations, and learn how to work effectively with others within an organizational context.

Agencies are always changing. Notice how shifts, increases, or cuts in funding cause changes in the services that can be provided. Observe how public attitudes and political forces shape the ways in which your agency functions. Your agency may go through some significant changes during your practicum. You may even observe the birth of a new agency, or perhaps the dismantling of one that has lost its support or outlived its usefulness. You will learn about the dynamic nature of a human services organization if you closely observe the functioning of your own agency and that of others in the community.

Learn about your agency's history, including the reasons why it was established, when it began, and how it has evolved over time. Find out if your agency began as a grassroots effort to address a social need or problem, and if so, whether it has changed its focus over the years of its existence.

Inquire about how your agency may have modified its original mission, changed its structure, and adapted to a changing community and political context. This will help you understand how agencies survive within an ever-changing environment and continually adjust and adapt their efforts to address the changing social problems and needs on which they focus.

Find out whether your agency was established as a response to state or federal legislation, and how that legislation has guided its development. If it began as a project of a religious organization, try to understand how specific values and religious beliefs may have influenced the agency's formation and operation.

Ask your field instructor about external forces that shape or limit your agency, such as funding priorities and sources, community attitudes, client feedback, regulatory bodies, political pressure, and research findings. Ask how much influence internal forces such as staff suggestions, changes in personnel, and staff morale have on the agency.

Read agency-related materials written by agency staff, including policies and procedures manuals, grant proposals, minutes of board meetings, financial reports, and public relations brochures. Each one will reveal a different facet of your agency, including its reason for being, its mission, its vision, the theories underpinning its programs, its accountability to funding sources, its problems, its effectiveness, its way of attracting financial supporters, and its method of attracting clients or consumers.

Notice how your agency's type (e.g., public or private, for-profit or nonprofit) affects its work. For instance, public agencies will tend to be quite attentive to the decisions of elected officials, sectarian agencies will reflect the values of the religious organizations that sponsor them, and for-profit organizations may at times focus on making a profit for their owners to the potential detriment of clients.

Observe how staff members are affected by the organizational structure of your agency. Social workers in bureaucratic settings often become frustrated because their agencies are overly structured, are unable to individualize interventions as much as the social workers think they should, and resist change. On the other hand, watch how some social workers seem able to provide high quality and personalized services to their clients, even within a system with many rules and regulations.

If your agency is less bureaucratic, watch to see if this structure has reduced staff frustration and results in services that are more individualized and responsive to clients. If possible, compare your agency's structure with that of another agency with a very different structure, observing how their structures affect both staff and clients.

Your agency will use one or more specific theories, models, or approaches in the design and provision of its services and programs. Determine what they are, and why they were chosen. Does your agency use a behavioral, psychodynamic, or family systems approach to counseling? Does your agency invest its resources in prevention, early intervention, or rehabilitation? Is the approach therapeutic or correctional? Does your agency hire generalist social workers or those with specializations in certain fields of practice? Does your agency see itself as working toward social change? Review courses you have taken and books you have read to help you understand why a particular approach was chosen by your agency to address the problem or concern identified. Consider what other theoretical approaches might also be used.

Become familiar with your agency's methods of evaluating its programs and services. Find out how your agency assesses its effectiveness, determines whether it is reaching its goals, measures client or community satisfaction, and decides whether it is making a difference. Your agency may use formal or informal methods of evaluation, process or outcome measures, and collect quantitative or qualitative data. Ask your field instructor whether he or she thinks these approaches or evaluation tools are valid and adequate. Ask what methods he or she would ideally recommend using to evaluate services provided enough time, money, and staff were available.

Agency Analysis: A Workbook Activity

1. Does your agency have an official mission statement? If yes, what is it?

_____

_____

_____

_____

2. What are your agency's goals and objectives?

_____

_____

_____

_____

3. List your agency's major programs and services.

_____

_____

_____

_____

4. Who is your agency's chief executive officer (i.e., director, administrator, or executive director)? How is this person hired or appointed?

_____

5. Is your agency a public agency? A private agency? A nonprofit agency? A for-profit agency?

_____

6. If your agency is a public agency, is it a federal, state, county, or city agency?

_____

7. If your agency is a public agency, what specific legislation or statute created the agency and assigned responsibilities to it? (Cite legal code.)

_____

_____

_____

_____

8. If your practicum is in a private, nonprofit agency, how many people serve on the board of directors? Do people want to serve on the agency's board or does the agency find it difficult to attract new board members?

   _____

   _____

9. If your practicum is in a private agency, how might the members of the board of directors be described in terms of such variables as their age, sex, ethnicity, race, socioeconomic class, occupation, and personal experiences with the agency's programs and services?

   _____

   _____

   _____

10. What percentage of the board of directors fall into the following categories:

    _____% Human services professionals

    _____% Business or community representatives

    _____% Current or former agency clients or consumers

11. If your practicum is in a private sectarian agency, with what religious organization or denomination is it affiliated?

    _____

12. If your practicum agency is a membership organization, how does someone become a member?

    _____

    _____

    _____

13. If it is a for-profit organization, who are its owners? For whom is it to make a profit (e.g., stockholders, another corporation, a partnership)?

    _____

    _____

    _____

14. Does your agency have an advisory board? If yes, what is its purpose? Who serves on this advisory board?

    _____

    _____

    _____

15. When was your agency first created or established? Has the agency or organization undergone a major reorganization within the last ten years?

    _____

16. What is your agency's overall or total operating budget for the current year?

    $ _____

    What is the budget for your department or program area?

    $ _____

17. Is the agency's budget or income fairly predictable and stable from year to year, or is it uncertain and unpredictable?

    _____

18. About what percentage of the budget is derived from each of the following sources:

    _____% Allocations by the U.S. Congress

    _____% Allocations by the state legislature

    _____% Allocations by the county commissioners

    _____% Allocations by the city council

    _____% Allocations by the United Way or other combined giving program

    _____% Grant from a federal agency

    _____% Grant from a state agency

    _____% Grant from a private foundation

    _____% Fees paid by the clients or consumers of services

    _____% Fees paid by a third party (e.g., insurance)

    _____% Purchase of a service contract

    _____% Private donation made directly to the agency

    _____% Other

19. What types of problems, concerns, or needs bring people to your agency or cause them to be brought to the attention of your agency (e.g., child abuse, delinquency, poverty, health concerns)?

    _____

    _____

    _____

20. Do the clients served by your agency often fall into certain demographic categories such as age, sex, ethnicity, socioeconomic class, level of education, religion, or language?

_____

_____

21. What statistics are recorded on a regular basis by agency personnel (e.g., number of clients served each month, number of cases opened and closed, or characteristics of clients)?

_____

_____

22. How does the agency determine if it is effective (e.g., recidivism, client's completion of treatment plans, number of clients served, level of client satisfaction, rate legislation passed, objectives achieved, social change)?

_____

_____

_____

23. Do your agency's clients or consumers participate in the evaluation process? If yes, in what way?

_____

_____

_____

24. Is your agency required to submit reports to a state or federal agency regarding its programs and services?

_____

If yes, what is the nature and the purpose of those reports?

_____

_____

_____

25. Is your agency regularly subjected to on-site inspections, surveys, or reviews by personnel from an oversight or regulatory body?

_____

If yes, what is the purpose of these reviews?

_____

_____

26. Is your agency accredited by a national organization (e.g., Joint Commission on the Accreditation of Health Care Organizations and Commission on Accreditation of Rehabilitation Facilities) or licensed by a state organization?

    _____

    If yes, what is the name of this accrediting body? How often is your agency reviewed by this accrediting body? How does your agency prepare for these reviews?

    _____

    _____

    _____

27. What community agencies frequently refer clients to your agency?

    _____

    _____

    _____

28. To what agencies does your agency frequently refer its clients?

    _____

    _____

    _____

29. Does your agency compete with other agencies for funding?

    _____

    If yes, with what other agencies?

    _____

    _____

30. In what interagency planning and coordinating bodies is your agency an active participant?

    _____

    _____

31. Of the professionals employed by your agency (division, department, or program), about what percentage have the following types and levels of education:

    _____ % DSW or Ph.D. in social work

    _____ % Doctoral degree in field other than social work

    _____ % Master's degree in social work

_____ % Master's degree in field other than social work

_____ % Bachelor's degree in social work

_____ % Bachelor's degree in field other than social work

_____ % A.A. degree in human services

_____ % Other

32. Do the employees in your agency belong to a union? If so, what is its name?

_____

If yes, what union represents the agency employees? In what ways does the existence of a union affect the operation of the agency and staff rights and benefits?

_____

_____

_____

_____

33. How do staff members describe the state of morale among agency personnel? What factors contribute to high or low morale? What is the rate of staff turnover?

_____

_____

_____

34. What efforts or programs are in place within the agency to help reduce job-related stress and worker burnout?

_____

_____

_____

35. Are the salaries paid by the agency lower, about the same, or higher than those paid by similar agencies in the community?

_____

36. To what extent and in what ways, if any, are unpaid volunteers used within your agency?

_____

_____

_____

37. Is the agency meeting its mission?

_____

_____

38. How effective is the agency in dealing with diversity?

_____

_____

_____

Additional notes and comments:

_____

_____

_____

_____

_____

_____

Suggested Learning Activities

- Study your agency's organizational chart. Locate on this chart your practicum supervisor and the department or unit in which he or she works.
- Ask your supervisor or other administrative personnel to explain how the agency's budget is established. Also ask about the problems faced by the agency in securing the funds it needs.
- Attend meetings of the agency's board of directors or advisory board and consider how the topics discussed relate to the agency's mission, goals, programs, and funding.
- Examine your agency's monthly, quarterly, or annual reports to better understand your agency's goals and performance.
- Find out how ordinary citizens or the general public view your agency. Speak with friends and acquaintances who know little about social work or the human services in your community and ask what they know or have heard about your agency.
- Attend public meetings sponsored by the United Way organization or other social welfare planning groups in order to better understand how your agency fits into the overall social welfare system.
- Accompany a client applying for services at another agency and identify attitudes reflected in how agency staff treat clients and handle client requests.
- Read about the Appreciative Inquiry approach to organizational change at David Cooperider's website (www.ovation.net.com/learning.htm). Click on Appreciative Inquiry Learning Tools.
- Visit other agencies that provide similar services to those of your agency and compare approaches and programs.

Additional Suggestions and Hints

- Ask for instruction and guidance on agency procedures, format and protocol related to record keeping, record storage, and client confidentiality.
- Collect a set of agency pamphlets, brochures, newsletters, and other materials used to inform the public about your agency and its services.
- In Sheafor and Horejsi (2006), read the sections entitled ""Preparing a Budget" (448–451) and "The Process of Agency Planning" (365–368).

Selected Bibliography

Cooperider, David, and Suresh Srivasta. *Appreciative Management and Leadership.* San Francisco: Jossey-Bass, 1990.

Edwards, Richard L., John A. Yankey, and Mary A. Altpeter. *Effective Management of Nonprofit Organizations.* Washington DC: NASW Press, 1998.

Gardella, Lorrie Greenhouse, and Karen S. Haynes. *A Dream and a Plan: A Woman's Path to Leadership in the Human Services.* NASW Press, 2004.

Haas, Richard N. *The Power to Persuade: How to Be Effective in Government, the Public Sector, or Any Unruly Organization.* Boston: Houghton-Mifflin, 1994.

Meenaghan, Thomas M., W. Eugene Gibbons, and John G. McNutt. *Generalist Practice in Larger Settings: Knowledge and Skill Concepts.* 2nd ed. Chicago: Lyceum Books, 2005.

Morales, Armando, and Bradford Sheafor. *Social Work: A Profession of Many Faces*. 10th ed. Boston: Allyn and Bacon, 2004.

Netting, F. Ellen, Peter Kettner, and Steven McMurtry. *Social Work Macro Practice*. 3rd ed. New York: Longman, 2004.

Rae, Ann, and Wanda Nicholas-Wolosuk. *Changing Agency Policy: An Incremental Approach*. Boston: Allyn and Bacon, 2003.

Weinbach, Robert. *The Social Worker as Manager: A Practical Guide to Success*. 4th ed. Boston: Allyn and Bacon, 2003.

9 | The Community Context of Practice

GOALS FOR LEARNING

- To identify and analyze community resources and needs
- To understand the impact of the community on the social functioning of clients
- To understand community forces that impede or support social change
- To develop community analysis and organization skills

Practicum agencies exist in and are influenced by the communities of which they are a part. Because of this, it is important to study the community in which your practicum agency is located. First, it is obvious that agencies do not exist in a vacuum. In fact, an agency's mission, programs, and operation are often a reflection of the community's characteristics, such as its values, politics, history, and special problems.

Second, most of your clients live and work in this community. It is not possible to understand your clients without understanding their wider social environment and both the positive and negative conditions and forces within that environment. If you work within a direct services agency, the client assessments and intervention plans you develop must consider your client's interactions with others in the community, as well as the resources available in the community.

Third, your informal study of the community will allow you to begin identifying unmet human needs as well as the gaps in the service network that should be addressed in order to better serve the people of the community. Finally, by gathering information about the community's values, history, power structure, economic base, demographics, and decision-making processes, you will be able to identify those groups or individuals who have the power and influence to either facilitate or block needed social change within the community.

Learning about a community takes time and effort. However, you will find this to be an invaluable and interesting experience. You will become fascinated as you begin to observe and understand the interplay between the functioning of individuals and families and their neighborhood and community. If your practicum is in an agency concerned mostly with micro-level practice, you will soon see how your clients' lives are either enriched or harmed by community factors. If your practicum is in an organization heavily involved in macro-level practice, you will come to understand that every community has its own personality, and that in order to deal effectively with social problems and bring about needed social change, you must understand and appreciate that uniqueness.

Background and Context

The term *community* refers to a group of people brought together by physical proximity or by a common identity based on shared experiences, interests, or culture. There are two major types of communities: communities of interest and identification and communities of place or location.

A *community of interest and identification* can be described as a group of individuals who share a sense of identity and belonging because they share a characteristic, interest, or life experience such as ethnicity, language, religion, sexual orientation, or occupation. We are referring to this type of community when we speak of the social work community, the business community, the gay community, the African American community, the Islamic community, the Catholic community, the university community, and so forth.

The second type of community, a *community of place or location,* is defined mostly by geography and specified boundaries. Such communities include neighborhoods, suburbs, barrios, towns, and cities. The boundaries of a community of place might be a legal definition, a river, or a street. They may have formal or informal names such as Woodlawn, the South Bronx, Orange County, the Blackfeet Indian Reservation, the university area, the west side, and the warehouse district. The people living in these areas or places may share some level of identification, but typically they are more diverse in terms of values, beliefs, and other characteristics than are the people of a community of interest and identification. Also, it is common for the people within this type of community to be in conflict over a variety of issues. Living in proximity to others, in and of itself, does not create a social bond and a sense of belonging. Within a given community of place, there may be many different communities of interest and identification.

It can be useful to examine communities of location in terms of their usual functions. Sheafor and Horejsi (2006, 242) describe these functions as follows:

- *Provision and distribution of goods and services.* Water, electricity, gas, food, housing, garbage disposal, medical care, education, transportation, recreation, social services, information, and the like are provided.
- *Location of business activity and employment.* Commerce and jobs exist from which people earn the money needed to purchase goods and services.
- *Public safety.* Protection from criminal behavior and hazards such as fires, floods, and toxic chemicals is provided.
- *Socialization.* Opportunities are available to communicate and interact with others and to develop a sense of identity and belonging beyond that provided by the family system.
- *Mutual support.* Tangible assistance and social supports beyond those provided by one's family are available.
- *Social control.* Rules and norms necessary to guide and control large numbers of people (e.g., laws, police, courts, traffic control, pollution control, etc.) are established and enforced.
- *Political organization and participation.* Governance and decision making related to local matters and public services are in place (e.g., streets, sewer, education, public welfare, public health, economic development, zoning of housing and businesses, etc.).

Social workers and social agencies must be knowledgeable about how power and influence are used in the community. *Power* is the ability to make others do what you want them to do, whereas *influence* is the capacity to increase the chances that others will do what you want. Successful efforts to develop a new agency program, pass a law, modify social policy, and bring about social change all depend on the skilled use of power and influence. By themselves, social workers may possess little power or influence. Thus, in order to promote social change, they must have access to and relationships with those individuals and organizations that have power and influence and are willing to use it on behalf of the social agency or its clients.

There are various forms of power and influence. Different types are more or less important, depending on the issue being addressed and the kind of change desired. Below are examples of various forms and sources of power and influence:

- Elected officials (e.g., mayor, members of city council, county commissioners, or state legislators)
- Those who control credit, loans, and investments (e.g., banks)
- Those who control information (e.g., newspapers or television stations)
- Executive directors of corporations that employ large numbers of people
- Respected religious and moral leaders
- Recognized experts in their profession or field
- Longtime and respected residents of the community
- Natural leaders (i.e., persons who are charismatic, articulate, and have attracted a loyal following)
- Advocacy organizations that are known for their solidarity, persistence, and devotion to a cause
- Membership or client groups that are skilled in self-advocacy

It is important to remember that the movers and shakers of a community (i.e., those with real power and influence) are not always the visible leaders. Many key decision makers work behind the scenes and hold no formal positions, but are capable of contributing greatly to social change.

Community dynamics differ depending on the size of a community. For example, in a large community, those with power tend to be more specialized and exercise their power only in relation to selected issues. By contrast, in smaller and more rural communities, those with power tend to become involved in a wide range of issues and decisions. These differences will impact the work of social agencies.

Community size also affects how individuals experience the push and pull of social forces and prevailing attitudes. For example, an individual who is gay or lesbian is more likely to experience discrimination and rejection in a small, rural community and feel more isolated than if he or she lived in an urban area. In a larger city, he or she may have access to a more clearly identified gay community to provide positive role models, socialization, and a nurturing environment that can buffer negative societal attitudes toward homosexuals.

Guidance and Direction

As you learn about the community context of practice, remember that we are all shaped in both positive and negative ways by our life experiences. We are supported or undermined, protected or put at risk, guided or controlled, served or stressed, and encouraged or discouraged by our interactions with the individuals, groups, and organizations that make up the communities in which we live. These interactions have a profound effect on our social functioning and quality of life.

Food for Thought

Individuals who are isolated, unaffiliated, with little knowledge, and without influence, often see themselves as "objects" susceptible to social forces and circumstances over which they have little or no control. These self-perceptions induce destructive social and psychological adaptations such as deprecatory self-images, anomie, and fatalism. Engagement in community life through political action can be the antidote by which such individuals gain a modicum of influence over some aspects of their lives. (Grosser and Mondros 1985, 159)

• • •

Environmental capital includes the natural features and resources of the area. *Physical capital* refers to things that have been added to the natural environment by human hands. This includes roads, buildings, and other forms of infrastructure. *Economic capital* comes in the form of financial wealth, as well as mechanisms for producing and exchanging things of monetary value. *Human capital* involves the storing of and access to the skills, talents, and health of the members of the community. *Political capital* involves access to the system of policy setting and enforcing in the community. *Information capital* is the generation, accumulation, storage, retrieval, and exchange of data, information, and knowledge. Research and educational activities help provide information capital. *Social capital* is the system of community norms and interrelationships that produce trust, collaborative action, and community consciousness. (Homan 2004, 40)

• • •

Each community has unmet needs. That is true. It is also true that no matter how poor or frightened or lacking in immediate power, each community has resources to meet many of these needs, including the most important resource, people. In fact, a crucial element for success is your ability to recognize and build on actual and potential capabilities that exist in your community. This, not concern over limitations, will be the foundation of your work. An overemphasis on liabilities is a serious error that colors problem solving in shades of inadequacy and dependence, undermining any attempt at empowerment. (Homan 1999, 121)

• • •

We know that people do not seem to talk to each other as much as they used to. Increasingly, we are overwhelmed by a mosaic of details that can seem useless because they are so unorganized. Managing the stresses of daily life may seem daunting, so planning ways to keep communities together will certainly feel overwhelming. (Perez-Koenig and Rock 2001, 214)

• • •

I have the audacity to believe that peoples everywhere can have three meals a day for their bodies, education and culture for their minds, and dignity, equality, and freedom for their spirits. I believe that what self-centered people have torn down, people-centered people can build up.

—*Martin Luther King, Jr.*

Always be conscious of the fact that the clients or consumers served by a social agency are members of a particular community of place and probably members of several communities of interest and identification. You need to understand the meaning of these groups for clients and the ways in which they impact clients both positively and negatively.

When working directly with clients, identify their social roles (e.g., spouse, parent, or employee) and then consider how specific community characteristics may make it easier or more difficult to fulfill those roles. As you examine the influence of a community on the social functioning of individuals and families, consider the following questions:

- Has my client had the benefits and opportunities provided by schools that are intellectually stimulating and physically safe?
- Does my client have adequate employment opportunities to support himself or herself and a family?
- Does my client live in adequate, safe, and affordable housing?
- Does my client feel safe when at home and on the street, and feel adequately protected by the law enforcement agencies of the community?

- Does my client feel encouraged, supported, and empowered by his or her interactions with others in the community?
- Is my client subjected to rejection, discrimination, or stereotyping by others in the community?
- Is my client's social functioning limited by a lack of public transportation, education and training, or accessible and affordable health care in the community?
- What services or programs are needed and wanted by my client but not available in the community?
- Is my client aware of groups or organizations in the community that can act as advocates for his or her needs?
- What natural helpers and informal resources of the community or neighborhood are used by or available to my client?
- Is my client a real or imagined threat to others in the community?
- Has my client chosen to live in this neighborhood or community? If so, why? If not, what social and economic circumstances necessitate that he or she live in a particular neighborhood or community?
- What significant life experiences have shaped my client's attitudes toward the community and toward my practicum agency, its services and programs?

Remember that your clients may view the community very differently than you or other members of the community do. If you have not been exposed to the negative aspects of community life as your clients may have been, acknowledge that your privileged position may make it difficult to understand your clients' views of the community.

As social work students gain experience and carefully observe and participate in a given community, they often become aware of factors that are common to many communities. For example, be alert to the following dynamics:

- All communities and neighborhoods have social support networks and informal helpers. However, special effort may be required to identify and access these resources for clients or social workers.
- There may be a degree of overlap and duplication in the functions and programs of various agencies in the community. Sometimes this duplication is unnecessary and wasteful, but in many cases the duplication is beneficial to clients and healthy for the total system of services.
- There may be "turf" issues and conflicts between agencies, brought on in part by their competition for funding, the differences in how they define and explain problems, and what they consider to be their territory.
- The people of a community expect agencies to cooperate and collaborate. However, this can be inherently difficult when the agencies must compete with each other for funding and because cooperation and collaboration are time consuming and labor intensive.
- An agency that has the support of powerful and influential individuals is able to secure funding and gain recognition, even when its mission and program may be less important and worthy than that of other agencies in the community.
- Negative community attitudes toward a certain client group or a certain type of agency can be a major obstacle to developing and providing needed services to a particular group.
- Certain groups in the community are better organized and better able to act as advocates for themselves than are others.
- Community attitudes and values can negatively or positively affect social agencies and their ability to carry out their mission.
- Communities under economic stress are sometimes ripe for the development of social problems, and may not be able to support their citizens in positive ways.

Work to understand how clients and those in need of the services provided by your agency perceive your organization and its work. Be cautious regarding the conclusions you reach about why the people of the community do not fully utilize the services available in the community, such as the ones offered by your agency. For example, you might assume that they are not fully informed or sufficiently motivated, when in reality they see your agency as culturally insensitive or irrelevant to their needs. Perhaps the agency's hours of operation do not mesh with their hours of employment or their lifestyle. They may also see your agency as representing a set of values and beliefs significantly different from their own. They may not even be aware that your organization exists.

Because it is vital to have an accurate and informed assessment of your community in order to practice effectively, make certain that your conclusions are well founded and not a result of first impressions, hasty judgments, faulty assumptions, or poor data gathering. It is as important to do good community assessments as it is to do good client assessments. Community level social work needs to be based on thorough, careful, and ongoing assessment.

Beginning a Community Analysis: A Workbook Activity

The following questions are designed to help you understand the community and its effects on your agency and its clients. Answer each one to the degree that you can, recognizing that you will obtain additional information over time. You can obtain some of this information from other social workers or administrators in your agency and some from organizations such as the U.S. Census Bureau, local chambers of commerce, and economic development groups.

1. What geographical area is served by your agency?

    _____

    _____

2. What are the names of the communities, neighborhoods, or areas served by your agency?

    _____

    _____

3. How many people live in the area served by your agency?

    _____

    _____

4. What is the population density of the area (i.e., people per square mile or per city block)?

    _____

    _____

5. Of the people in the community, about what percentage are in various age groups (e.g., preschool, grade school, teen, young adult, middle age, and old age)?

    _____

    _____

    _____

6. About what percentage fall into the various categories used to identify racial and ethnic background or identity? (Note: The categories listed below were used in U.S. Census 2000 materials.)

    _____% White (Caucasian)

    _____% Black (African American)

    _____% American Indian or Alaska Native

    _____% Mexican, Mexican American, Chicano

_____% Puerto Rican

_____% Cuban

_____% Other Spanish/Hispanic/Latino_____

_____% Asian Indian

_____% Chinese

_____% Filipino

_____% Japanese

_____% Korean

_____% Vietnamese

_____% Other Asian_____

_____% Native Hawaiian

_____% Guamanian or Chamorro

_____% Samoan

_____% Other Pacific Islander

_____% Other_____

7. What languages are spoken by the people of the community?

_____

_____

8. Of the people living in the area served by your agency, what can be said about their income levels?

Median per person income

_____

Median household income

_____

Percentage of families receiving some form of public assistance

_____

9. How do these data on income compare with the state and national averages?

_____

_____

10. How does the cost of living in this community compare with communities or cities of similar size in the state or region?

_____

_____

11. What are the rates of unemployment in the community? How do these compare with figures for the state, region, and nation?

_____

_____

12. How many people in the community live below the poverty line?

_____

_____

13. What is considered a living wage in the community?

_____

_____

14. Of the adults living in the community, about what percentage are in each of the following categories of educational achievement? (Consult U.S. Census data.)

_____% 8th grade or less

_____% 12th grade or less (no diploma)

_____% High school graduate

_____% Some college

_____% Associate arts degree

_____% Bachelor's degree

_____% Graduate degree

15. What groups wield considerable power and influence in the community? What is the source of their power and influence?

_____

_____

_____

16. Are certain ethnic, racial, or religious groups particularly influential in the community?

_____

_____

_____

17. What groups are underrepresented in the community's decision-making process and structures? Why?

_____

_____

_____

18. Does one political party or a particular ideology dominate decision making at the community level?

_____

_____

19. What significant problems (e.g., crime, pollution, lack of affordable housing, poverty) is the community experiencing?

_____

_____

_____

_____

20. To what extent has the community experienced intergroup conflict related to differences in race, ethnicity, religion, language, and social class?

_____

_____

_____

_____

21. Of what is the community especially proud (e.g., physical beauty, history, climate, schools, sports teams)?

_____

_____

_____

22. Has anyone completed community asset mapping in your community? If so, what were its results?

_____

_____

_____

23. Have community capacity building efforts taken place in your community? If so, what were their results?

_____

_____

_____

24. About what is the community especially fearful or embarrassed (e.g., environmental problems, corruption, violence, poor roads, high taxes)?

_____

_____

_____

25. What minority groups live within the community, including refugees and immigrants? What special services, if any, are available to them?

_____

_____

_____

26. What community welfare planning councils or interagency coordinating bodies exist in the community? How might you observe or participate in their work?

_____

_____

_____

_____

27. What mutual aid or self-help groups exist in the community that might be especially helpful to the clients you serve in your practicum agency (e.g., Alcoholics Anonymous, fetal alcohol syndrome support group, Alliance for the Mentally Ill, Lambda Alliance, Alzheimer's support group)? Can you attend and observe their meetings?

_____

_____

_____

_____

28. Does your community have a United Way or another combined fund-raising program that raises money for numerous human service agencies? By what process does this fund-raising organization decide which agencies it will support?

_____

_____

_____

_____

29. What significant gaps exist in the array of human services and programs within the community? Why do they exist?

_____

_____

_____

_____

_____

30. Are there significant, unnecessary, or wasteful duplications among the human service programs of the community? If yes, what are they and why does this situation exist?

_____

_____

_____

_____

_____

31. What "turf" conflicts and unhealthy competitions exist between human services agencies within the community? How do they affect your clients?

_____

_____

_____

_____

32. In the opinion of experienced human services professionals and experts of the community, how adequate are the following community elements?

Housing

_____

_____

Schools

_____

_____

Police and fire protection

_____

_____

Recreational programs

_____

_____

Public transportation

_____

_____

Health care and hospitals

_____

_____

Mental health services

_____

_____

Day care centers for children

_____

_____

Family support programs

_____

_____

Programs for the treatment of alcoholism and drug abuse

_____

_____

Programs for troubled youth

_____

_____

Programs for persons with disabilities

_____

_____

Programs for the elderly

_____

_____

Additional notes and comments:

_____

_____

_____

_____

Suggested Learning Activities

- Participate in interagency committees or task groups that are made up of representatives of various community organizations.
- Read grant proposals and reports written by your agency to see how they claim to meet community needs.
- Locate and study community resource directories, census data, and historical materials to help deepen your understanding of a particular social problem addressed by your agency.
- Use the Internet to examine census data related to the area served by your agency. The home page for the U.S. Census Bureau is www.census.gov. Once there, click on Access Tools, then click on American FactFinder.
- Attend meetings of support groups whose goals are related to the problems addressed by your agency.

Additional Suggestions and Hints

- In Sheafor and Horejsi (2006), read the sections entitled "Learning about Your Community" (241–245) and "Community Decision-Making Analysis" (331–332).

Selected Bibliography

Fisher, Robert, and Howard Jacob Karger. *Social Work and Community in a Private World: Getting Out in Public.* New York: Longman, 1997.

Grosser, Charles, and Jacqueline Mondros. "Pluralism and Participation: The Political Action Approach." In *Theory and Practice of Community Social Work.* Ed. Samuel Taylor and Robert Roberts. Irvington, NY: Columbia University Press, 1985.

Hardcastle, David, Stanley Wenocur, and Patricia Powers. *Community Practice: Theories and Skills for Social Workers.* 2nd ed. New York: Oxford University Press, 2004.

Hardina, Donna. *Analytical Skills for Community Organization and Practice.* New York: Columbia University Press, 2002.

Homan, Mark. *Promoting Community Change.* 2nd ed. Pacific Grove, CA: Brooks/Cole, 1999.

Homan, Mark. *Promoting Community Change: Making It Happen in the Real World.* 3rd ed. Belmont, CA: Brooks/Cole, 2004.

Lohmann, Nancy. *Rural Social Work Practice.* New York: Columbia University Press, 2005.

Perez-Koenig, Rosa, and Barry Rock, eds. *Social Work in the Era of Devolution: Toward a Just Practice.* New York: Fordham University Press, 2001.

Sheafor, Bradford, and Charles Horejsi. *Techniques and Guidelines in Social Work Practice.* 7th ed. Boston: Allyn and Bacon, 2006.

Weil, Maria. *The Handbook of Community Practice.* Thousand Oaks, CA: Sage Publications, 2005.

10 | The Social Problem Context of Practice

GOALS FOR LEARNING

- To understand the social conditions, needs, and problems faced by your clients
- To understand the social conditions, needs, and problems that are addressed by your practicum agency
- To understand how various theories concerning the cause of social problems influence the development of social policies and social programs
- To understand how particular theories of causation may influence the operation of human services organizations
- To understand how political power and influence can determine whether a particular condition comes to be defined as a social problem

Most of the agencies and organizations that employ social workers were created in response to a specific social problem or need as perceived and understood by elected officials (in the case of public agencies), by powerful and committed community leaders (in the case of private nonprofit agencies), or by investors (in the case of for-profit organizations). In order for you to understand your agency's purpose, policies, and operation, it is important to carefully examine the social problems or conditions on which it focuses its attention and resources.

The definition and conceptualization of a social problem is a complex process that is shaped by historical, political, and cultural forces as well as by existing scientific knowledge. There can be intense disagreement over whether a particular condition is to be defined as a problem. Even when there is agreement that a problem exists, there can be much debate over its cause, its severity, and over what can and should be done about it. There can also be great disagreement over whether those experiencing a social problem are to be blamed or held accountable for their situation or are to be supported by others as they attempt to cope with or change their situation.

For example, one segment of society may view the situation of intimate partner violence as the responsibility of the person being battered, whereas another segment may see the interaction between sociocultural attitudes, socialization, and personal attributes as better explanations of why victims of intimate partner violence are not able to leave their situations.

How a problem is defined and the predominant beliefs about its causation have a profound effect on the formulation of social policies and the design of social programs that are intended to address the problem. Moreover, as our understanding of the problem changes, agencies must modify their guiding principles and adapt their services and interventions to these new interpretations.

Background and Context

A *social condition* is a factual reality. Examples include the fact that about 50 percent of marriages in the United States end in divorce, the fact that between two and three million people in the U.S. are homeless, the fact that about one in four high school students (mostly minorities) never graduate, the fact that many teenagers have babies, and the fact that many children are beaten and injured by their parents. These are facts, but are they actually social problems? If yes, why? Who decides that a particular condition is a problem that requires action by the community or government? Whose values, norms, and beliefs are to be used in forming a judgment?

A *social problem* can be defined as a social condition that negatively impacts individuals or communities, and as a situation in which the welfare and well-being of society may be threatened. A social problem is considered as such because many people believe that its existence is wrong, harmful, or immoral. Some people may view a given condition as a problem that violates the values they hold dear and that demands collective action and an investment of resources, whereas others presume that it is simply an acceptable part of life that requires no special response. A condition becomes a problem when it threatens the values, the sense of morality, the security, or safety of those in a community or a society who have the power and influence to bring forth collective action and, eventually, the new policies, programs, and agencies that will address this problem. For example, teenage pregnancy may be defined as a social problem because it is associated with increased high school dropout rates and reliance on public assistance.

When powerful and influential individuals and groups come to view a social phenomena or condition as a problem and a threat to what they value, they must decide what social policies and actions are needed to solve this problem or lessen its negative impact. Many different solutions or actions may be proposed. Each will rest on a particular set of assumptions and beliefs about the cause of the problem and what interventions will be feasible and effective. There may be several competing theories of causation, each of which purports to explain why the problem exists and what can and should be done about it.

Those in decision-making positions may sponsor research into the causes of the problem and seek the advice of experts, but in the final analysis, the decisions about the nature and cause of the problem will be heavily political and will reflect the views and preferences of those who have power and influence. That is why social workers must become competent in the political and social policy arena if they are to expect change in the social policies that impact their clients. For example, in recent years powerful political forces have redefined poverty as a problem caused by an unwillingness of people to work and by the existence of welfare programs thought to create dependency. Their approach is to reduce access to welfare benefits and to place limits on those benefits. Not addressed in this approach are questions of whether jobs exist, whether those who are poor have the education and skills needed to obtain and hold such jobs, and whether the available jobs provide health insurance and pay a wage high enough to support economic independence.

The decisions made concerning which actions should be taken to address a social problem eventually give rise to specific *social policies*. In turn, these shape the programs and services provided by social agencies and other human services organizations. Many of the social agencies that serve as social work practicum settings have the responsibility of carrying out these social policies and designing specific programs and interventions to solve the problem.

The specific actions by agency employees can be viewed as their *practices*. The relationship between a social condition, a social policy, a social program, and practices is outlined in Figure 10.1.

Guidance and Direction

In any community or society, there is great variety in the perspectives of its members as they seek to understand and explain the social problems they observe and experience. These different viewpoints will be based on personal experiences, attitudes, values, information, misinformation, and stereotypes. You may think that some of these perspectives are biased or uninformed, but it is important to realize that the beliefs make sense and seem valid to those who hold them.

These different viewpoints and the political debate that arises from them will sometimes result in social policy that you support and, at other times, in policy

SOCIAL CONDITION An existing situation or phenomenon is observed, measured, and acknowledged by a community or society.

SOCIAL PROBLEM

The people of a community or society judge the social condition to be unacceptable and are motivated to do something about it. The condition is now perceived as a social problem. For a condition to "become" a social problem, its existence must somehow threaten or disturb those groups that have the power or influence to bring about a collective and political response and move others to address the problem.

SOCIAL POLICIES

The existence of a social problem calls forth or requires some type of action. A social policy is an agreed upon course of action. Policy makers propose various policy options based on their values, beliefs, and knowledge about the nature and cause of the problem.
A political process determines which of the possible options is chosen. These policies are then expressed in laws, in administrative rules and regulations, and in the budgeting process and the allocations of monies.
Policies change over time in response to new knowledge or a shifting political climate.

SOCIAL PROGRAMS

Social programs flow from, social policy. A program is a planned and organized effort that reflects the social policies. A program is designed to accomplish a certain outcome.
A program exists as an organization or as a component of a formal organization. Programs require funds for staff, office space, travel, training, equipment, and client services.

PRACTICES

Practices are actions performed by those hired to perform the tasks and activities required by the social policies and social programs.

Figure 10.1   The Evolution of Policies, Programs, and Practices

Food for Thought

The United States today is a society in which a major segment has been systematically marginalized, a rich society in which income and wealth disparities are nonetheless widening at an unprecedented pace, in which poor minority-group members are headed away from material betterment and political empowerment and toward destitution, incarceration, and despair. (Perez-Koenig and Rock 2001, 9)

• • •

The action we take to remedy social problems . . . depends largely on whether we find the causes of those problems within individuals or in the contexts in which the individuals live. (Becker 2005, 138)

• • •

The current American system in which health care is linked to employment is creating a caste of the chronically ill, infirm, and marginally employed. Because health care is so tightly linked to employment, once an individual or a family is caught in the death spiral, it is nearly impossible to find a way out. (Sered and Fernandopulle 2005, 15)

• • •

The media's description of poverty is risky because the words used to represent the poor are often projections of class fears, such as "lazy," "promiscuous," "dirty," "ugly," and "stupid." Among the middle class, such depictions confirm their differences from the poor and, to the rich, their wisdom and generosity. A seemingly alternative description includes such terms as "depressed," "insane," "dysfunctional," "unsanitary," "unsuited for marriage," "poorly educated," and "having a low IQ." This second list merely parrots the first but with fancier language that presumes to express openmindedness, understanding, even compassion. Both are misleading and deceptive. (Roth 2002, 49)

• • •

The oppressed receive the euphemistic title of "welfare recipients." They are treated as individual cases, as marginal men who deviate from the general configuration of a "good, organized, and just" society. The oppressed are regarded as the pathology of the healthy society, which must therefore adjust these "incompetent and lazy" fold to its own patterns by changing their mentality. These marginals need to be "integrated," "incorporated" into the healthy society

that they have "forsaken." The truth is, however, that the oppressed are not "marginals," not men living "outside" society. They have always been "inside"— inside the structure which made them "beings for others." The solution is not to "integrate" them into the structure of oppression, but to transform that structure so that they can become "beings for themselves." (Freire 1970, 110)

• • •

One of the defining elements of social work practice is that social workers are trained to see the connections between problems that affect individuals and problems that affect larger numbers of people because of organizational or governmental policies that impose costs, monetary and otherwise, on or deny services to people in need. (Hoefer 2006, 1)

• • •

Definitions of social problems are expressed in terms that describe the condition, reflect attitudes toward the condition, and give numerous other hints as to how that condition is considered offensive or problematic. Groups vie for control of the definition of a problem. When one group wins, its vocabulary may be adopted and institutionalized while the concepts of the opposing group fall into obscurity. When terminology changes, when new terms are invented, or existing terms are given new meaning, these actions signal that something important has happened to the career or history of a social problem. (Spector and Kitsuse 2001, 8)

• • •

A good society . . . creates a sense of economic security for all its members. It damages us all that the United States leads the industrialized world in rates of homelessness, child poverty, lack of health care, infant mortality, inequality of wealth, and nearly every other index of desperation among the voiceless and vulnerable. Even if we own our own homes, have decent jobs, and possess a modicum of financial comfort, we're demeaned by our society's radical economic polarization. Having to avert our eyes on the street, avoid certain neighborhoods, and mistrust other human beings who might take what we've got is "tacky," as preacher Will Campbell would say, and we know it. (Loeb 1999, 295)

that you see as ineffective or harmful. Remember that the democratic political process is influenced by public attitudes, values, information, and power. In order to influence the process, you will need to venture into the process and use your skills to advocate for social policies that benefit those you serve. This will rarely be easy because of the strongly held beliefs of everyone involved in the issue and because those negatively impacted by existing social problems or policies may not have access to power.

As our society becomes more diverse and pluralistic, there will be even more differences in how people think about social conditions and social problems. Strive to understand perspectives that are different from your own. Expect increasing numbers of lively discussions, heated debates, and serious conflicts between groups with very different views about what constitutes social problems and what ought to be done about them. If you wish to address social problems at the community or societal level, you will need to contribute reason, solid data, and political influence to this debate.

To a large extent, your understanding of social conditions and social problems will be rooted in your liberal arts background and in course work in sociology, psychology, economics, political science, anthropology, and history. You may also have had personal experiences that deepen your understanding of certain problems, or perhaps these experiences serve to bias your viewpoint, particularly if the associated pain and conflict have not been satisfactorily resolved at an emotional level. Strive to develop an awareness of what you truly believe and why.

It is important to remember that clients who are experiencing problems first-hand may view them very differently from the way you do. A situation that you or other professionals define as a problem may not seem like a problem to your client or vice versa.

If you have never struggled with poverty, were not raised in an unsafe home or neighborhood, or have not been affected by racism, you may not fully appreciate the profound effects these experiences can have on people. Listen sensitively to client accounts of their life experiences so that you can better understand their importance and the impact on their lives.

Continually deepen your knowledge about how social problems such as poverty, violence, or racism develop not only so you can help clients improve their social functioning, but also so you can work toward the prevention of these social problems. If you are familiar with the multitude of interrelated individual, family, community, and economic factors associated with various social problems, you will be better equipped to devise effective strategies of intervention and prevention.

Draw on your understanding of the ecosystems perspective and social systems theory to examine how social problems develop and change over time. Identify the many factors, conditions, and circumstances that interact to create a social problem. As you gain experience, you will see more clearly how one social problem can lead to or exacerbate others, or how several problems clustered together can overwhelm clients or communities and have devastating consequences. You will also see that social change at the macro level must take place in order to enhance the social functioning of individual clients and families.

Think hard about the concept of prevention and the ways in which you could become involved in preventing the social problems you are attempting to address. What changes at the community and societal level are needed in order to prevent adverse conditions and social problems from developing in the first place? Do existing prevention programs appear to be effective? Do we have the knowledge, the resources, and the political will to launch effective programs of prevention? What would various solutions cost and from where would this money come? As you ponder various strategies, consider the advantages, disadvantages, feasibility, and probable effectiveness of various prevention efforts at the micro, mezzo, and macro levels. What groups might oppose prevention programs and why?

During your practicum, you will most likely meet clients who are truly remarkable, positive human beings despite the fact that they grew up in very challenging or destructive environments. For reasons that we are just beginning to understand, some individuals are resilient and able to resist the negative influences of a corrosive environment. There may have been social supports available to these individuals in addition to their individual strengths and coping skills that allowed them to function well in spite of their experiences. Seek to understand why the same environment affects people differently. Learn from your clients about the strengths and resiliency factors that have made it possible for them to overcome adversity.

Finally, begin to identify ways in which you as a social worker might be able to impact the identification of a social problem by a community in order for it to be addressed. Find ways to empower your clients to articulate their experiences effectively so their needs are not ignored or their views discounted.

The Problems and Needs Addressed by Your Agency: A Workbook Activity

1. What specific social conditions, needs, or problems does your practicum agency address?

   _____

   _____

   _____

2. Within the geographical area served by your agency, how many people are estimated to have the specific condition(s), problem(s), or need(s) addressed by your agency?

   _____

3. How do these numbers and data compare with state and national statistics regarding the prevalence of this social problem or condition? If the numbers are higher for your area, to what do you attribute the severity of this problem?

   _____

   _____

   _____

   _____

4. What particular subpopulations are most likely to experience these problems, needs, or conditions? For example, is there a particular age group, gender, ethnic group, socioeconomic class, or occupational group that is most likely to experience the problems or conditions addressed by your agency?

   _____

   _____

   _____

   _____

5. How will the community be harmed if these conditions or problems grow larger and more serious?

   _____

   _____

   _____

   _____

6. What groups and organizations in your community have argued that the concerns or conditions addressed by your agency should indeed be defined as problems that require action in the form of programs, services, and interventions? In other words, who believes in and supports what your agency is trying to do?

_____

_____

_____

7. What groups and organizations in your community have argued that the concerns or conditions addressed by your agency should not be viewed as real or significant problems and that the programs and services provided by your agency are unnecessary, misdirected, or of low priority? In other words, who does not believe in and support what your agency is trying to do?

_____

_____

_____

8. What groups, individuals, or organizations, if any, stand to benefit economically or politically (e.g., by access to a low income employee pool or lower taxes) from the continued existence of these social conditions, problems, and needs?

_____

_____

_____

9. What groups or organizations, if any, might be penalized or in some way harmed (e.g., by higher taxes and loss of power or status) by an extensive effort to eliminate or reduce these social conditions, problems, and needs?

_____

_____

_____

10. Has the problem or concern addressed by your agency become more or less serious in the past ten years?

_____

_____

_____

_____

11. What criteria or measures are used to document the seriousness of the problem or condition?

_____

_____

_____

_____

12. Are there different opinions and perspectives about the seriousness of the problem? If so, are these differences based on different definitions of the problem, different statistics, or differences in attitudes toward the problem?

_____

_____

_____

_____

13. How are the problems and concerns addressed by your agency related to other broad social problems such as poverty, crime, racism, violence, high rates of divorce, substance abuse, lack of affordable health care, lack of jobs, or changes in societal values and attitudes?

_____

_____

_____

_____

14. What differing opinions, beliefs, and theories of causation are offered to explain the existence of the human and social conditions, problems, and needs that are addressed by your agency (e.g., individual responsibility or societal and economic contributors to social problems)?

_____

_____

_____

15. How do various professional groups in the community and society differ in their explanation of and the solutions proposed for the problems and concerns addressed by your agency (e.g., the views of physicians, nurses, lawyers, police, economists, business people, psychologists, clergy, teachers, sociologists, and social workers)? On what points do they agree?

_____

_____

_____

_____

16. In what ways, if any, are new research findings in the social and behavioral sciences changing the way your agency conceptualizes and explains the problems, conditions, and needs that it attempts to address?

_____

_____

_____

_____

17. Given the results of various demonstration programs, experimental approaches, and research projects around the country, what approaches to these problems, conditions, and needs appear to be most effective and efficient?

_____

_____

_____

_____

18. What specific steps and actions would be needed to prevent these problems or conditions?

_____

_____

_____

_____

19. What specific research or demonstration projects would you recommend be done in order to build knowledge about the social problems your agency addresses (e.g., long term effects of welfare reform, genetic influences on mental illness, principles of violence prevention)?

   _____

   _____

   _____

20. What local, state, or federal monies or funding programs are available to combat the problem your agency addresses (e.g., United Way funding, government grants, line items in state budgets, private foundations, service organizations with specific human service priorities)?

   _____

   _____

   _____

21. What national resources or associations address or provide help for this social problem (e.g., clearinghouses, advocacy groups, toll free hotlines)?

   _____

   _____

   _____

   Additional notes and comments:

   _____

   _____

   _____

   _____

   _____

   _____

Suggested Learning Activities

- Conduct interviews with experienced professionals within the agency to better understand the theories of causation that shape the agency's programs, procedures, and staff interactions with the agency's clients and consumers.
- Attend public meetings (e.g., city council meetings) and read the letters to the editor of the local newspaper in order to better understand the various ways in which people explain the existence of social problems and the variety of solutions that may make sense and seem logical to them.
- Attend the meetings of a group or organization that defines the problem addressed by your agency much differently than does your agency. Try to understand the basis for their views.
- Identify a self-help group that addresses the social problem your agency addresses. Attend a meeting or read about its views to determine if it explains the social problem and its solution differently from your agency.

Additional Suggestions and Hints

- Look through several textbooks that focus on human and social problems in search of information about the problems and conditions addressed by your practicum agency. For example, if your agency provides services to abused children, read chapters that present various theories that have been developed to explain the growing problem of child abuse and neglect.
- Examine the *Encyclopedia of Social Work* for chapters that offer summaries of basic information related to the various problems addressed by social workers and social agencies.
- Examine the most recent edition of the *Social Work Almanac* or a similar book that presents national statistics to determine how the problem addressed by your agency at the community level fits into a larger context at the national level.
- Locate websites that monitor and publish findings about certain populations (e.g., www.unicef.org, which monitors the state of the world's children).
- Read print and electronic media descriptions of social problems. Pay attention to whether the media takes a strengths perspective on these social problems.

Selected Bibliography

Becker, Dana. *The Myth of Empowerment: Women and the Therapeutic Culture in America.* New York: New York University Press, 2005.

Berlaget, Gai, and William Egelman. *Understanding Social Issues: Critical Analysis and Thinking.* 6th ed. Boston: Allyn and Bacon, 2003.

Edwards, Richard L., ed. *Encyclopedia of Social Work.* 19th ed. Washington, DC: NASW Press, 1995. See also 1997 and 2003 supplements to the *Encyclopedia of Social Work.*

Eitzen, D. Stanley, and Craig S. Leedham. *Solutions to Social Problems: Lessons from Other Societies.* 3rd ed. Boston: Allyn and Bacon, 2004.

Eitzen, D. Stanley, and Maxine Baca Zinn. *Social Problems.* 9th ed. Boston: Allyn and Bacon, 2003.

Freire, Paulo. *Pedagogy of the Oppressed.* New York: Herder and Herder, 1970.

Ginsberg, Leon. *Social Work Almanac.* Washington, DC: NASW Press, 1995.

Hoefer, Richard. *Advocacy Practice for Social Justice.* Chicago: Lyceum Books, 2006.

Loeb, Paul Rogat. *Soul of a Citizen: Living with Conviction in a Cynical Time.* New York: St. Martin's Griffin Press, 1999.

Perez-Koenig, and Barry Rock. *Social Work in the Era of Devolution: Toward a Just Practice.* New York: Fordham University Press, 2001.

Roth, William. *The Assault on Social Policy.* New York: Columbia University Press, 2002.

Sered, Susan Starr, and Rushika Fernandopulle. *Uninsured in America: Life and Death in the Land of Opportunity.* Berkeley, University of California Press, 2005.

Spector, Malcolm, and John Kitsuse. *Constructing Social Problems.* New Brunswick, NJ: Transaction Publishers, 2001.

Sullivan, Thomas. *Social Problems.* 6th ed. Boston: Allyn and Bacon, 2003.

Zastrow, Charles. *Social Problems.* 5th ed. Belmont, CA: Wadsworth, 2000.

11

The Social Policy Context of Practice

GOALS FOR LEARNING

- To identify, become familiar with, and analyze the social policies that most directly affect the clients or consumers served by your agency
- To identify, become familiar with, and analyze the social policies that most directly influence the operation and activities of your practicum agency
- To become aware of the difference between an agency policy and a social policy, and of the interplay between these two types of policy
- To understand how social policies are formed and change over time
- To understand the concept of social policy practice

Previous chapters focused on the agency context, the community context, and the social problem context of social work practice. This chapter examines a fourth context, the social policy context. The clients or consumers served by your practicum agency, the other social workers and staff within this agency, and even your practicum experiences are affected by social policy.

The study of social policy can be an exciting activity because it involves the examination of what we as a society believe about people, the problems experienced by people, and what can and should be done about these problems. It forces us to carefully examine our own beliefs and values and in the process we are sometimes surprised by what we discover about ourselves. Although stimulating, the study of social policy is also a complex undertaking. For example, the analysis of a particular social policy requires students to know how to locate relevant governmental documents and legal codes, understand the legislative process, and acquire a basic understanding of the many historic, political, cultural, and economic forces that shaped the development of a particular policy.

This chapter attempts to clarify the nature of social policy by defining and distinguishing between various terms and by explaining the impact of social policy on a social agency and on those that it serves. In addition, specific suggestions are offered on how you can identify and locate information concerning the social policies most relevant to your practicum setting.

Background and Context

Soon after beginning your practicum, you may discover that the typical human services agency has an abundance of policies and procedures. Very often, as a matter of fact, one of the first assignments a student receives from his or her field instructor is to read the agency's policy manual. It is important to recognize the difference between the policy statements found in an agency's policy manual and a formal social policy. In many settings, agency policies will be influenced by social policies, but an agency policy is not a social policy.

For purposes of this chapter, *social policy* is defined as a decision made by public or governmental authorities regarding the assignment and allocation of resources, rights, and responsibilities and expressed in laws and governmental regulations. In this definition, the term *resources* refers to various social and economic benefits and opportunities, both tangible and intangible. The use of the terms *assignment* and *allocation* implies that a policy may either offer or curtail these resources for all people or for certain individuals. The term *responsibilities* refers to such matters as tax burdens, service in the military, payment for public services, and other duties common to citizenship. The term *rights* refers to the protection of guaranteed freedoms or entitlements.

Needless to say, lawmakers and government officials formulate policies on a wide variety of topics. Thus, there are public policies on international relations, economics and the monetary system, the tax structure, interstate and international commerce, military and defense, highways, public lands, environmental safety, education, and the like. For the most part, social policies address matters or issues related to the social well-being of people and the relationships between various groups within society. Thus, social policies focus on such concerns as marriage, divorce, adoption, domestic abuse, the special needs of the elderly, juvenile delinquency, mental health, discrimination against minority groups, training and job opportunities for the disadvantaged, economic assistance to the poor, availability of affordable housing, immigration, and other similar concerns. The term *social welfare policy* is often applied to those social policies that focus primarily on the distribution of economic benefits to those in need (e.g., public assistance, food stamps, subsidized housing, Medicaid, or subsidized child care).

Lowy (1991, 377–379) explains that public social policies are derived from four dichotomous approaches to the legislative process:

1. *Generic versus categorical approach.*   A generic approach to social policy development seeks a particular outcome for an entire population, such as health care or housing for all people in society. By contrast, a categorical approach focuses on only one segment of the population, such as housing for the elderly or health care for children.
2. *Holistic versus segmented approach.*   A holistic approach to policy development attempts to address the needs or concerns of the total person or the whole family, while a segmented approach focuses on only a single factor, such as an individual's income or nutrition. A segmented approach gives rise to a fragmented and confusing service system in which clients must approach several different agencies in order to secure the services or results they need.
3. *Rational versus crisis approach.*   The rational approach places a heavy emphasis on deriving social policy from a careful and thorough study of the problem and issues. By contrast, the crisis approach creates policy as a hurried and usually highly political reaction to a crisis or serious problem. Very few of our country's social policies have grown out of the rational planning process.
4. *Future planning versus political context approach.*   The future planning approach gives careful consideration to social trends and probable future developments and tries to anticipate how the various policy options would fit with what can be expected in the future. By contrast, the political context approach is mostly concerned with solving an immediate problem and allows the policy to be determined mostly by popular opinion, political interests, and pragmatic assumptions about what will be supported and tolerated by dominant forces in society.

It could be said that social policy planning would be most effective if the generic, holistic, rational, and future planning approaches were all used because the resulting policies would be more broad and more carefully conceived and based on current or future needs. The reality, however, is that most social policies are a result of the categorical, segmented, crisis, and political context approaches. This is because of limited vision and information, monetary constraints, political motivation and power, and a tendency to only enact social policy when social needs reach the crisis stage.

A social policy is created when a legislative body enacts a law, usually at the federal or state level but in some cases, at the county or city level. Once the law is enacted, high-level governmental officials and various governmental legal departments will usually prepare a set of rules and regulations that clarify the provisions of the law and describe in detail how the law is to be implemented. These directives are often called *administrative rules and regulations*. Subsequently, key provisions of the law and many of the rules and regulations are written into a public agency's manual of policy and procedure that guides its day-by-day operation and the decisions and actions of agency staff.

Statements of social policy are found in legal codes, in executive orders issued by the president and governors, in administrative rules and regulations issued by governmental officials, and sometimes in statements and speeches made by high-ranking public officials. In some instances, legal decisions handed down by appellate courts have the effect of creating social policy.

As indicated previously, an agency policy is not a social policy, but social policies do filter down to the level of a local or community agency and find their way into the agency's policy manual. At the local level, social policies have a significant impact on an agency's services and programs and on what a social worker actually does or does not do in his or her work with clients. The impact of social policy on agency policy is most evident in the operation of a public agency in which one will find that many of the statements found in the manual are direct responses to specific legal codes and various governmental rules and regulations.

Food for Thought

Suffice it to say that solving the welfare problem is not the answer to solving the poverty problem, as policymakers often imply. Rather, solving—or at least dealing with—the poverty problem is the answer to solving the welfare problem. (Popple and Leighninger 2004, 181)

• • •

Social policy addresses fundamental values of social inclusion, equity, human rights and widening of human capabilities: It is important that these intrinsic values are always at the forefront of thinking about social policy. (Mkandawire 2004, 31)

• • •

The problem is that U.S. society no longer exhibits . . . commitment, and its political leadership has moved with alarming speed to disassemble the meager vestiges of past concern for the poor. Rather than "working" the system harder on behalf of their clients' immediate needs, social workers must now seek to work *against* a system that is intent upon denial of moral responsibility for responding to those same needs. (Perez-Koenig and Rock 2001, 10)

• • •

Social welfare policies are not created in a vacuum, but are imbedded in the social fabric of the society of which they are a part. The very social and personal values which give them life and meaning at one point in history may be their undoing later on. In hard times when public hysteria is voiced against welfare mothers, criminals, and illegal immigrants, the political pendulum shifts. Social welfare policy makers are under pressure to "reform welfare as we know it." New legislation is introduced, and if there is no mass counter-attack by concerned parties, the legislation passes. (van Wormer 1997, 51)

• • •

Policy advocates need perspective to avoid pessimism and self-recrimination in the wake of defeats or partial successes. No single person or group is likely to prevail on the complex playing field of policy deliberations. Advocates must realize that defeats are more likely when people champion the needs of stigmatized and relatively powerless groups, which lack the clout of more powerful interests. (Jansson 1999, 23)

The far-reaching and sometimes subtle effects of a national or state level social policy on a social agency, on the practice of social work in that agency, on the individual social worker employed by the agency, and on the agency's clients are illustrated in the following sequence of concerns, decisions, and responses:

- The problems, concerns, and unmet needs of people and various political responses and economic considerations at the state and national level give rise to a social policy.
- The nature of the social policy shapes the programs that are created to respond to human needs and problems.
- The nature and purpose of the programs shape the function, structure, and funding of those agencies or organizations that are to administer the programs.
- Organizational function, structure, and the funding mechanisms and restrictions shape the formation of the agency's policies, operational procedures, and the writing of the agency manual to be followed by the agency's personnel (i.e., the social workers employed by the agency).
- Agency policy and procedure shape and influence the social worker's selection of a practitioner role, theoretical frameworks for practice, tasks to be performed, professional values on which to focus, and the relative priorities among those professional tasks and activities.
- The roles, tasks, and activities of the social worker shape and influence the relationships he or she forms with the agency's clients or consumers and the nature of the services provided to them.
- The services provided by the social worker shape and influence the behavior and needs of clients and consumers.
- The social problems affecting clients are reduced, resolved, or made worse as a result of the social policies designed to lessen them.

Social policies are a reflection of values and what is believed to be right and wrong, desirable and undesirable. They are mostly shaped by those having power and influence. The formulation of social policy is basically a political process and politics are primarily about power. It is the art of gaining, exercising, and retaining power in order to influence and enact social policies that are believed to be right and effective. Hopefully the effectiveness of social policies is monitored, measured, and evaluated, and results are shared with policy makers so that social policies can be continually improved in order to address social problems more effectively.

If social policies are ill conceived, because the decision makers either do not understand the problem or have erroneous beliefs about its causes, the resulting social programs will also be flawed. Those who understand the concerns being addressed and understand the inadequacies of existing policies and programs, have both an obligation and an opportunity to provide accurate information to the decision makers so they can develop appropriate and effective social policies. In the absence of such information, policy makers will assume that social policies are addressing the needs they were intended to address. Social workers can thus be extremely influential in not only providing needed information, but also lobbying for just, equitable, and effective social policy changes.

Guidance and Direction

You may be surprised at the degree to which your work is impacted by social policy. You will need to learn about social policy so that you can take part in its formulation. You may be excited at the prospect of working at the macro level to design social policies and social programs that could improve the lives of many people.

You may see social change and social policy development as the most efficient and exciting way to help large numbers of people and promote social justice. This level of practice is referred to as *social policy practice*.

On the other hand, you may see yourself primarily as a direct services provider and you may prefer to help clients and families one by one and in a very personal way. The idea of becoming involved in political action and social change efforts may not be the focus of your emerging practice. However, it is still imperative for you to understand social policy and how it affects your clients, positively or negatively. In order to be an informed advocate for your clients and a skilled provider of direct services, you must understand specific social policies, their strengths and limitations, and why they exist in their current forms.

Depending on your practicum setting, you will need to become familiar with a cluster of social policy issues and concerns. You must acquire a basic or working understanding of the social policies that most directly influence the operation of your agency, its own agency policies, your role and its clients or consumers. Below is a list of social policy domains that are of interest to many social workers and many social agencies.

Abortion
Adolescent pregnancy
Adult protection (abuse and
  neglect of older persons)
Child care
Child protection (abuse and
  neglect of children)
Child support
Community and neighbor-
  hood development
Discrimination and racism
Economic development
Family planning
Foster care and adoption
Health care and rehabilitation
Homelessness

Housing
Immigration and refugee
  issues
Intimate partner violence
Job creation and unemployment
Juvenile delinquency and adult
  crime
Long-term care
Marriage and divorce
Mental health and mental illness
Physical and mental disabilities
Preschool, elementary, and
  secondary education
Public assistance/welfare
Public health and safety
Substance abuse

Social policy is constantly evolving as a result of changing societal needs, changing values, changes in financial resources available to implement policy, and, of course, political forces. You will need to keep abreast of proposed legislative changes and find ways to have input in the political process. During your practicum, make a special effort to involve yourself in the following activities:

1. Participating in task forces or committees working to pass a law
2. Participating in grassroots or advocacy groups seeking to change social policy
3. Observing and giving testimony at public meetings or legislative hearings that solicit public input before social policy decisions are made

Be aware of the fact that when social workers do not engage in the politics of forming social welfare policy and allocating funding for social welfare programs, many client needs and concerns are overlooked by the decision makers, and the insights and values of the social work profession are omitted from the policy development process. Your knowledge and skills are needed in the ongoing work of social policy development.

You will need to develop and utilize a model or conceptual framework to guide your examination and analysis of the social policies that impact the operation of your agency and either support or undermine the social functioning of your clients. Examples of such social policy analysis models can be found in textbooks on social welfare policy. The questions listed in the workbook activity in this chapter are ones often addressed in the various models and conceptual frameworks used in policy analysis. Learn to view such models as tools to help you understand and assess the effectiveness of social policies with which you work. Recognize that these frameworks will not only guide your evaluation of social policy, but can also provide you with the insights needed to improve social policy.

Sources of information regarding a social policy include the original code or statute, administrative rules and regulations, and other governmental documents that describe and explain the policy. Various professional and advocacy organizations (e.g., Child Welfare League of America, National Association of Social Workers, American Association of Retired Persons, Children's Defense Fund, American Public Welfare Association, American Hospital Association, Urban League, Southern Poverty Law Center) distribute reports of their analysis of social policies relevant to their particular concerns. In addition, the observations of social workers and of clients will give you insight into how a given policy affects the lives of individuals and families. The social workers in your agency will have opinions about how social policy could be improved, how it benefits or harms clients, and how it complements or conflicts with other social policies. Clients may also have insights based on their experiences with effective or ineffective social policies.

As a way of learning about social policy, identify a social problem (e.g., unemployment) that your agency addresses. Next, identify a specific social policy related to that problem (e.g., public assistance laws, unemployment compensation laws). Using the questions found in the workbook activity, analyze this social policy and determine if it is adequate, effective, and positive in its effects.

During your analysis, consider the following categories of social policies, each of which reflects a philosophy, a set of values, and a belief system about how society should deal with social problems:

- *Policies of social and financial support* are those intended to help or encourage people to carry out their roles and responsibilities and meet their basic needs for food, shelter, and so on. Examples include policies related to financial assistance, medical care for the poor, and subsidized day care for the children of parents who are poor.
- *Policies of protection* are those that seek to protect people from harm and exploitation, especially those who are most vulnerable. Examples are policies related to child abuse and neglect, domestic violence, the frail elderly, and to groups often subjected to discrimination and oppression.
- *Policies of rehabilitation and remediation* are those intended to correct or minimize the impact of certain disabling conditions such as serious mental illness, severe physical disabilities, developmental disabilities, and chronic illness.
- *Policies of prevention* are those that attempt to prevent certain social and health problems from developing or increasing. Examples are those that encourage economic development, immunizations, parent education, family planning, proper nutrition, and curfews for youth.
- *Policies of punishment and correction* are those that seek to punish and control persons who violate laws and societal norms. Examples are policies related to crime and delinquency, probation and parole, and the monitoring of convicted sex offenders.

The social policy you are analyzing will probably be one of these types, and thinking about it this way will help you understand the overall intent of the policy, the values that drive it, and how it may reflect public attitudes and political ideology.

As you study a social policy, you will soon be able to describe it in terms of the following social policy analysis factors:

- Its authority and auspices (federal, state, or local law)
- Its history and the reasons for its development
- Its stated purpose and goals
- Its key principles and main provisions
- Its impact on your agency's operation
- Its impact on your clients
- Its positive effects and advantages
- Its negative effects and disadvantages
- Its relationship to other social policies

After you have become familiar with a specific social policy and its effects, consider how it could be improved and what steps or actions would be necessary to achieve those improvements, such as changes in existing legislation, changes in administrative rules, or the creation of incentives to adhere to the policy.

Social Policy Analysis: A Workbook Activity

Identify one public social policy that has a significant impact on the operation of your agency and/or on the clients or consumers served by your agency. Then, in relation to that specific policy, answer the questions presented below.

1. What is the official name of the social policy being studied?

   _____

2. What is the legal citation of the policy (e.g., public law number or state statute code number)?

   _____

3. When was the social policy enacted or established and when was it significantly modified?

   _____

   _____

   _____

4. What programs are commonly associated with or mandated by this policy?

   _____

   _____

   _____

   _____

   _____

5. What conditions, problems, or needs does this social policy address (e.g., violence, poverty, homelessness, addictions, unemployment)?

   _____

   _____

6. What are the overall goals of this social policy (e.g., protection of a vulnerable population, provision of public assistance, or social control)?

   _____

   _____

7. Does this social policy apply to all people in society or to only a segment of society? If only certain people, which ones?

   _____

   _____

8. If this policy creates certain benefits or services, what are the criteria for eligibility? Why do some people receive benefits, services, or protection while others do not?

_____

_____

_____

_____

9. What underlying values, beliefs, or assumptions about people and their needs or problems are reflected in this policy? How do these values fit or not fit with the values of the social work profession?

_____

_____

_____

_____

10. Who benefits from this social policy?

_____

_____

11. Who loses or is placed at a disadvantage as a result of this social policy?

_____

_____

12. What is the source of the funds used to provide these benefits or services (e.g., federal or state income taxes, property tax, sales tax, or voluntary donations)?

_____

_____

13. Does the funding required to implement this social policy need to be reauthorized regularly (e.g., each year or every two years)?

_____

14. Is this social policy doing what it is supposed to do? If not, why?

_____

_____

_____

_____

15. In what ways could this social policy be changed to better address the needs and concerns of those it is designed to assist (e.g., close gaps in services, coordinate with related programs, increase funding, and change eligibility criteria)?

_____

_____

_____

_____

16. What would it take to actually change this policy (e.g., legislation, amendments, coalition building, or lobbying)?

_____

_____

_____

17. Does one political party support this policy more than another? If yes, why?

_____

_____

_____

18. Who opposes this policy and would like to change or eliminate it? Why?

_____

_____

_____

19. What interest groups, advocacy groups, or grassroots organizations support this social policy? Why?

_____

_____

_____

20. What interest groups, advocacy groups, or grassroots organizations oppose this social policy? Why?

_____

_____

_____

21. How are the roles and duties of social workers in your agency shaped, constrained, or expanded by this social policy?

_____

_____

_____

_____

22. To what degree and in what ways do agency staff at the local level have an opportunity to use professional judgment and discretion in deciding to whom and how the protections, services, and benefits associated with this policy are made available to clients and consumers?

_____

_____

_____

_____

23. What other social policies are interrelated with this particular policy? Do they fit together well or are they in conflict with each other?

_____

_____

_____

_____

Additional notes and comments:

_____

_____

_____

_____

_____

_____

Suggested Learning Activities

- Interview a social worker in your agency about a social policy that most directly affects his or her clients and obtain his or her recommendations for improving the social policy.
- Review the NASW *Code of Ethics* (1999) guidelines regarding the social worker's responsibility in the area of social policy (www.socialworkers.org).
- Examine the most recent edition of *Social Work Speaks*, which describes NASW's stance or position on a wide variety of social issues.
- Attend legislative or public hearings that gather public input before a social policy is enacted or modified.
- Identify your personal position regarding a controversial area of social policy, such as abortion. Attend meetings of an organization that takes an opposing position to try to understand that perspective, including the values, beliefs, knowledge, and assumptions on which it is based.
- Invite a state legislator to discuss the process by which social legislation is proposed, developed, and passed into law.
- Engage in a discussion with another social worker or student about a social policy you feel strongly about. Argue the opposite of your opinion in order to understand another perspective.

Additional Suggestions and Hints

- Use the Internet to monitor the progress of a bill before the U.S. Congress or your state legislature. For information on federal legislation relevant to social work, explore NASW's legislative page at http://naswca.org/legis.html.
- Identify grass roots advocacy organizations that support or oppose legislation that impacts your clients.
- Explore the websites of organizations that monitor social policy, such as the Electronic Policy Network (http://epn.org), Social Policy (www.socialpolicy.org), U.S. Department of Health and Human Services (www.os.dhhs.gov), World Wide Web Resources for Social Workers (www.nyu.edu/socialwork/ip).

Selected Bibliography

DiNitto, Diana, and Linda Cummins. *Social Welfare: Politics and Public Policy*. 6th ed. Boston: Allyn and Bacon, 2005.

Faherty, Sara. *Welfare Reform*. New York: Chelsea House, 2005.

Flynn, John. *Social Agency Policy*. 2nd ed. Chicago: Nelson-Hall, 1992.

Gilbert, Neil, and Paul Terrell. *Dimensions of Social Welfare Policy*. 5th ed. Boston: Allyn and Bacon, 2002.

Ginsberg, Leon. *Conservative Social Welfare Policy*. Chicago: Nelson-Hall, 1998.

Heffernan, W. Joseph. *Social Welfare Policy*. New York: Longman, 1992.

Jansson, Bruce. *Becoming an Effective Policy Advocate*. 3rd ed. Pacific Grove, CA: Brooks/Cole, 1999.

Long, Dennis D., Carolyn J. Tice, and John D. Morrison. *Macro Social Work Practice: A Strengths Perspective*. Belmont, CA: Thomson Brooks/Cole, 2006.

Lowy, Louis. *Social Work with the Aging*. 2nd ed. Prospect Heights, IL: Waveland, 1991.

Mkandawire, Thandika. *Social Policy in a Developmental Context*. New York: Palgrave Macmillan, 2004.

National Association of Social Workers. *Code of Ethics*. Washington, DC: NASW Press, 1999.

National Association of Social Workers. *Social Work Speaks: NASW Policy Statements 2003–2006*. 6th ed. Washington, DC: NASW Press, 2003.

Perez-Koenig, Rosa, and Barry Rock, eds. *Social Work in the Era of Devolution: Toward a Just Practice*. New York: Fordham University, 2001.

Popple, Philip R., and Leslie Leighninger. *The Policy-Based Profession: An Introduction to Social Welfare Policy Analysis for Social Workers*. Boston: Allyn and Bacon, 2004.

Rodgers, Harrell R. *American Poverty in a New Era of Reform*. 2nd ed. Armonk, NY: M. E. Sharpe, 2006.

Roth, William. *The Assault on Social Policy*. New York: Columbia University Press, 2001.

Schroeder, Leila. *The Legal Environment of Social Work*. Washington, DC: NASW, 1995.

Seccombe, Karen. *So You Think I Drive a Cadillac? Welfare Recipients' Perspective on the System and Its Reform*. Boston: Allyn and Bacon, 1999.

Sherraden, Michael, ed. *Inclusion in the American Dream: Assets, Poverty and Public Policy*. New York: Oxford University Press, 2001.

van Wormer, Katherine. *Social Welfare: A World View*. Chicago: Nelson-Hall Publishers, 1997.

12 | Diversity

GOALS FOR LEARNING

- To learn how human services agencies and programs adapt programs and practices to address the concerns and needs of diverse clients
- To understand how client experiences with minority status and discrimination might influence their lives and their use of human services and programs
- To become aware of the legal and ethical prohibitions against discrimination
- To understand your own values and beliefs and how they might affect relationships with persons from different backgrounds

We live in an increasingly diverse and pluralistic society. Our nation is made up of many distinct ethnic, religious, and cultural groups. Consequently, its people have different values, beliefs, traditions, and languages. Social workers and social services agencies are being challenged to find ways of recognizing, respecting, and accommodating differences while treating all clients and consumers with fairness and equality under the law.

Members of the social work profession believe that all people have worth, simply because they are human beings. All possess certain fundamental human rights and all have basic responsibilities, including the responsibility to treat others with respect, dignity, and fairness. These beliefs are prerequisites to peaceful relations among people, to social justice, and to the effective and proper operation of human services organizations.

Public and private human services agencies must be thoughtful and fair as they make decisions concerning who is eligible for the services they offer and how best to allocate limited resources. In keeping with federal law, agencies must avoid discrimination based on race, color, sex, national origin, age, religion, creed, and physical and mental disability.

Background and Context

Culture refers to the learned patterns of thought and behavior that are passed from generation to generation. One's culture consists of the unspoken and unquestioned assumptions and ideas about the nature of reality, the human condition, and how life should be lived. Everything we do, or think about doing, is influenced by the ways of thinking, values, beliefs, expectations, and customs that make up our culture. All of our professional knowledge and practice, all legal codes, and all agency policies and procedures are shaped by culture. Broadly defined, culture can include not only references to ethnicity or background, but also the influence of such variables as age, disability, and sexual orientation. Each of these forms of diversity shapes clients' thoughts, behavior, and world views.

Whittaker and Tracy (1989) observe that every contact between a social worker and client is, at some level, a cross-cultural encounter.

> On the one hand, the worker brings a particular knowledge base, set of value components, and methods of helping—all of which have been shaped in part by his or her own cultural background, by that of the dominant culture, and by the values and ethics of the professional helping community. These influences shape the manner in which a social worker will define social problems, what aspects will be considered relevant to assess, and what specific interventions will be employed to ameliorate the problem. On the other hand, the client also brings cultural elements to the social work relationship, including culturally determined patterns of help seeking and service utilization. (147)

Ethnocentrism is the tendency to assume that one's own culture, including one's beliefs and way of life, is normal and even superior and an appropriate standard for judging the beliefs and behaviors of other people. Needless to say, we cannot avoid being ethnocentric to some degree because our own beliefs, values, and patterns feel natural and normal and seem rooted in common sense and our daily lives. These are such an integral part of us that it is difficult to realize that there can be other ways of thinking and living. However, we must strive to become more aware of how our own culture is influencing our thoughts, decisions, and actions in order to avoid misunderstanding our clients and failing to recognize and respect their unique culture.

Most people are prejudiced to some degree. The word *prejudice* means to prejudge or to judge before one has a factual basis for forming a judgment. It refers to evaluating a person in a negative way, simply because that person belongs to a group or category, such as an ethnic minority.

Prejudice can breed *discrimination*, which refers to decisions, behaviors, or actions that deprive an individual or a whole group of certain rights and opportunities. It should be noted that prejudiced beliefs and attitudes do not always give rise to discriminatory behavior. Moreover, it is possible to engage in discrimination without being prejudiced, as in the case of an employee or a professional who follows a culturally insensitive and unjust policy or is truly ignorant of how his or her decisions and behaviors are causing harm to a group.

Discrimination can be either intentional or unintentional, depending on whether it was motivated by prejudice and the intent to harm. Discrimination can be personal or institutional. In *personal discrimination,* an individual behaves in ways that cause harm to the members of a group. In *institutional discrimination,* the harm is the result of the beliefs and practices that are embedded in law, in social and economic systems, and in governmental or organizational policy. Examples of laws that seem discriminatory to many people and that are used as examples of institutional racism include those requiring English as a primary language, those restricting refugees' or illegal immigrants' access to basic services, and those that disallow insurance and governmental benefits to domestic or same sex partners.

For both legal and ethical reasons, social workers must avoid discriminating. Section 4.02 of the NASW *Code of Ethics* (1999, 22–23) states that:

> Social workers should not practice, condone, facilitate, or collaborate with any form of discrimination on the basis of race, ethnicity, national origin, color, sex, sexual orientation, age, marital status, political belief, religion, or mental or physical disability.

People tend to be ethnocentric—that is, they assume that their way of life is a superior or appropriate standard for judging others. It is difficult to completely rid oneself of the prejudice acquired during his or her upbringing, but social workers must constantly guard against falling into the ethnocentric trap when assessing and working with clients. The professional helper should watch for these following signals that his or her thinking is racist or otherwise prejudiced:

Sheafor and Horejsi (2006) explain that ethnocentrism exists when:

- Stereotyped explanations are given for the behavior of persons of a specific ethnic or minority group.
- The same helping strategies are used for all clients who are members of a particular ethnic or minority group.
- The importance of culture and ethnicity in a person's life are minimized, or at the other extreme, used to explain nearly all behavior. (175)

Clients' membership in a minority group may have a more significant influence on their interaction with a social worker or agency than does their membership in a specific cultural group. A *minority group* is one whose members have significantly less power and control over their lives than the members of the dominant or majority groups of the society. Typically, the members of a minority group experience some level of discrimination and, according to Schaefer (2004, 6), "a narrowing of life's opportunities—for success, education, wealth, the pursuit of happiness—that goes beyond any personal shortcoming he or she may have."

Schaefer (2005) identifies several characteristics of a minority group. For example:

1. Members . . . experience unequal treatment and have less power over their lives than members of a dominant group have over theirs. Social inequality may be created or maintained by prejudice, discrimination, segregation, or even extermination.
2. Members . . . share physical or cultural characteristics that distinguish them from the dominant group such as skin color or language. . . .
3. Members . . . are born into the group. [Membership is not voluntary.]
4. Members . . . have a strong sense of group solidarity. [They] make strong distinctions between members of their own group (the in-group) and everyone else (the out-group). When a group is the object of long-term prejudice and discrimination, the feeling of "us versus them" can and often does become extremely intense. (7)

Minority status is not simply a function of numbers. In a given society, a particular group may be in the majority in terms of percentage of the overall population, but still have minority status. For example, even though females are slightly more numerous than males, women are often considered a minority group because they have less power and control over their lives than do men, and because they experience prejudice and discrimination based on gender. Minority status may also be tied to age, sexual orientation, physical or mental disability, socioeconomic status, educational background, or religion. If people perceive themselves as different from others or as less powerful and more vulnerable, these perceptions have an impact on help-seeking behavior, on how they expect to be treated, and on what they consider to be a useful and relevant service or program.

Social agencies vary in their capacity to respond effectively to culturally diverse clients. Cross (1988, 1–4) suggests that the various levels of cultural competency and cultural sensitivity among human services agencies exist along a continuum. Six levels are identified on this continuum. Consider, based on your observations

Food for Thought

In spite of their training, behavioral science students, researchers, and practitioners are no more immune to racism than is the average person. (Lum 1992, 133)

• • •

If practitioners do not incorporate culturally competent skills and knowledge in their assessment, diagnosis, and treatment, many minority patients will fall victim to the "culturally encapsulated" practitioner. (Lecca et al. 1998, 7)

• • •

While living within one's culture and sharing a history with the majority society, one takes both culture and history for granted. History and culture shape and provide the boundaries and context of one's identity, and it is only when one is removed from the familiarity of these boundaries, and when one's culture is challenged, that one consciously attempts to adhere to the once familiar or begins to critically examine it. (Lieberman and Lester 2004, 298)

• • •

When providing culturally sensitive practice social workers must avoid applying a narrow cultural "lens" that can interpret client system traditions and problem-solving processes as abnormal or dysfunctional. (Colby and Dziegielewski 2004, 135)

• • •

The biases that may be the most difficult for us to detect are those that relate to our taken-for-granted cultural norms. Most theory, by its very nature as a scientific endeavor, is permeated with Western value assumptions that we rarely think to question. (Robbins et al. 2006, 23)

• • •

It is the rare individual who swims in this culture of homophobia and heterosexism and stays dry. (Fish and Harvey 2005, 98)

• • •

Once systems of oppression are in place, they are self-perpetuating. (Adams et al. 1997, 17)

• • •

Cultural competence necessitates working with the idiosyncratic differences between cultures but also requires the essential skills of advocacy and negotiation so that groups that have been oppressed and stripped of their self-confidence struggle through the complexities of the majority society. (Lieberman and Lester 2004, 303)

• • •

The world view of the culturally different client who comes to counseling boils down to one important question: "What makes you, a counselor/therapist, any different from all the others out there who have oppressed and discriminated against me?" (Sue and Sue 1990, 6)

• • •

Cultural self-awareness is a vital skill for social work practice. This includes recognition of one's own cultural influences upon values, beliefs and judgments, as well as the same influences derived from the professional culture of social work. Awareness of the effects of these personal and professional influences upon client relations is necessary for the implementation of an ethnic sensitive approach. Without self-awareness, biases will be unconsciously imposed and client self-determination will be compromised. The commitment of the social work profession to equal treatment of all groups requires an approach which is not "color blind," but rather sensitive to the particular situations of each individual, including the impact of their group membership on their lives. (Winkelman 1999, 7)

or formal evaluations of your agency, where your organization might fall on this continuum.

1. *Destructiveness*—The agency's policies, programs, practices, and attitudes are destructive to cultures and hence, to the individuals of the culture. The agency is aware of its negative effect on the peoples' culture and believes its actions are desirable or justified.
2. *Incapacity*—The agency's policies, programs, and practices are destructive but these negative effects are unintended and unrecognized.
3. *Blindness*—The agency does not recognize important differences. It assumes that all people are the same and that all clients can and should be treated the same without consideration of different customs and belief systems.

4. *Pre-Competence*—The agency recognizes its inability to properly serve minorities or those who are culturally different and is working to improve service to a specific population. Efforts may include recruiting minority personnel, seeking cultural knowledge, and building linkages with the minority community.

5. *Basic Competence*—The agency recognizes and respects cultural differences and conducts ongoing self-assessments of its policies and practices and continually works to expand its cultural knowledge and the special resources needed to adequately serve minority groups.

6. *Advanced Competence*—In addition to activities of basic competence, the agency strives to develop new knowledge of culturally competent practice and is an advocate for changes within the wider human services system and throughout society.

Guidance and Direction

In an effort to see your agency from the perspective of diverse individuals, examine its physical environment, its written materials, and its staffing patterns. Assess whether your agency is accessible to persons with disabilities. Look to see if reading material, posters, and artwork would appeal to diverse groups of people, including language adaptations and visual representations of people from a variety of backgrounds. Read agency written materials to determine if they are free of bias and whether they use inclusive language. Finally, learn if the agency staff is diverse and represents people of various ages, cultures, sexual orientations, and other backgrounds.

Many social work students work hard at being culturally sensitive and respectful of differences among people. However, they, like other people, may not always recognize their own biases, prejudices, or ignorance regarding diverse groups. The practicum offers an important opportunity for self-examination and self-correction in terms of such personal limitations.

You may believe that people are more alike than different, and also that treating all clients alike is fair and reasonable. However, these beliefs do not recognize the importance of diversity, and may cause you to overlook unique aspects of a client's background and the powerful impact of minority status. Although it is true that people have much in common, it is also true that there are differences and these can greatly affect social work practice. Sue and Sue (1990, 165) remind us that "In counseling, equal treatment may be discriminatory."

Recognize the positive experiences resulting from minority group status, such as ethnic pride, bilingual abilities, community solidarity, extended family cohesion, and a strong sense of history. These experiences are strengths on which a professional relationship and a possible intervention can be built. Do not assume that membership in a minority group has only negative implications.

Work to understand any negative experiences your clients may have had because of their minority status, such as discrimination in school, housing, or employment, inappropriate placement in foster homes, or threats and violence in the form of hate crimes. Remember that many personal problems such as depression, poverty, dropping out of school, substance abuse, suicide, and even physical illness may have some roots in the stress and inner turmoil a person feels when subjected to discrimination or oppression.

If you are the member of a minority group, you may be better able to understand the effects of prejudice and discrimination, as well as the unique benefits that are a result of such membership. It is also important for you to have satisfactorily resolved any related personal issues, anger, and resentment in order to be objective and to perceive the uniqueness of every situation and individual. A social worker who, for whatever reason, is bitter and has a personal agenda will be of little help to clients. However, such negative experiences of personal discrimination or marginalization can provide motivation and passion for the work you may do with others who are experiencing oppression.

Social work with diverse clients is complex and demanding. Simple and stereotypical adaptations of usual approaches or slight changes in the agency's standard operating procedures are not likely to be effective. Rather, you will need to develop distinct methods that are acceptable, relevant to, and appropriate for the specific group with which you are working.

If the clients you serve are more comfortable with a language different from your own, make a genuine effort to learn at least some of their language and to locate an interpreter when needed. This demonstrates your respect for their language and your desire to understand and communicate.

Be alert to the fact that misunderstandings and misinterpretations in cross-cultural interactions can occur in many areas and situations including:

- Spoken language (e.g., misunderstanding words, accent, and nuances)
- Nonverbal communication (e.g., misunderstanding gestures, facial expressions, touch, and tone of voice)
- Judgments concerning what is an appropriate level of directness, assertiveness, and disclosure of personal information
- Male–female relations and judgments concerning what is appropriate touching and appropriate expressions of attraction for another person
- Judgments concerning appropriate dress, body decorations, and level of modesty
- Importance assigned to punctuality, use of time, and planning ahead
- Work habits, ways of organizing and approaching work to be done, and level of formality in communication between employees in an organization
- Use of physical space and judgment as to what is an appropriate distance between people
- Ways of learning and teaching and giving and taking direction
- Ways of negotiating, handling conflict, and expressing emotion
- Ways of seeking and utilizing professional or culturally valued helpers
- Differences in definition of family and the involvement of family in social work interventions

Learn about client differences in worldview and how you and your clients may differ in the value and meaning assigned to, for example, loyalty and obligation to family and friends, time, money, mealtimes, independence, health and wellness, and religious practices.

Seek to understand your clients' beliefs about the appropriateness of asking for help and receiving help from professionals and agencies. The members of some ethnic groups may believe that personal and family problems should not be discussed with a person outside the family. Some may feel great shame if they must seek help from a stranger. Others may prefer to seek help from religious leaders, and some may view social workers with mistrust for historical reasons.

Recognize that different groups may hold very different beliefs about the nature and cause of personal problems. For example, some ethnic groups may view depression or physical illness as primarily a problem of spirituality (e.g., a consequence of eating a taboo food, having broken one's relationship with God, or of a lack of balance between one's spirit and body).

Appreciate that different groups have different ideas about what constitutes an appropriate method of helping and about who has the capacity and authority to help with or treat certain types of problems. For example, some people may choose to use informal helpers and spiritual leaders, prayer, purification ceremonies, and religious rituals rather than the services of a professional helper. As a professional you will need to learn how to work cooperatively with spiritual leaders, healers, and clergy. Expect to learn from them about approaches to helping that are valued by your clients.

Be alert to the fact that clients from a minority group may have had or may expect negative experiences when they must have contact with social workers or social agencies, based on their group's history with the dominant culture. Clients may also be fearful of interacting with social workers because they fear legal recrimination for themselves (e.g., illegal immigrants and homosexual clients living in states that have laws prohibiting homosexual sexual activity). Their fears may be a barrier to their development of trust and their willingness to invest themselves in a professional helping relationship. Be careful not to interpret such mistrust, fear, or anger as client resistance. Do not automatically interpret client quietness, reticence, or anxiety as pathology or dysfunction. When appropriate, acknowledge to your client that you recognize the differences that separate you, and show your appreciation for their struggles by validating their experiences. Attempt to bridge the gap between you by developing culturally competent practice.

Developing competence in working with diverse populations and acquiring the knowledge about diverse client groups required for truly effective practice will be a long-term, perhaps lifelong process. Relish the possibilities available to you as you venture into work with clients and communities who are very different from you, and remain aware of the limitations of your ability to understand others' experiences and interpretations of their world. Even the most skilled and experienced social workers cannot know the intricacies of every culture or minority group, so try to learn about the world of others in an authentic way.

Work to understand as many facets of working with individuals with disabilities as you can. This includes knowing the laws pertaining to accessibility, treating persons with disabilities as individuals, and using language that avoids labels and emphasizes the person before his or her disability. Strike a balance between acknowledging the disability and not allowing it to color your entire view of the person's abilities and limitations.

Develop what social workers call a *dual perspective*, which is the consciously used ability to focus simultaneously on the attitudes, values, and customs of the larger, perhaps dominant society and the attitudes, values, and customs of the individual client or family. Doing this while also being aware of the impact of your own values, attitudes, and customs will allow you to more effectively relate to diverse clients, understand how they are impacted by the larger social system, and at least partially view your clients' experiences from their point of view and not just your own.

Watch for what can be described as agency efforts for "cooling out" diverse clients (Alle-Corliss and Alle-Corliss, 2006).

- *Ambiguous standards.* There is no consistency or uniformity, which creates confusion for clients. Clients may feel ambivalent about returning for further assistance.
- *Status differential.* Workers may use a large vocabulary and pose as having a higher status than their clients. Clients feel inferior and reluctant to return for help.
- *Inappropriate use of inquiry.* Workers may ask clients to share information when they are not ready, willing, or capable. This approach is insensitive to the clients' needs and capacities.
- *Inflexible approach to helping:* The worker demands that clients comply with his or her or the agency's expectations.

- *Being tentative about services.* The worker or agency may be tentative about providing services, unsure about how to help, and reluctant to engage fully with the client. This behavior may create a sense of futility in the client.
- *Gradual disengagement.* Helpers may gradually disengage from clients in an effort to discourage them from continuing treatment.
- *Sidetracking.* The worker or agency may prematurely refer clients elsewhere, for a variety of reasons—not feeling comfortable with certain clients, not knowing how to help clients, not believing clients are capable of changing.
- *Denial of services.* Clients are denied services because of the worker's or agency's discomfort with or negative views of the client's group. (150)

Work to broaden what Anderson and Carter (2003, 154–155) call *cultural borderlands,* which refer to the area of overlap between the social worker's cultural identity and the client's cultural identity. This can be done by expanding your knowledge of diverse people, increasing your awareness of the impact of your own cultural identity on your work, and recognizing that your communication with your clients and their communication with you are both seen through personal and cultural filters.

Identity and Self-Awareness: A Workbook Activity

1. How would you describe yourself in terms of gender? Race? Ethnicity? Socio-economic class? Religion? Age group? Minority group? Sexual orientation?

_____

_____

_____

_____

2. Describe your earliest memories of realizing your own identity in terms of your gender, race, ethnicity, socioeconomic class, and religion.

_____

_____

_____

_____

3. What positive and negative characteristics were ascribed to your gender, race, ethnicity, socioeconomic class, and religion by your family? Your relatives? Your neighbors? Your classmates in elementary school and high school?

_____

_____

_____

_____

4. What are the positive aspects of each of these group identities or memberships for you?

_____

_____

_____

_____

5. What are the negative aspects of each of these group identities or memberships for you?

_____

_____

_____

_____

6. How might your identity, characteristics, and membership in particular groups affect your work with clients who are different from you?

_____

_____

_____

_____

7. Describe a time and place when you were in the minority in terms of your race, skin color, ethnicity, or religion (i.e., most others present were of a different group). What were your feelings about this experience?

_____

_____

_____

_____

8. What are your most common thoughts and feelings when you encounter people who are different from yourself?

_____

_____

_____

_____

_____

9. What biases and stereotypes, if any, have you identified within yourself as you have encountered clients who are different from you? What can you do to ensure that these do not color your work?

_____

_____

_____

_____

10. What steps can you take to improve your skills in working with diverse clients?

_____

_____

_____

_____

Additional notes and comments:

_____

_____

_____

_____

_____

_____

Awareness in Your Agency: A Workbook Activity

1. What specific actions has your agency taken to make sure it is in compliance with federal law that prohibits discrimination on the basis of race, color, sex, national origin, age, religion, creed, physical or mental disability, and familial status?

   _____

   _____

   _____

   _____

2. In what ways does your agency make accommodations for clients or consumers who have a physical or mental disability or limitation?

   _____

   _____

   _____

   _____

3. In what ways does your agency make accommodations for clients who are not fluent in or comfortable with the English language?

   _____

   _____

   _____

   _____

4. About what percentage of your agency's clients could be described as members of a cultural, ethnic, religious, or racial minority?

   _____

   What groups are they?

   _____

   _____

   _____

   _____

5. What special efforts has your practicum agency made to reach out to and provide relevant services or programs to members of minority groups?

_____

_____

_____

_____

6. What specific actions, if any, has your agency taken to make sure it does not discriminate on the basis of sexual orientation? On the basis of clients' political beliefs, religion, or age?

_____

_____

_____

_____

7. To what extent are members of minority groups represented on your agency's board of directors or on advisory boards?

_____

_____

_____

8. What culturally sensitive assessment instruments or practice techniques, if any, does your agency use with clients who are members of minority groups?

_____

_____

_____

9. Is there anything about your agency that might discourage minorities from using its services (e.g., the racial, ethnic, or gender makeup of staff; location; office hours and days of operation; reputation in community; costs; perceived attitude toward minorities)?

_____

_____

_____

_____

10. What state or federal laws or regulations may affect minority clients negatively (e.g., anti-immigration laws and laws that prohibit same-sex marriage)?

   _____

   _____

   _____

   _____

11. What grievance procedures are available to clients or consumers if they believe they have experienced discrimination by the agency or its staff?

   _____

   _____

   _____

   _____

12. About what percent of the personnel assigned to professional and administrative jobs within your agency are:

   _____% Members of a racial or ethnic minority

   _____% Persons with physical or mental disabilities

   _____% Women

   _____% Members of a religious minority

   _____% Over 65 years of age

   _____% Fluent in a second language

   _____% Persons of a sexual minority

13. Does your agency or organization have an affirmative action program that is applied when hiring new staff? If yes, does the program achieve its purpose?

   _____

   _____

   _____

   _____

14. Where on the cross-cultural continuum described by Cross (see Background and Context section) would you place your agency? Why?

   _____

   _____

   _____

Additional notes and comments:

_____

_____

_____

_____

_____

_____

Diversity in Client Behavior: Situations to Discuss

Many factors influence the behavior and decisions of clients. One important set of factors, but certainly not the only one, is the client's cultural and ethnic background. Below is a list of situations that a social worker might encounter. Read each one carefully and answer each of the following questions about each situation.

- What diverse beliefs, values, or customs might be operating in this situation that would explain or clarify the client's behavior or choices?
- How might these situations be misunderstood if you do not understand the beliefs and customs of the client?
- What else would you need to know in order to be competent in this situation?
- What individual or family strengths might be identified if you understood the client's culture, beliefs, customs, experiences, and spirituality?

1. A couple with six children hopes to have additional children. They live in a small and crowded house and have great difficulty paying their bills and handling expenses related to food, rent, and health care.

_____

_____

_____

_____

_____

2. A man who needs his job and wants to keep it did not report to work today. Instead, he drove 200 miles to be with a relative who had phoned him last night and requested his assistance.

_____

_____

_____

_____

3. A client did not appear for a scheduled appointment and did not submit an application form, even though these two actions are prerequisites for receiving government benefits that the client wants and desperately needs.

_____

_____

_____

_____

_____

_____

4. A client brings two of her relatives to a scheduled individual counseling session and assumes that they will be included.

_____

_____

_____

_____

_____

5. A family in need of counseling chooses to use indigenous healers, spiritual leaders, and cultural advisors rather than social workers or other professional helpers.

_____

_____

_____

_____

_____

6. The father and mother of a 16-year-old girl become very angry when their daughter asks if she can go on a date with a 17-year-old boy who is a high school classmate. The parents then restrict the daughter from all social activities for three months.

_____

_____

_____

_____

_____

7. The adults in a family that immigrated to this country three years ago avoid learning the English language, even though this decision erects a serious barrier to their economic advancement.

_____

_____

_____

_____

_____

8. During the first meeting with a social worker, a client asks the worker many personal questions about the worker's parents, children, marriage, religion, and family history.

_____

_____

_____

_____

_____

9. A client who lives in near poverty and expresses a strong desire to obtain a decent job, refuses to take a well-paying job in another city 100 miles away.

_____

_____

_____

_____

_____

10. A woman whose husband restricts her movement, and verbally and physically abuses her, returns to live with her husband after seeking shelter for herself and her children in a domestic violence shelter.

_____

_____

_____

_____

_____

11. A husband and wife have been caring for the husband's elderly father for six years. The father is very ill and dependent, and requires around the clock care and supervision. A doctor and medical social worker suggest that the couple seek the help of a home attendant or consider placing the father in a nursing home. The couple becomes very angry and flatly refuses to even discuss such options.

_____

_____

_____

_____

_____

12. Parents who recently immigrated to this country refuse to authorize recommended corrective surgery for their daughter, a decision that will result in permanent disability.

_____

_____

_____

_____

_____

13. A woman whose 12-year-old daughter was sexually molested and impregnated by the child's uncle refuses to report this matter to authorities and wants to avoid making an issue out of the situation.

_____

_____

_____

_____

_____

14. An immigrant family who was robbed of several valuable possessions refuses to report the crime or speak with police.

_____

_____

_____

_____

_____

_____

15. An enrolled member of an American Indian tribe is in need of social services, but is reluctant to accept them from an agency that provides these services to individuals and families from many different backgrounds.

_____

_____

_____

_____

_____

_____

16. A family that is eligible for needed social services that are available on proof of citizenship chooses not to use these services.

_____

_____

_____

_____

_____

_____

17. An elderly woman who could benefit from mental health services declines them.

_____

_____

_____

_____

_____

_____

18. A person involved in a same-sex relationship is experiencing intimate violence at the hands of his or her partner, but declines to seek legal protection.

_____

_____

_____

_____

_____

_____

19. A family whose child is in grave danger of dying without a blood transfusion recommended by a team of physicians refuses to allow their child to undergo this procedure.

_____

_____

_____

_____

_____

_____

20. A student with a severe learning disability refuses university-provided accommodations, and is in danger of being placed on academic probation because her grade point average is below the university requirement for good academic standing.

_____

_____

_____

_____

_____

_____

21. A client with a severe mental illness cannot maintain employment or stable housing because of his symptoms when not on his prescribed medications, but he refuses to take them.

_____

_____

_____

_____

_____

_____

Suggested Learning Activities

- Attend cultural and religious celebrations and activities that are meaningful to many of the clients or consumers served by your agency (e.g., powwows, religious ceremonies, and gay pride events).
- Invite respected members of various ethnic and religious groups to explain how cultural and religious factors might influence clients' perceptions of the agency's programs and services and whether they would be inclined to use those services.
- Listen to music and read books and poetry by members of cultural or minority groups served by your agency.
- Study the history of the diverse groups your agency serves.
- Visit agencies that specifically serve members of minority groups (e.g., refugee programs, women's centers, gay and lesbian community centers, and advocacy groups for persons with disabilities). Ask how their programs differ from yours.
- Seek special training designed to help human services personnel respond more effectively to diverse clients.
- Examine assessment tools used in your agency to determine if they could be considered culture bound or culturally inappropriate.

Additional Suggestions and Hints

- In Sheafor and Horejsi (2006) read the section entitled "Applying Cultural Competence to Helping" (172–180).
- Read articles in the *Journal of Multicultural Social Work* and *Journal of Gay and Lesbian Services.*
- Read the novel about head injuries from the perspective of a client titled *Every Good Boy Does Fine* (see bibliography).

Selected Bibliography

Adams, Marianne, Lee Anne Bell, and Pat Griffin, eds. *Teaching for Diversity and Social Justice: A Sourcebook.* New York: Routledge, 1997.

Alle-Corliss, Lupe, and Randy Alle-Corliss. *Human Services Agencies: An Orientation To Fieldwork.* Belmont, CA: Thomson Brooks/Cole, 2006.

Anderson, Joseph, and Robin Wiggins Carter, eds. *Diversity Perspectives for Social Work Practice.* Boston: Allyn and Bacon, 2003.

Appleby, George Allen, and Jeane W. Anastas. *Not Just a Passing Phase: Social Work with Gay, Lesbian and Bisexual People.* New York: Columbia University Press, 1998.

Child Welfare League of America. *Cultural Competence Self-Assessment Instrument.* Washington, DC: Child Welfare League of America, 2002.

Colby, Ira, and Sophia Dziegielewski. *An Introduction to Social Work: The People's Profession.* 2nd ed. Chicago: Lyceum Books, 2004.

Cross, Terry. "Services to Minority Populations: Cultural Competence Continuum." *Focal Point* 3.1 (Fall 1988): 1–4.

Dhooper, Sirjit Singh, and Sharon S. Moore. *Social Work Practice with Culturally Diverse People.* Thousand Oaks, CA: Sage Publications, 2001.

Egan, Gerald. *Skilled Helping around the World: Addressing Diversity and Multiculturalism.* Belmont, CA: Thomson Brooks/Cole, 2006.

Fish, Linda Stone, and Rebecca G. Harvey. *Nurturing Queer Youth: Family Therapy Transformed.* New York: W. W. Norton, 2005.

Laskowski, Timothy. *Every Good Boy Does Fine.* Dallas: Southern Methodist University, 2003.

Lecca, Pedro J., Ivan Quervalu, Joao V. Nunes, and Hector F. Gonzales. *Cultural Competency in Health, Social, and Human Services: Directions for the Twenty-First Century.* New York: Garland Publishing, 1998.

Lieberman, Alice A., and Cheryl B. Lester. *Social Work Practice with a Difference: Stores, Essays, Cases, and Commentaries.* Boston: Allyn and Bacon, 2004.

Lum, Doman. *Social Work Practice with People of Color: A Process-Stage Approach.* 4th ed. Pacific Grove, CA: Thomson Brooks/Cole, 2004.

Potocky-Tripodi, Miriam. *Best Practices for Social Work with Refugees and Immigrants.* New York: Columbia University Press, 2002.

Robbins, Susan P., Pranab Chatterjee, and Edward R. Canda. *Contemporary Human Behavior Theory: A Critical Perspective for Social Work.* Boston: Allyn and Bacon, 2006.

Shaefer, Richard. *Racial and Ethnic Groups.* 9th ed. Upper Saddle River, NJ: Prentice-Hall, 2004.

Sheafor, Bradford, and Charles Horejsi. *Techniques and Guidelines for Social Work Practice.* 7th ed. Boston: Allyn and Bacon, 2006.

Sue, Donald, and David Sue. *Counseling the Culturally Different: Theory and Practice.* 3rd ed. New York: John Wiley and Sons, Inc., 1999.

Whittaker, James, and Elizabeth Tracy. *Social Treatment.* 2nd ed. New York: Aldine De Gruyter, 1989.

13 | Professional Social Work

GOALS FOR LEARNING

- To understand the purpose, mission, and nature of the social work profession
- To clarify how social work is similar to and different from other helping professions
- To distinguish between professional and nonprofessional behavior
- To become aware of the challenges of adhering to principles of professional practice within a bureaucratic agency with many regulations and restrictions

Social workers see themselves as professionals and they describe their occupation as a profession. As a social work student you are expected to behave in a professional manner during your practicum, but what exactly is a profession and what does professional behavior look like? How does one decide whether clients are being treated in a truly professional manner and receiving a truly professional service? Does the presence of professionally trained social workers in an agency have an observable and positive effect on the nature and quality of the services received by clients or consumers?

Social work is one of many helping professions. Social workers often work closely with other helpers such as physicians, nurses, speech therapists, psychologists, substance abuse counselors, school counselors, and others. What do social workers do that is not done by the members of other helping professions? Is there anything unique or special about what social workers know or do? How is social work different?

This chapter will review basic information about the unique nature of our profession and offer criteria for judging whether your own work and the work you observe in your practicum setting is of a professional nature.

Background and Context

All professions and all professionals *profess* to have special and unique knowledge and skills. They profess to understand certain phenomena better than those who do not have this special training. Because they profess to adhere to a code of ethical conduct, they expect to be trusted by their clients and by the public at large. They profess to be accountable for their decisions and actions. Professionals lay claim to a certain domain of activities. This is the basis for professional licensing and certification. It is important to know that the requirements for licensing and certification vary from state to state. From a legal perspective, professionals are responsible for providing their clients with a certain standard of care, and if they fail to do so, they may be sued for malpractice or professional negligence.

Broadly speaking, a *profession* is an occupation that possesses certain characteristics:

- A unique body of knowledge and theoretical underpinnings from which special skills and techniques are derived
- Methods of teaching this body of knowledge and skills to persons entering the profession
- Recognition by society that the members of the profession possess a special expertise
- Sanction by the community or state to perform certain activities
- Practitioners who share a distinct culture, specialized language or terminology, sense of purpose, identity, history, and set of values
- A written code of ethics that guides practice activities
- A professional organization whose members are bound together by a common purpose
- Capacity and authority, usually by law, to regulate practice
- Ability to control the admission of new members to the profession
- A sense of "calling" to the profession by those entering it by virtue of their values, interests, or natural abilities

The National Association of Social Workers (1970, 2) defines *social work* as "the professional activity of helping individuals, groups, or communities enhance or restore their capacity for social functioning and creating societal conditions favorable to this goal." The term *social functioning* refers, in general, to the social well-being of people and especially their capacity and opportunity to meet their basic needs such as food, shelter, safety, self-worth, and to satisfactorily perform their social roles such as spouse, parent, student, employee, and citizen.

Social work professionals focus primarily on the interactions or transactions between the individual and his or her social environment. That environment is composed of a multitude of units and systems such as family; support networks; neighborhood and community groups and organizations; workplace; and various legal, educational, health, and human services systems. This is often referred to as the *person-in-environment* focus of the social work profession. Social workers often focus on how well the social environment supports individuals and families, and what clients can do to enhance the social systems of which they are a part.

The Council on Social Work Education (2003) explains that professional social work practice serves the following purposes:

- To enhance human well-being and alleviate poverty, oppression, and other forms of social injustice
- To enhance the social functioning and interactions of individuals, families, groups, organizations, and communities by involving them in accomplishing goals, developing resources, and preventing and alleviating distress
- To formulate and implement social policies, services, and programs that meet basic human needs and support the development of human capacities
- To pursue policies, services, and resources through advocacy and social or political actions that promote social and economic justice
- To develop and use research, knowledge, and skills that advance social work practice
- To develop and apply practice in the context of diverse cultures (31)

The first two of these purposes is concerned with enhancing social functioning and preventing impediments to effective social functioning. The other four seek to create conditions and social policies that ensure that people receive appropriate human services when needed and to prevent social problems from developing. Stated somewhat differently, we can say that a social worker will perform tasks and activities aimed at achieving the following:

- Restoring and maintaining the social functioning of people
- Enhancing the problem-solving and coping capacities of people
- Preventing the occurrence of serious personal and social problems
- Linking people with those systems and resources that can provide needed support, services, and opportunities
- Protecting the community from persons who consistently behave in ways that harm others
- Promoting humane and effective social policy and social services programs
- Planning, developing, and administering social agencies and social programs
- Promoting the effective and humane operation and administration of organizations and human services delivery systems that provide people with resources, services, and opportunities
- Protecting the most vulnerable members of society from destructive social influences
- Conducting research, developing and disseminating knowledge relevant to the practice of social work

Social work is often described as a value-driven profession because so much of what a social worker does is guided by a particular set of core values. However, all professions are rooted in a particular set of values. For example, the medical profession values health and physical wellness and the education profession values learning and academic success. Thus, the physician strives to develop knowledge and methods that can be used to maintain and restore health, and the educator strives to develop knowledge and methods that facilitate learning.

A profession can be viewed as an organized effort to actualize its core values. This idea is reflected in the definition of *social work practice* offered by *The Social Work Dictionary* (Barker 1995, 95): "The use of social work knowledge and social work skills to implement society's mandate to provide social services in ways that are consistent with social work values."

The NASW *Code of Ethics* (1999, 5–6) identifies six core values that should inform and guide the decisions and actions of a social worker. These values and their implications are described as follows:

Value: Service

Ethical Principle: Social workers' primary goal is to help people in need and to address social problems.

Social workers elevate service to others above self-interest. Social workers draw on their knowledge, values, and skills to help people in need and to address social problems. Social workers are encouraged to volunteer some portion of their professional skills with no expectation of significant financial return (pro bono service).

Value: Social Justice

Ethical Principle: Social workers challenge social injustice.

Social workers pursue social change, particularly with and on behalf of vulnerable and oppressed individuals and groups of people. Social workers' social change efforts are focused primarily on issues of poverty, unemployment, discrimination, and other forms of social injustice. These activities seek to promote sensitivity to and knowledge about oppression and cultural and ethnic diversity. Social workers strive to ensure access to needed information, services, and resources; equality of opportunity; and meaningful participation in decision making for all people.

Value: Dignity and Worth of the Person

Ethical Principle: Social workers respect the inherent dignity and worth of the person.

Social workers treat each person in a caring and respectful fashion, mindful of individual differences and cultural and ethnic diversity. Social workers promote clients' socially responsible self-determination. Social workers seek to enhance clients' capacity and opportunity to change and to address their own needs. Social workers are cognizant of their dual responsibility to clients and to the broader society. They seek to resolve conflicts between clients' interests and the broader society's interest in a socially responsible manner consistent with the values, ethical principles, and ethical standards of the profession.

Value: Importance of Human Relationships

Ethical Principle: Social workers recognize the central importance of human relationships.

Social workers understand that relationships between and among people are an important vehicle for change. Social workers engage people as partners in the helping process. Social workers seek to strengthen relationships among people in a purposeful effort to promote, restore, maintain, and enhance the well-being of individuals, families, social groups, organizations, and communities.

Value: Integrity

Ethical Principle: Social workers behave in a trustworthy manner.

Social workers are continually aware of the profession's mission, values, ethical principles, and ethical standards and practice in a manner consistent with them. Social workers act honestly and responsibly and promote ethical practices on the part of the organizations with which they are affiliated.

Value: Competence

Ethical Principle: Social workers practice within their areas of competence and develop and enhance their professional expertise.

Social workers continually strive to increase their professional knowledge and skills and to apply them in practice. Social workers should aspire to contribute to the knowledge base of the profession.

These six core values are the foundation of social work practice.

Although social work is a profession, social workers may or may not behave in a professional manner. Nonprofessional behavior leads to diminished quality of services and may also violate the NASW *Code of Ethics.* Sheafor and Horejsi (2006, 166) offer a comparison of professional and nonprofessional behavior in Table 13.1.

Social workers must be alert to the possibility of *professional drift.* This occurs when a social worker begins to neglect or avoid traditional social work values, purposes, and functions in favor of ones associated with another helping profession or discipline. This is evident, for example, when social workers abandon or avoid the title of social worker and prefer to be identified as psychotherapists. Shulman (1991, 10) explains that when social workers align themselves with the purposes and knowledge base of another profession that gives little attention to issues of

TABLE 13.1   Professional and Nonprofessional Behavior

Professional Behavior	Nonprofessional Behavior
Views social work as a calling and a lifetime commitment to certain values and action	Views social work simply as a job that can be easily abandoned if something better comes along
Bases practice on a body of knowledge and research findings that have been learned through a process of formal education and training	Bases practice on personal opinions or on agency rules and regulations
Bases decisions on facts, analysis, and critical thinking	Bases decisions on feelings and habits
Follows principles of good practice, regardless of other pressures	Allows political and fiscal pressures to dictate decisions and actions
Uses the profession's values, principles, and *Code of Ethics* to identify and resolve ethical issues	Lets many ethical concerns go unrecognized or be ignored; uses only personal moral judgments to resolve ethical issues
Upgrades knowledge and skills continually so that services to clients can be improved	Learns only what is required to keep the job
Takes responsibility for creating new knowledge and sharing it with peers	Does not see self as responsible for development of new knowledge
Assumes personal responsibility for examining the quality of services provided and for working to make agency, program, or policy changes that will improve services to the client	Is concerned only about doing the job as assigned or described by others; does not see self as responsible for agency, policy, or program changes
Expects and invites review of performance by peers	Avoids peer review
Keeps accurate and complete records of decisions and actions	Avoids recordkeeping; records are incomplete or inaccurate
Has the well-being and needs of the client as primary concern; does not expect to meet his or her own needs within work-related relationships	Has own well-being and needs as primary concern; expects to have his own needs met within work-related relationships
Develops a relationship with the client that is purposeful and goal oriented	Develops a relationship with the client that lacks a sense of direction and resembles a friendship
Exercises self-discipline; keeps emotions under control	Lacks self-discipline; expresses emotions in thoughtless and hurtful manner
Does not take client's expressions of negative emotion personally; seeks to understand the reasons behind the client's frustration and anger	Takes the client's frustrations and anger personally

Source: Sheafor, Bradford, and Charles Horejsi. *Techniques and Guidelines for Social Work Practice.* 7th ed. Boston: Allyn and Bacon, 2006. Copyright © 2000 by Pearson Education. Reprinted by permission of the publisher.

social justice and service to disadvantaged groups, it results in social workers ". . . who adopt a view of themselves as therapists first and social workers second, or not even social workers at all." Professional social workers, including those who perform the roles of counselor and psychotherapist, want to be known as social workers and identified with the social work profession.

For the most part, social work is an agency-based profession. Most social workers are employed by some type of social agency or social welfare–related organization. Social workers often experience a push and pull between loyalty to their organization and its managers and loyalty to their profession and its values and principles. On the one hand, they want the benefits that come from being an employee within an organization, and on the other hand they want the freedom and status that come from being an independent professional. This tension is illustrated in Table 13.2.

TABLE 13.2   Employee versus Professional Orientation to Social Work Practice

Employee Orientation	Professional Orientation
Employees are to follow all policies and rules.	Rules and policies may need to be adapted and changed to serve the best interests of clients.
Salary is to be determined by years of service to organization.	Salary is to be determined by level of knowledge, skill, and performance.
Loyalty and duty to superiors and organization are highest value.	Duty to clients is highest value.
Employees place their jobs in jeopardy if they openly criticize agency's operation and policy.	Professionals must speak out and question agency operations and policy if necessary to better serve clients.
All employees are to be supervised, and major decisions require approval from a higher level.	Professionals must have and are entitled to autonomy in their decisions and practice. Supervision is not always needed or appropriate.

Much of what a social worker does is shaped—and sometimes driven—by agency policy. For this reason, social workers must be attentive to the nature and purpose of their agency's policies and how these impact clients. From the perspective of professional social work, an agency policy should have the following characteristics:

- It promotes the well-being of clients and of the community as a whole.
- It is respectful and fair to those most directly affected by the policy.
- It serves to empower clients and it recognizes and builds on their strengths.
- It promotes social and economic justice, directly or indirectly.
- It is consistent with the core values and principles found in the *Code of Ethics*.
- It reflects the principle of effective social work based in current knowledge and research findings.
- It holds social workers and other agency employees accountable for the work they perform and the services they provide.
- It is clearly written, realistic, and consistent with relevant legal codes and regulations.

Guidance and Direction

A primary purpose of the practicum experience is to help you develop a professional identity as a social worker. To possess this identity means that you have a clear understanding of the purpose of the profession, your roles and responsibilities as a social worker, the profession's core values and ethical guidelines, and the skills and knowledge needed to perform social work tasks and activities. Most students begin developing a professional identity by observing other social workers and reflecting on their behavior, decisions, and attitudes.

As you meet social workers employed in various agencies, consider whether they possess the hallmarks of a professional with a philosophy of practice.

Food for Thought

A calling without professionalization is bumbling, ineffective, and even dangerous. A profession without a calling, however, has no taps of moral and humane rootage to keep motivation alive, to keep human sensitivities and sensibilities alert, and to nourish a proper sense of self-fulfillment. Nor does a profession without a calling easily envision the larger ends and purposes of human good that our individual efforts can serve. (Gustafson 1982, 502–503)

• • •

Social justice work challenges us to examine the social construction of reality, that is, the ways we use our cultural capacities to give *meaning* to social experience. It guides us to look at the *context* of social problems and question relations of *power*, domination and inequality that shape the way knowledge of the world is produced and whose view counts. It forces us to recognize the importance of *history* and a historical perspective to provide a window into how definitions of social problems and the structuring and shaping of institutions and individuals are time specific and contextually imbedded. Finally, social justice work opens up the *possibility* for new ways of looking at and thinking about programs, policies, and practices, and to envision the people with whom we work and ourselves as active participants in social transformation toward a more just world. (Finn and Jacobson 2003, 32)

• • •

Social work is one of the final protectors of the collective social trust. . . . (Reid and Popple 1992, 5)

• • •

No one likes to ask for anything. It is easier to ask an organization for help than to ask an individual. Ironically, social workers generally like to be relied on, like people to ask them for help, and feel great when they can help others. Here we are, wanting to be in the powerful position of making a difference in people's lives, while at the same time we realize how awful it makes most people feel to have to receive help with life's tasks. People often feel even worse to have to ask for help with things that they think they should be able to do themselves. They feel they should be able to take care of themselves and those who depend on them. Acknowledging the difficulty of asking for help and truly listening to the struggle clients have in asking is a gift one can extend. Seldom in North American culture do people take the time to truly listen and attempt to understand another's experience. This is the gift social workers offer. Seldom are people expected to share their innermost thoughts and fears and make themselves vulnerable in another's presence. This is the gift that clients offer. Recognition of this two-way gift exchange goes far in promoting a partnership in the helping relationship. (Kerson 2002, 177)

Drawing on ideas presented by Gambrill (2006, 12–15), these hallmarks include the following:

- Social workers are responsible for their decisions.
- Social workers help their clients attain outcomes of value to them.
- Social workers do not harm their clients.
- Social workers use the least restrictive and intrusive methods possible.
- Social workers fully inform their clients of and involve their clients in decisions.
- Social workers assume responsibility for maintaining up-to-date knowledge and skills.
- Social workers make well-reasoned decisions.
- Social workers value truth and recognize their ignorance and prejudice.
- Social workers engage in critical discussion and testing of claims.
- Social workers base decisions on both empirical data and theory.
- Social workers consider individual differences and challenge biases and stereotypes.
- Social workers develop self-knowledge.
- Social workers' words correspond to their actions.

Read the job description for social workers in your agency, and determine if it is consistent with the profession's stated purposes, values, and practice roles. Watch for variation between how social workers define their own roles and responsibilities and how their roles may be defined by administrators or funding sources. Ask your field instructor or other social workers how they attempt to meet the expectations of high-level administrators and fiscal managers while still adhering to the mission and purpose of the profession and fulfilling their obligations to their clients.

Review your social work practice courses to recall the variety of social work roles and activities described in social work textbooks. Common social work roles include counselor, broker, advocate, community organizer, facilitator, case manager, mediator, program planner, and policy analyst or researcher. Because BSW-level social workers and many MSW-level social workers are expected to be generalists, we recommend that you gain experience in many of these roles and learn to move between them as client needs dictate.

Identify the roles that the social workers in your agency perform and observe how social workers may select and shift their practice roles in response to individual situations and client needs. Become skilled at moving from one role to another, matching your actions to each situation and its requirements.

Strive to clarify how the values, knowledge base, and approach of the social work professional are different from those of other helping professionals such as clinical psychologists, nurses, school counselors, physicians, occupational therapists, and vocational counselors. Social work's uniqueness will become apparent if you truly understand the profession's core values and ethical principles, as well as the concept of social functioning. You will discover that social work's uniqueness lies in its commitment to the overall social functioning of people as well as its commitment to working for social change and social justice. However, contrary to the beliefs of many social work students, social work is not unique because it pays attention to the "whole person," the client's environment, and the ecological perspective. These are ideas also commonly discussed in textbooks for nursing, education, counseling, and occupational therapy. Social work's distinctive identity comes from its commitment to both enhancing the social functioning of clients and to creating social environments, conditions, and social policies that promote positive social functioning.

You are likely to encounter stereotypes and misconceptions about social workers and the social work profession, just as you would for any other profession, and you will need to learn how to respond to them appropriately. Such stereotypes may include ideas such as:

- Social workers like to meddle in other people's lives.
- Social workers create dependency in their clients.
- Social workers remove children from their homes and hand out welfare checks to the poor.
- Social workers are softheaded, low-level bureaucrats, and wild-eyed liberals.
- Anyone can do social work, including nonprofessionals and those with degrees in other related fields.
- Because many social workers are generalists, they are jacks of all trades and masters of none.

Hearing these misconceptions about your chosen profession will be frustrating. You may need to inform others about the profession's real purposes and values, as well as about the level of education required for professional social work. You might also ask yourself where these perceptions of social work originated, and consider whether some social workers may speak or behave in ways that perpetuate the stereotypes.

Negative images of the profession are often based on limited information about social work and sometimes on experiences with ineffective or unethical social workers. They could also be based on negative experiences with persons who are assumed to be social workers, but who do not have a degree in social work. While in your practicum, give careful thought to whether social workers are recognized and respected as true professionals within your agency and community. Consider why the social workers in certain agencies behave and are viewed as professionals, whereas in other agencies they neither behave as professionals, nor are they treated as professionals. Do what you can to enhance the image of the profession by purposefully using the title social worker to describe your work, by committing to practicing in the most competent and ethical manner possible, and by taking opportunities to inform the public about the profession.

Finally, you will probably find it helpful to remember that for all the emphasis on social work knowledge, theory, and research, you will not be effective if you do not pay close attention to what many consider the "art" of social work. As Sheafor and Horejsi (2006, 38–44) note, the "social worker as artist" has several components:

- *Compassion and courage.* You will daily confront the pain of others, and must join with them in a compassionate manner. You must also develop the inner strength to repeatedly face human suffering and frustration without being consumed by it.
- *Professional relationship.* Your most fundamental tool in practice is the capacity to build meaningful and productive professional relationships, which is rooted in your capacity for demonstrating empathy, genuineness, and nonpossessive warmth.
- *Creativity.* You must be innovative, imaginative, flexible, and persistent as you work to overcome barriers to change.
- *Hopefulness and energy.* You will need to believe in the basic goodness and ability of people, to continue working without becoming discouraged, and to bounce back from failures and mistakes.
- *Judgment.* You will need to develop sound judgment, critical thinking skills, thoughtful decision-making abilities, and the ability to reflect on and learn from successes and failures.
- *Personal values.* Your personal values must be compatible with the core values of social work, including respect for basic rights, a sense of social responsibility, commitment to individual freedom, and support for self-determination.
- *Professional style.* Because you are the instrument of change in practice, you will need to develop your own professional style, which is a combination of professional knowledge and your own personality and personal gifts.

The social worker's professional identity is formed as he or she blends these artistic elements with the science of the profession. Sheafor and Horejsi (2006) explain that:

the social worker must combine his or her personal qualities, creative abilities, and social concern with the profession's knowledge in order to help clients enhance their social functioning or prevent social problems from developing. Each person has unique personal qualities that represent the artistic component of social work practice. Professional education cannot teach these artistic features, although it can help the learner identify such strengths and develop the ability to focus on and apply them in work with clients. Professional education can also assist the learner in developing a beginning understanding of the knowledge (or science) that is necessary for effective practice. This merging and blending of one's art and the profession's science is initiated in social work education programs, but it is a lifelong activity, as social work knowledge is constantly expanding and the worker is being continually changed by life experiences. (37)

The Image and Impact of Social Work: A Workbook Activity

It is important to examine the impact of the profession's values, ethical code, practice principles, and knowledge base on the behavior and performance of the social workers in your practicum agency. In light of this, respond to the following questions.

1. Is the NASW *Code of Ethics* posted and frequently mentioned and discussed by the social workers in your practicum agency?

   _____

2. Does the NASW *Code of Ethics* appear to have a significant impact on decision making and practices within your practicum agency? If yes, in what ways? If no, why not?

   _____

   _____

   _____

   _____

3. To what extent and in what ways, if any, do conflicts between personal and professional values, political pressures, and a push to hold down operating costs keep agency staff from following principles of good social work practice and adhering to basic principles of the NASW *Code of Ethics?*

   _____

   _____

   _____

   _____

4. In what ways and to what degree are the six core values of the social work profession reflected in the mission of your agency and in the behavior of the social workers you observe (see Background and Context in this chapter)?

   _____

   _____

   _____

   _____

5. Which of social work's purposes are most apparent in the goals and activities of your agency and its social workers (see p. 164)?

   _____

   _____

   _____

6. Which of the six core values of social work are most lacking in your agency (see pp. 165–166)?

_____

_____

7. Which of the six core social work values are most central to your own practice?

_____

_____

_____

8. Which of the following social work roles are most often assumed by the social workers in your agency?

_____ Broker of services

_____ Case manager

_____ Advocate

_____ Social activist

_____ Counselor/therapist

_____ Collaborator/networker

_____ Group leader/facilitator

_____ Program planner

_____ Educator/trainer

_____ Community organizer

_____ Social policy analyst

_____ Researcher/program evaluator

_____ Administrator/manager/supervisor

_____ Other (specify)

_____

9. About what percentage of the social workers in your agency are members of NASW?

_____

About what percentage are active members of NASW?

_____

What are the requirements for obtaining and retaining a social work license in your state (e.g., degree required, examination, years of experience, and hours of supervised practice)?

_____

_____

_____

About what percentage of the social workers in your agency have a social work license?

_____

10. What governmental body issues social work licenses and receives complaints about the practice of social workers?

_____

_____

11. Does your agency require a social work degree (BSW or MSW) as preparation for certain positions or jobs? If yes, for what jobs?

_____

_____

_____

12. Do the administrators of your agency prefer to hire persons with degrees in social work rather than persons with training in other fields? If yes, why? If no, why not?

_____

_____

_____

13. Do the employees in your agency who have degrees in social work call themselves social workers?

_____

If not, why not? If they do not use the title social worker, what title do they use (e.g., therapist, case manager, program coordinator, client advocate) and why?

_____

_____

_____

_____

14. Do you see evidence of "professional drift" in your agency? If yes, describe and explain (see p. 166).

_____

_____

_____

_____

15. What professional journals do the social workers in your agency read on a regular basis?

_____

_____

_____

_____

16. What is the public image of social workers in your community? What forces and experiences have shaped this image?

_____

_____

_____

_____

17. What agency policies, procedures, and expectations reinforce and encourage social work professionalism within your agency (e.g., continuing education is expected and rewarded, workers are expected to take personal responsibility for decisions and actions, constant attention is given to professional ethics)?

_____

_____

_____

_____

18. What, if any, agency policies, procedures, and behavioral norms tend to undermine and discourage social work professionalism within your agency (e.g., lack of sanctions for sloppy work, political concerns driving decision making, or bureaucratic regulations taking precedence over individual client needs)?

_____

_____

_____

_____

19. What other professionals do you work with in your agency? How do you perceive your role and code of ethics to be similar to or different from theirs?

_____

_____

_____

Additional notes and comments:

_____

_____

_____

_____

_____

_____

Suggested Learning Activities

- Attend local chapter meetings of the NASW or the meetings of other social work–related professional organizations and decide what issues are of greatest concern to the social workers in your community.
- Review announcements of social work conferences and workshops to determine what topics are of interest to social workers.
- Watch for media portrayals of social workers in newspapers, magazines, and on television to determine how social work is described and whether it is usually presented in a positive or negative light.
- Join the National Association of Social Workers as a student member, which will allow you to keep abreast of professional social work issues and programs.

Additional Suggestions and Hints

- In Sheafor and Horejsi (2006), read and discuss the section entitled "Improving the Social Work Image" (625–626).
- Investigate a variety of social work membership organizations, such as Association for Community Organization and Administration, the National Association of Black Social Workers, the Association of Oncology Social Workers, the National Association of Puerto Rican/Hispanic Social Workers, the Clinical Social Work Federation, the National Indian Child Welfare Association, the Rural Social Work Caucus, the Society for Spirituality in Social Work Practice, the North American Association of Christians in Social Work, International Federation of Social Workers, and the Social Welfare Action Alliance.

Selected Bibliography

Barker, Robert L. *The Social Work Dictionary*. 3rd ed. Washington, DC: NASW Press, 1995.

Council on Social Work Education. *Handbook of Accreditation Standards and Procedures*. 5th ed. Alexandria, VA: CSWE, 2003.

DuBois, Brenda, and Karla Miley. *Social Work: An Empowering Profession*. 5th ed. Boston: Allyn and Bacon, 2005.

Finn, Janet L., and Maxine Jacobson. *Just Practice: A Social Justice Approach to Social Work*. Peosta, IA: Eddie Bowers Publishing, 2003.

Gambrill, Eileen. *Social Work Practice. A Critical Thinker's Guide*. 2nd ed. New York: Oxford University Press, 2006.

Gustafson, James F. "Professions as 'Callings,'" *Social Services Review* 56 (1982): 502–503.

Hokenstad, M. C., and James Midgley. *Lessons from Abroad: Adapting International Social Welfare Innovations*. Washington, DC: NASW Press, 2004.

Kerson, Toba Schwaber. *Boundary Spanning: An Ecological Reinterpretation of Social Work Practice in Health and Mental Health Systems*. New York: Columbia University Press, 2002.

National Association of Social Workers. *Code of Ethics*. Washington, DC: NASW Press, 1999.

Payne, Malcolm. *Modern Social Work Theory*. 3rd ed. Chicago: Lyceum, 2005.

Reid, P. Nelson, and Philip R. Popple. *The Moral Purposes of Social Work: The Character and Intentions of a Profession*. Chicago: Nelson-Hall Publishers, 1992.

Sheafor, Bradford, and Charles Horejsi. *Techniques and Guidelines for Social Work Practice*. 7th ed. Boston: Allyn and Bacon, 2006.

Shulman, Lawrence. *The Skills of Helping Individuals, Families, Groups, and Communities*. 5th ed. Chicago: Thomson/Wadsworth, 2006.

Specht, Harry, and Mark Courtney. *Unfaithful Angels: How Social Work Has Abandoned Its Mission*. New York: Free Press, 1994.

14

Social Work Ethics

GOALS FOR LEARNING

- To understand the definition of an ethical dilemma
- To identify the ethical questions and dilemmas that arise most frequently in your practicum setting
- To articulate various ethical positions and principles that are related to an ethical question or dilemma
- To become familiar with how your agency and its staff attempt to resolve ethical dilemmas
- To become aware of how the NASW *Code of Ethics* may affect the decisions and actions of social workers within your agency setting
- To become aware of how your own moral and ethical standards may differ from those identified in the NASW *Code of Ethics*

Every day, social workers make decisions and take actions based on ethical principles. These principles have a profound and far-reaching impact on practice. They also have a significant impact on a student's social work practicum.

Prior to beginning your social work practicum, you have studied the NASW *Code of Ethics* and devoted classroom time to the discussion of ethical questions and issues. Up to this point, the topic of professional ethics may have seemed rather abstract. In your practicum you will meet these questions and dilemmas face to face.

This chapter briefly reviews the nature of professional values and ethics, discusses the content of the NASW *Code of Ethics,* and offers guidance on resolving ethical dilemmas. The workbook activity will heighten your awareness of ethical concerns within your practicum setting.

Background and Context

The National Association of Social Workers was formed in 1955 by the merging of several separate social work organizations, some of which had developed a code of ethics for their members. In 1960, the NASW adopted its first *Code of Ethics.* It has been revised several times. In this section I will be referring to the NASW *Code of Ethics* that became effective in 1999.

Ruggiero (1992) explains that

> Ethics is the study of right and wrong conduct. . . . The focus of ethics is moral situations—that is, those situations in which there is a choice of behavior involving human values. [Values] are those qualities that are regarded as good and desirable. (4–5)

Social work ethics are rooted in six values (listed in Chapter 13). A *value* can be defined as a consistent preference that affects one's decisions and actions and is based on one's deepest beliefs and commitments. A value reflects one's fundamental beliefs about what is right and wrong. Typically, emotions are attached to our values. Thus, if we do not experience a stirring of our emotions when we think or speak about our values, we are probably not talking about a genuine value.

According to NASW (1999), the *Code of Ethics* serves six purposes:

1. Identifies core values on which social work's mission is based
2. Summarizes broad ethical principles that reflect the profession's core values and establishes a set of specific ethical standards that should be used to guide social work practice
3. Is designed to help social workers identify relevant considerations when professional obligations conflict or ethical uncertainties arise
4. Provides ethical standards to which the general public can hold the social work profession accountable
5. Socializes practitioners new to the field to social work's mission, values, ethical principles, and ethical standards
6. Articulates standards that the social work profession itself can use to assess whether social workers have engaged in unethical conduct (2)

NASW (1999) explains that although the *Code of Ethics* provides principles and standards, it

> does not provide a set of rules that prescribe how social workers should act in all situations. Specific applications of the *Code* must take into account the context in which it is being considered and the possibility of conflicts among the *Code*'s values, principles, and standards. (2–3)

Included in the *Code of Ethics* are hundreds of separate statements of general principle, some of which may be in conflict in a specific practice situation. The term *ethical dilemma* describes a situation in which the social worker has two or more ethical obligations (e.g., to take action to protect the client from imminent harm and also to protect the client's right to privacy) but cannot adhere to one principle without violating another because of their mutually exclusive nature. The *Code of Ethics* does not offer guidance on how to resolve an ethical dilemma. NASW (1999) explains that its ethical code

> does not specify which values, principles, and standards are most important and ought to outweigh others in instances when they conflict. Reasonable differences of opinion can and do exist among social workers with respect to the ways in which values, ethical principles, and ethical standards should be rank ordered when they conflict. (3)

Because much of the *Code of Ethics* focuses on the social worker's responsibilities to clients, every application of the *Code* must begin by answering the question: Who is my client? Sometimes that question is difficult to answer, especially when working with an involuntary client or with a group that has been targeted for change but has not requested specific services. A dictionary might define a *client* as the party for whom professional services are rendered and/or a customer or patron. Thus, the social work client is the person, group, or organization who has requested the social worker's services and expects to benefit from what the worker does.

Thus far, the NASW *Code of Ethics* has been discussed as one set of principles and values that may govern a social worker's behavior. There are two others of importance to the social worker. A worker's *moral code* consists of his or her personal beliefs and judgments as to what is right and wrong. In addition, there is a *legal code* that regulates practice.

The social worker must sometimes struggle to sort out the relevant issues and resolve conflicts related to the interplay of these three standards of behavior. Often there is an overlap among these codes. For example, the act of murder would violate all three codes. However, a social worker may view a specific action as immoral even though it is legal. Examples might be abortion, capital punishment, depriving someone of welfare benefits, and paying taxes that finance a war. On the other hand, a social worker might find nothing wrong or immoral with some acts that are illegal (e.g., certain forms of drug use, assisted suicide, and the theft of needed food). On a personal level, a social worker might not see anything wrong with having sex with a client, but such an action is a very clear violation of the NASW *Code of Ethics*. Because of these potential conflicts between a social worker's personal values and the profession's *Code of Ethics*, social workers must constantly strive to reconcile the two in order to practice ethically and honestly.

Food for Thought

Social workers cannot be non-judgmental and they should not attempt to be. They are merchants of morality and should acknowledge this fact openly. (Pilseker 1978, 55)

• • •

The reason we should avoid the extremes of absolutism and relativism is that they both trivialize the subject of ethics. (Ruggiero 2001, 70)

• • •

The concept of an ethics audit is consistent with social work's enduring efforts to protect clients and prevent ethics-related breaches. Such systematic attempts to highlight, address, and monitor the ethical dimensions of social work practice will, in the final analysis, strengthen the profession's integrity. (Reamer 2001, 41)

• • •

Ignorance of ethics code provisions is not a defense to unethical acts or omissions and will not lessen damages awarded. (Bernstein and Hartsell 2000, 173)

• • •

For many years, the practice principle of value neutrality found wide acceptance among social workers. There are also critical questions about this value-neutral stance that must be considered. Many have asked whether value neutrality or value suspension is a realistic option for social workers. They point out that social workers are human beings, not robots. What are they to do with the values they hold when working with clients who hold contrary values? Can they really avoid imposing their own values by either subtle or nonverbal communications? . . .

There is no escaping moral and ethical issues at each step of social work processes. . . . [Can] we honestly say that we do not care what a client does? Can we accept child molestation, neglect, violence, cheating, stealing, or lying? Dare social workers not condemn physical and sexual abuse, rape and beatings, irresponsible sexual activities, and similar antisocial behaviors? (Dolgoff, Loewenberg, and Harrington 2005, 114–115)

Guidance and Direction

Read the NASW *Code of Ethics* carefully and often. Pay particular attention to those ethical principles that apply most directly to your agency setting. If you do not understand a principle or its application, seek consultation from your field instructor or faculty supervisor.

Ask your field instructor to identify the ethical concerns most often encountered in the agency. It is important to recognize that many ethical concerns and questions have been anticipated by the agency, and guidance on how to handle them has been written into the agency's policy manual or employee handbook. Ask your field instructor whether your agency has had an ethics audit, which is a rigorous self-assessment of the extent to which agency policies, procedures, and staff members protect clients while also identifying and managing the risks of ethical situations in order to minimize harm or avoid lawsuits.

Inquire about the agency's process or procedures for resolving ethical dilemmas. These procedures may be written or informal. Your agency may use ethics committees, staff discussions, and outside legal and ethics consultations to help staff members make difficult decisions. Observe and participate in such meetings as often as possible, because this will help you develop awareness of and skill in identifying and resolving ethical dilemmas.

It is very likely that you will observe disagreements over situations involving ethics. Each situation is unique to some degree, and there is seldom only one right way to deal with it. Over time, you will become more comfortable with this uncertainty and be better able to sort out the competing values and potential consequences of each decision. Baird (1996) reminds us that

> ethics cannot be boiled down to a simple "cookbook" of dos and don'ts. Ethical conduct requires a continuous process of self-monitoring, reflection, and careful thought. . . . As a professional it is incumbent upon you to know and understand not only the letter of the ethical codes, but their spirit, rationale, and practical implications. (30)

When you encounter an ethical dilemma, we recommend that you consider the guidelines offered by Sheafor and Horejsi (2006, 167–168) and begin by seeking answers to questions such as the following:

- Who is your primary client (i.e., usually the person, group, or organization that requested the social worker's services and expects to benefit from them)?
- What aspects of the agency's activity or worker's roles and duties give rise to the dilemma (e.g., legal mandates, job requirements, agency policy, questions of efficient use of resources, possible harm caused by an intervention, etc.)?
- Who can or should resolve this dilemma? Is it rightfully a decision to be made by the client? Other family members? The worker? The agency administrator?
- For each decision possible, what are the short-term and long-term consequences for the client, family, worker, agency, community, and so on?
- Who stands to gain and who stands to lose from each possible choice or action? Are those who stand to gain or lose of equal or of unequal power (e.g., child vs. adult)? Do those who are most vulnerable or those with little power require special consideration?
- When harm to someone cannot be avoided, what decision will cause the least harm or a type of harm with fewest long-term consequences? Who of those that might be harmed is least able to recover from the harm?

- Will a particular resolution to this dilemma set an undesirable precedent for future decision making concerning other clients?
- What ethical principles and obligations apply in this situation?
- Which, if any, ethical principles are in conflict in this situation and therefore create an ethical dilemma?
- In this situation, are certain ethical obligations more important than others?

It is likely that you will encounter some very troublesome situations in which all available choices or options are in some way and to some degree harmful and destructive to your client and other people. In such cases you must decide which option is the least harmful. Essentially, you are forced to choose the lesser of two or more evils.

In order to function effectively as a social worker you must be able to distinguish between your values and morals and those of the client. As a general principle, you should not impose your values and beliefs on the client. However, this is a challenging principle of practice because the social work profession and social agencies are built on and represent a set of values and beliefs about what is good for people and desirable in human relationships. Moreover, some clients engage in behaviors that are clearly wrong and a danger to themselves and others (e.g., assault, rape, robbery, child neglect). In such situations, attempting to be value free or value neutral is extremely dangerous, irresponsible, and possibly unethical.

Avoiding the imposition of one's own values on a client is especially difficult when the client's perspective and behavior is rooted in uncommon or unusual cultural or religious beliefs. For example, parents may decline needed medical treatment or surgery for their child because of their religious beliefs, and you may have to decide between honoring the family's religious beliefs and requesting legal action to protect the physical well-being of the child. Fundamentally, the resolution of this dilemma revolves around the answer to these questions: Who is my client? Will a certain decision or action cause significant harm to another person? What is my role?

You may find that your personal moral code conflicts with the values of your clients, your field instructor, your agency, or even the NASW *Code of Ethics*. For example, you and your client or you and other professionals may hold very different views on the morality of abortion or of placing an elder in a nursing home. When you encounter such conflicts, do not ignore them. They are important questions and dilemmas that must be faced honestly and squarely. You will need to decide when you can and cannot suspend your personal moral code.

When you encounter a troublesome practice situation, you must be able to distinguish between questions of preferred method and questions of ethics. The former has to do with ideas about what actions will work best in a given situation to bring about a desired change. Ethical questions are about what is right and wrong from a moral perspective. Many of the conflicts and disagreements between professionals have to do with differences of opinion about the intervention method and are not true ethical dilemmas.

There may be times when you conclude that your agency violates certain ethical principles or violates the rights of certain clients. If this occurs, discuss your concerns with your field instructor or faculty supervisor in order to sort out the issues and determine whether an ethical principle is being violated.

In general, practicum students tend to make mistakes in several areas. Guard against errors in the following areas of ethical conduct:

- *Violating client autonomy and self-determination.*   Be careful not to violate your clients' right to autonomy by overprotecting vulnerable populations. Be prepared to accept your clients' choices, even when you disagree with them.

- *Violating client confidentiality and privacy.*   Do not release information regarding your clients without their consent, or reveal their identity by carelessness in casual conversation or in how you handle and store written documentation.
- *Violating client right to information and informed consent.*   Do not withhold information that clients request and are entitled to have. Keep your clients fully informed of decisions and plans that will have a significant impact on their situation.
- *Violating client right to competent services.*   Be careful not to practice beyond your abilities or knowledge level. When a situation calls for knowledge and skills that you do not possess, consult your field instructor and consider referral to someone who can provide the needed service.
- *Entering into dual relationships.* Maintain a proper professional relationship with your clients. Be friendly, but realize that a professional relationship is not a friendship. Never date or become romantically involved with a client. Do not enter into a buying, selling, lending, or renting agreement with a client.

An ethical area of special concern for you may be the limits to client confidentiality. Clients have a right to privacy. However, this right is not absolute; there are limits and exceptions to a client's right to confidentiality. You may need to release client information, without your client's permission, in the following situations:

- Your client is abusing or neglecting a child or an elderly person.
- Your client is planning or has committed a serious and dangerous illegal act that places others in danger.
- Your client is threatening to harm him- or herself or another person.
- You receive a court order requiring the release of client information.
- You are required by contract to share information with third party entities (e.g., managed care and insurance) that pay for the services received by your client.
- Your client is a minor.

When you encounter these or similar situations, consult with your field instructor on how to handle the matter.

Be certain that you understand the federal and state laws that apply to confidentiality as well as related agency policy on this matter. Make sure that you also understand the concept of privileged communication so you can accurately explain to your client whether client information can ever be revealed to others.

Values, Ethics, and Your Practicum: A Workbook Activity

1. What are two or three ethical concerns or dilemmas most frequently encountered in your practicum setting?

_____

_____

_____

2. How do the personnel in your agency go about dealing with ethical questions and resolving ethical dilemmas (e.g., discussions at a staff meeting, presentations to an ethics committee, consultations with experts)?

_____

_____

_____

3. Does your agency have its own code of ethics or a code of conduct for its employees? If yes, how is it similar to and different from the NASW *Code of Ethics?*

_____

_____

_____

_____

4. To what degree and in what way does the NASW *Code of Ethics* influence the decisions and behavior of the social workers employed by your agency (e.g., is the *Code of Ethics* referred to during case conferences and staff meetings and do the social workers have a copy of the *Code of Ethics* in their office)?

_____

_____

_____

_____

5. Are there specific items or sections in the NASW *Code of Ethics* that are particularly difficult to follow in your agency? If yes, what are they and why are they difficult to follow?

_____

_____

_____

_____

6. Are there particular issues or concerns that are not addressed by the NASW *Code of Ethics* but, in your opinion, should be included? If yes, what are they?

_____

_____

_____

_____

_____

7. Does your agency have policies that, in your opinion, are in violation of the NASW *Code of Ethics?* If yes, describe how these policies are in conflict with specific provisions of the NASW *Code of Ethics.*

_____

_____

_____

_____

_____

8. Are there specific items or sections in the NASW *Code of Ethics* that appear to be in conflict with the state or federal laws and regulations that your agency is expected to follow? If so, describe the conflict and explain how you and other agency social workers attempt to resolve this matter.

_____

_____

_____

_____

_____

9. Section 1.01 of the NASW *Code of Ethics* (1999) states that the social worker's primary responsibility is the well-being of his or her clients. As you observe the day-to-day operation of your agency and the day-to-day activities of the social workers in your agency, does it appear as if the well-being of the client is the primary concern? On what basis do you reach this conclusion?

_____

_____

_____

_____

_____

10. How does your agency handle reports of ethics violations on the part of its staff (e.g., written incident reports, temporary suspensions of staff, formal investigations, grievance policies, reports to state licensing bodies)?

_____

_____

_____

11. Within the past five years, have any agency social workers or other agency personnel been dismissed or reprimanded for ethics violations? If so, what was the nature and type of misconduct?

_____

_____

_____

12. Does your agency have policies that are in conflict with your personal moral code? If yes, how will you handle or resolve these conflicts?

_____

_____

_____

_____

13. Are there statements or sections in the NASW *Code of Ethics* that are in conflict with your personal moral and ethical standards? If yes, how you will attempt to resolve this conflict?

_____

_____

_____

_____

14. What ethical principles in the NASW *Code of Ethics* do you feel most strongly about? Why?

_____

_____

_____

_____

15. What is the name of the agency in your state that is responsible for handling formal complaints about ethics violations by licensed social workers?

_____

_____

16. What process was used by this agency to investigate possible ethics violations?

_____

_____

_____

_____

17. What are the possible sanctions in your state for social workers who commit ethics violations (e.g., loss of license, civil action for monetary damages, criminal prosecution, sanctions by the NASW)?

_____

_____

Additional notes and comments:

_____

_____

_____

_____

_____

_____

Suggested Learning Activities

- Read and study the NASW *Code of Ethics*. It can be downloaded from the NASW's website (http://www.naswdc.org).
- If members of other professions (e.g., psychologists, nurses, or teachers) work in your practicum setting, secure a copy of their profession's code of ethics and compare it to the NASW *Code of Ethics*.
- Conduct interviews with experienced social workers and ask them to describe the ethical issues they most often encounter and the issues that are especially difficult for them to resolve.
- Review your agency's policy manual and identify policy principles that are very similar to the NASW *Code of Ethics*. Identify policies that appear to be in opposition to the *Code of Ethics*.
- In a small group of students and social workers, discuss and share your beliefs regarding the following questions:

  1. How do you decide when the good of the community is more important than the good of the individual?
  2. What is your image of a truly ethical social worker?
  3. What should a social worker do when his or her personal morals are in conflict with agency policy? With the NASW *Code of Ethics?*

Additional Suggestions and Hints

- In Sheafor and Horejsi (2006), read the section entitled "Making Ethical Decisions" (167–168).

Selected Bibliography

Baird, Brian N. *The Internship, Practicum, and Field Placement Handbook: A Guide for the Helping Professions.* Upper Saddle River, NJ: Prentice Hall, 1996.

Baird, Brian N. *The Internship, Practicum, and Field Placement Handbook: A Guide for the Helping Professions.* 4th ed. Upper Saddle River, NJ: Prentice Hall, 2005.

Bernstein, Barton E., and Thomas L. Hartsell. *The Portable Ethicist for Mental Health Professionals: An A–Z Guide to Responsible Practice.* New York: John Wiley and Sons, 2000.

Corey, Gerald, Marianne Schneider, and Patrick Callahan. *Issues and Ethics in the Helping Professions.* 6th ed. Pacific Grove, CA: Brooks/Cole, 2003.

Dolgoff, Ralph, Frank Loewenberg, and Donna Harrington. *Ethical Decisions for Social Work Practice.* Belmont, CA: Thomson Brooks/Cole, 2005.

Galper, Jeffrey. "Code of Ethics for Radical Social Service." In *The Politics of Social Services.* Englewood Cliffs, NJ: Prentice Hall, 1975.

National Association of Social Workers. *Code of Ethics.* Washington, DC: NASW Press, 1999.

Pilseker, C. "Values: A Problem for Everyone." *Social Work* 23 (1978): 54–57.

Reamer, Frederic G. *The Social Work Ethics Audit: A Risk Management Tool.* Washington, DC: NASW Press, 2001.

Ruggiero, Vincent. *Thinking Critically about Ethical Issues.* 3rd ed. Mountain View, CA: Mayfield, 1992.

Ruggiero, Vincent. *Thinking Critically about Ethical Issues.* 5th ed. Boston: McGraw Hill, 2001.

Sheafor, Bradford, and Charles Horejsi. *Techniques and Guidelines for Social Work Practice.* 7th ed. Boston: Allyn and Bacon, 2006.

15

Legal Concerns

GOALS FOR LEARNING

- To become familiar with the specific state and federal statutes (codes) that are relevant to your practicum setting and its programs and services
- To become familiar with the legal terminology frequently used within your practicum setting
- To become aware of the types of practice situations that could give rise to an allegation of wrongdoing or professional negligence
- To become aware of precautionary steps that may reduce the chances of being named in a malpractice suit

Social work, like all professions, is guided and impacted greatly by the law. Every social services agency and program is shaped and guided by specific codes or legal considerations. Some agencies were formed in response to a law requiring states or the federal government to provide specific programs and services. In some agencies, a client's eligibility for services is defined by law. In many instances, a social worker's actions are dictated by law, as in the case of mandated reporting of child abuse. Many social workers are licensed by state law and must conform their practice to the provisions of that law.

The social work practicum student must understand the legal context of his or her professional practice. He or she must be alert to the actions that may violate the law and to the types of situations that might give rise to a lawsuit against an agency, a professional social worker, and even a social work student.

Background and Context

There are three broad categories of laws which guide, direct, and sometimes mandate the actions of social workers and agencies:

1. *Laws regulating services or actions related to a specific client.* Such laws may determine whether a client is eligible to receive a certain service or benefit, whether a specific client can be forced to accept intervention (e.g., involuntary hospitalization), or whether a particular family situation can be defined as suspected child or elder abuse or neglect that must be reported to the authorities.
2. *Laws regulating a field of practice or type of social services program.* Specific social work arenas may have laws that affect the clients served by agencies providing services in this arena. For example, if an agency provides service to

youth, many of its policies and procedures for dealing with young clients will be shaped by laws related to the notification of parents regarding services to be provided to their children. In hospitals, such laws as those related to informed consent, release of patient records, and durable power of attorney for health care are daily concerns to a medical social worker. Social workers who provide services to refugees and immigrants must understand laws relating to refugee and immigration status.

3. *Laws regulating the professional practice of social work.* Laws guiding professional social work practice dictate how social workers must conduct themselves in order to practice competently. These laws may deal with matters such as confidentiality, privileged communication, informed consent, duties to clients, duty to warn, and requirements for obtaining a social work license.

Because laws directly impact social workers and clients, social workers must acquire a basic understanding of the laws and legal procedures that most directly impact their practice setting and clients served. In addition, they must become familiar with specific laws related to their practice roles, duties, and job description. For example, if a social worker functions as a case manager, he or she must be conversant in the laws relating to sharing of confidential information and the eligibility requirements for services needed by clients.

Social workers must be familiar with the court system and know proper conduct when testifying in court. Practitioners in the fields of child welfare and in probation and parole may testify in court on at least a weekly basis. However, all social workers, regardless of field of practice or agency setting, can expect to be occasional witnesses in court proceedings.

Because of that, practitioners and social work students must operate on the assumption that any of their professional records, case notes, reports, and correspondence may eventually become the target of a subpoena, gathered and reviewed by attorneys, and read in court. They need to be thoughtful and cautious about what they put into a written record and how they write it, for at some point they may be asked to explain and defend their statements.

A growing number of social workers are being sued for malpractice. This reality must be considered daily, even as a practicum student. Malpractice and professional negligence fall under a category of law known as tort law. A *tort* is a private or civil wrong or injury that results from actions other than the breach of a formal legal contract and the commission of a crime.

The person who alleges the negligence and brings a malpractice lawsuit against a social worker or agency is termed the *plaintiff*. In this instance, the social worker or agency would be termed the *defendant*.

In order for the plaintiff (e.g., the social worker's client or former client) to be successful in this type of lawsuit, the plaintiff's attorney must prove four points:

1. The social worker had a professional obligation or duty to provide the plaintiff with a certain level of service, a certain standard of care, or a certain manner of professional conduct.
2. The social worker was negligent or derelict in his or her professional role because he or she did not live up to this recognized obligation or duty, standard of care, or expected professional conduct.
3. The plaintiff suffered injury or harm (e.g., physical, mental, emotional, or financial) as a result of what the social worker did (act) or did not do (omission) and this act or omission had a foreseeable harmful consequence for the plaintiff.

4. The social worker's act or omission was a direct or proximate cause of the harm experienced by the plaintiff.

Sheafor and Horejsi (2006) explain how the actions of social workers are judged:

> Whether a breach of duty has occurred is determined by measuring the allegedly harmful act or omission against published standards of practice, agency policy, and the performance of social workers in similar settings. The client's injury must be one that would not have occurred had it not been for the social worker's negligence. Despite this traditional *proximate cause* requirement, juries are increasingly finding liability without fault (i.e., finding providers of health and social services negligent even when they are not the proximate cause of the injury). (596)

A wide variety of acts or omissions can place social workers or the agencies for which they work at risk of being sued and held liable for causing harm to their clients or to individuals harmed by their clients. For example:

- Failure to outline duties of social worker and client
- Sexual or romantic involvement with a current or former client
- Failure to warn others when a client discloses clear intent to inflict serious physical harm on someone
- Failure to alert others when a client discloses intent to harm self
- Failure to attempt to prevent a client's suicide
- Failure to properly diagnose and treat a client
- Failure to provide proper and appropriate treatment and services to a client
- Failure to ensure continuity of service to a client under the care of a worker or agency
- Failure to maintain and protect confidentiality
- Failure to maintain accurate professional records and a proper accounting of client fees, payments, and reimbursements
- Misrepresentation of professional training, experience, and credentials
- Accepting gifts from a client
- Breach of client civil rights
- Failure to refer clients to other services or professionals when indicated
- Use of harmful or ineffective interventions
- Failure to protect a client from harm caused by other clients in a group, program, or facility
- Failure to report suspected child or elder abuse, neglect, or exploitation

Clients in certain situations place social workers and agencies at a higher risk of being sued. These clients and situations may include:

- Clients who have a history of alleging malpractice and negligence and bringing suits against various professionals
- Clients who are a real physical danger to others
- Clients who have been separated from their child because of actions taken by the social worker or agency (e.g., foster care placement and custody evaluations)
- Clients with complex personal circumstances and intense needs requiring social workers to provide highly technical and competent services
- Clients who may commit suicide
- Clients who are very suspicious of others and quick to blame and accuse others of some wrongdoing
- Clients who are very manipulative and deceptive
- Clients who have a history of using sex as a way of manipulating others

Food for Thought

Even if one's practice is perfectly within standards, there is no guarantee that a lawsuit will not be filed or that one would emerge unscathed from such a suit. A practitioner who is successfully sued could be required to pay damages as high or higher than hundreds of thousands of dollars. Furthermore, regardless of income, the process of defending against the suit can be financially and emotionally expensive. (Baird, 2005, 51)

• • •

Even a social worker employed in settings that provide group liability coverage should seriously consider obtaining their own individual coverage. When both a social worker and the worker's employer are named in a liability claim, the employer could argue that the social worker, and not the employing agency, was negligent. Individual coverage would thus protect workers who find themselves at odds with their employers in relation to a liability claim. (Reamer 1994, 24)

• • •

The recent recognition of social work's autonomous professional stature by the government, insurance companies, courts of law, and the public has helped create new forms of exposure and greater risk in practice. (Edwards et al. 1998, 407)

• • •

The victory for social work is a mixed blessing. Legal regulation may mean more jobs, income, opportunities to serve all clients, and public acceptance; it also means more scrutiny and higher risks. Social workers become subject to the same controls that the public exercises over other professions—at a time when the public has grown increasingly litigious. (Barker and Branson 2000, 9)

Guidance and Direction

Make a special effort to become familiar with the laws relevant to your practicum setting, including the laws that regulate the services your agency provides and the laws that regulate professional social work practice.

Depending on the nature and purpose of your agency, you will need to become familiar with federal and state codes, and sometimes local ordinances, that apply to your clients and the services your agency provides. Your clients' lives are affected directly and indirectly by such laws. For example, you may need to understand laws pertaining to the following:

- Marriage and parenthood
- Divorce and child custody
- Partner violence and abuse
- Voluntary and involuntary termination of parental rights
- Foster care and adoption
- Guardianship, conservatorship, power of attorney, durable power of attorney for health care
- Child or elder abuse and neglect
- Involuntary hospitalization of persons with mental illness

- Detention or involuntary hospitalization of persons who are suicidal or a threat to others
- Prosecution and punishment of adult offenders
- Parental notification regarding treatment for minors
- Probation and parole
- Adjudication and treatment of juvenile offenders
- Crime victims assistance
- Immigration and refugee status
- Health care (e.g., managed care, Medicaid, Medicare)
- Substance abuse and treatment of chemical dependency
- Buying and selling of illegal drugs
- Public assistance
- Family planning
- Abortion
- Education of children with disabilities
- Discrimination in employment and housing
- Social Security and Supplemental Security Income
- Confidentiality in health care settings
- Reporting of contagious diseases and public health hazards
- Personal debt and bankruptcy
- Disability accommodation

Social work administrators will need a basic understanding of laws related to employee matters, financial management, and the like. Watch for opportunities to learn about laws pertaining to:

- Contracts
- Leases and rental agreements
- Property and liability insurance
- Employee compensation and benefits
- Workers compensation and unemployment insurance
- Hiring and dismissal of employees
- Employee unions
- Financial record keeping
- Receipt of charitable contributions
- Accessibility for persons with disabilities
- Job classification related to public employees
- Restrictions on political action and lobbying by public employees
- Nonprofit corporations
- Sexual harassment
- Drug-free workplaces
- Affirmative action

If social workers in your agency commonly appear in court, request the opportunity to observe their testimony. Determine their role and function in court, how they prepare for a court appearance, what types of questions they are asked by attorneys, what written documents they provide the court, and if their recommendations tend to be followed by judges. Give special thought to legal and ethical issues that may arise when social workers advocate for their clients, when they are asked to participate in involuntary treatment of clients, or when they must testify on behalf of one client and against another. Identify the social work interventions that follow those documents and orders. Learn about social workers who testify as expert witnesses and what is required of them.

If possible, read the case records of clients whose cases are heard in court. Read the petitions and other legal documents filed on behalf of or against your agency's clients. Read the court orders found in client records. If you have questions about what these records mean, ask your field instructor to explain their significance and what is expected of social workers in these situations.

Learn about the types of situations and clients that present the highest legal risk to social workers in your agency. Ask how often lawsuits are threatened or actually filed against social workers or the agency. Ask about your agency's policy regarding legal defense expenses for employees who are sued. Find out if practicum students who are sued are covered in your agency's liability or malpractice insurance policy. If not, obtain liability insurance for yourself that will cover you for a possible malpractice suit.

An agency's manual of policy and procedure generally describes a standard of care and service owed to, and expected by, the client. Thus, in a malpractice lawsuit, a social worker's failure to follow agency policy may be used as evidence of professional negligence. An agency places itself at higher legal risk when it has an official policy that is not or cannot be regularly followed by its employees. Agency policies will not protect social workers who do not abide by them. The best way to avoid becoming involved in a malpractice lawsuit is to be proactive in learning about and acting on the following guidelines:

- Read the NASW *Code of Ethics* regularly and abide by its guidelines.
- Adhere to agency policy, procedure, and protocol.
- Make every effort to practice competently and avoid situations beyond your level of competence.
- Utilize supervision regularly to ensure that your approaches and techniques are legal, ethical, and therapeutically sound.
- Refer clients to other professionals and programs when you are unable to provide the services they require and document your efforts to make a referral.
- Recognize situations of high legal risk.
- Consult with your agency's legal counsel whenever confronted with troublesome legal issues or questions.
- Obtain malpractice insurance if your agency does not provide it for you.
- Avoid dual relationships with clients.
- Protect client confidentiality.
- Inform clients about the limits of confidentiality.
- Maintain up-to-date, accurate, and complete client records.
- Create client records that are free of judgmental language and hearsay.
- Obtain written permission from clients to release information about them to others.
- Document any client complaints or grievances, and the steps you took to resolve them.
- Understand the concept of privileged communication for social workers and the laws governing this in your state.
- Abide by all mandatory reporting laws requiring you to report suspected abuse or neglect.

You are not likely to become entangled in a malpractice lawsuit if you follow the guidelines described above. Adhere to what would be considered reasonable, customary, and prudent practices. The actions you take on behalf of clients must be fair, in good faith, and in keeping with how other professionals would tend to act. If you need clarification in any particular area, seek guidance and consultation from your social work supervisor and/or agency legal counsel.

Legal Issues and Concerns: A Workbook Activity

The following questions are designed to heighten your awareness of the legal context of social work practice and the legal considerations that are relevant to your practicum agency. Discuss these questions and issues with your field instructor and with experienced social workers in your agency. Your agency may have a legal department and staff attorneys who can respond to your questions and explain legal principles.

1. Is eligibility for your agency's services in any way defined by law? If so, what statutes, legal rules, and regulations are used to determine who is and is not eligible?

   _____

   _____

   _____

   _____

2. Are certain individuals legally required or mandated to obtain services from your agency (e.g., those on probation and subject to court-ordered treatment or those whose children are in foster care)? If so, what specific statutes apply to these individuals and situations?

   _____

   _____

   _____

   _____

3. Do those individuals who are pressured to make use of your agency have a right to refuse to participate? If so, do they face any consequences for that action?

   _____

   _____

   _____

   _____

4. Is your agency licensed by the state (e.g., a licensed child placing agency, licensed hospital, and licensed residential center for youth)? If yes, identify the specific license(s) and the laws and regulations that apply to these licensures.

   _____

   _____

   _____

   _____

5. What outside agencies or organizations (e.g., governmental agencies, accrediting bodies, and citizen review boards) are authorized to interview staff about their practices and review the records kept by your agency (e.g., client records, client services, and financial records)?

_____

_____

_____

_____

6. What percentage of the social workers in your agency hold a state social work license?

_____

Another type of professional license?

_____

7. Does your agency have liability insurance that provides employees with legal defense against allegations of wrongdoing and/or pay the assessed damages if found guilty? If so, what limitations and restrictions apply (e.g., must the employee be following agency policy and behave in an ethical manner before he or she can use the insurance policy)?

_____

_____

_____

_____

8. Does the agency's liability insurance cover the actions of social work practicum students? The actions of volunteers? If yes, what limitations and restrictions apply?

_____

_____

_____

_____

9. What are the possible legal consequences for a social worker who takes action that conflicts with or violates the agency's written policy?

_____

_____

_____

_____

10. Within the past ten years, has the agency or any staff member been sued for negligence or malpractice? If yes, what was the nature of the allegation(s) and the outcome of the lawsuit(s)?

_____

_____

_____

_____

_____

11. Within the context of your agency, what types of clients and what types of situations are associated with high legal risk (i.e., cases most likely to result in a lawsuit alleging agency wrongdoing or professional malpractice)?

_____

_____

_____

_____

_____

12. What attorneys or law firms represent your agency or its staff when someone alleges wrongdoing or professional negligence?

_____

_____

_____

_____

13. What agency policies apply in the following situations that raise legal questions?

a. The client who appears to be a threat to self (e.g., possible suicide)

_____

_____

b. The client who appears to be a threat to others (e.g., verbal threats, previous violent behavior)

_____

_____

c. The client who may not be mentally competent to make legal, medical, or financial decisions

_____

_____

    d. The client who is a minor

_____

_____

    e. The client who is injured while in your agency or while participating in an agency program

_____

_____

    f. The client who insists on withdrawing from a treatment program or another agency service when doing so will place him or her at risk of harm

_____

_____

    g. The client who threatens harm to a social worker or other staff member

_____

_____

    h. The client who is suspected of or known to have committed a serious crime

_____

_____

    i. The client who appears to need legal counsel or representation

_____

_____

    j. The client who has been ordered by a court to receive certain services from your agency (e.g., assessment, treatment, and intervention)

_____

_____

    k. The client who has clearly lied, withheld information, or falsified an application in order to become eligible for the benefits or services provided by your agency

_____

_____

    l. The client who states he or she intends to bring a lawsuit against a social worker or the agency

_____

_____

14. What policies apply when you or others encounter the following situations and legal questions?

    a. How to proceed when a client requests the opportunity to read or copy the records in his or her case file

    _____

    _____

    b. How to obtain a client's permission to release his or her records to another agency or professional

    _____

    _____

    c. How to report suspected child or elder abuse and neglect

    _____

    _____

    d. How to obtain a client's informed consent to participate in certain programs and services

    _____

    _____

    e. How to handle and record the receipt of gifts from a client or donations to the agency

    _____

    _____

    f. How to respond when one receives a subpoena for client records or to be a witness in a trial or court action

    _____

    _____

Additional notes and comments:

_____

_____

_____

_____

_____

Suggested Learning Activities

- Examine your agency's policy manual and identify policies that refer to the need for staff to conform with specific legal codes or requirements.
- Identify situations in which there might be a conflict between what is required by the NASW *Code of Ethics* and the requirements of a specific state or federal law.
- Observe court proceedings, especially ones in which your agency is involved.
- Determine whether your agency has a staff attorney. If so, familiarize yourself with the legal services provided by the attorney to staff social workers.

Additional Suggestions and Hints

- In Sheafor and Horejsi (2006), read the sections entitled "Avoiding Malpractice Suits" (595–600) and "Testifying in Court" (600–602).
- Read contracts and legal documents that affect services provided or that are part of your agency's purchase of services agreements (e.g., a state agency agrees to pay your agency for certain services to provide to clients or agreements with managed care companies).
- Familiarize yourself with the 2003 privacy rule and standards for security of electronic health information of the Health Insurance Portability and Accountability Act (HIPAA) of 1996.

Selected Bibliography

Albert, Raymond. *Law and Social Work Practice: A Legal Systems Approach*. 2nd ed. New York: Springer Publishing Company, 2000.

Baird, Brian N. *The Internship, Practicum, and Field Placement Handbook: A Guide for the Helping Professions*. 4th ed. Upper Saddle River, NJ: Prentice Hall, 2005.

Barker, Robert, and Douglas Branson. *Forensic Social Work: Legal Aspects of Professional Practice*. 2nd ed. New York: Haworth, 2000.

Bernstein, Barton E., and Thomas L. Hartsell, Jr. *The Portable Guide to Testifying in Court for Mental Health Professionals: An A–Z Guide to Being an Effective Witness*. Hoboken, NJ: John Wiley and Sons, 2005.

Bullis, Ronald. *Clinical Social Worker Misconduct*. Chicago: Nelson-Hall, 1995.

Edwards, Richard L., John A. Yankey, and Mary A. Altpeter, eds. *Effective Management of Non-Profit Organizations*. Washington, DC: NASW Press, 1998.

Houston-Vega, Mary K., Elane M. Nuehring, and Elizabeth R. Daguio. *Prudent Practice: A Guide for Managing Malpractice Risk*. Washington, DC: NASW Press, 1997.

Kurzman, Paul A. "Managing Risk in Nonprofit Settings." In *Skills for Effective Management of Nonprofit Organizations*. Washington, DC: NASW Press, 1998.

National Association of Social Workers. *Code of Ethics*. Washington, DC: NASW Press, 1997.

Pollack, Daniel. *Social Work and the Courts*. 2nd ed. New York: Garland, 2003.

Reamer, Frederic. *Social Work Malpractice and Liability*. New York: Columbia University Press, 1994.

Reamer, Frederic. *Social Work Malpractice and Liability*. 2nd ed. New York: Columbia University Press, 2003.

Schroeder, Leila. *The Legal Environment of Social Work*. Washington, DC: NASW Press, 1995.

Sheafor, Bradford, and Charles Horejsi. *Techniques and Guidelines for Social Work Practice*. 7th ed. Boston: Allyn and Bacon, 2006.

16

Social Work Practice as Planned Change

GOALS FOR LEARNING

- To become aware of the fundamental beliefs about change that may inform and guide your agency's services and programs and the actions of its social workers
- To become aware of the various practice frameworks (perspectives, models, and theories) that are used to plan and guide intervention and agency programs
- To become aware of the data-gathering and assessment tools used in your agency
- To become aware of commonly used interventions in your agency
- To become aware of how the effectiveness of social work interventions is evaluated in your agency

Fundamentally, the practice of social work is about the process of planned change. The verb *process* means to advance, to progress, to move onward. In the practice of social work, the worker takes deliberate and specific steps to encourage and facilitate movement toward a certain goal. Your practicum offers an excellent opportunity to observe and critically examine the values, beliefs, ethical principles, and knowledge base that guide a social worker's efforts to bring about a desired change.

This chapter encourages you to think about the nature of change. All social agencies are committed to and structured around deep-seated beliefs about how clients, communities, or broad social conditions change. Strive to identify the assumptions about change that are embedded in your agency's programs and policies as well as in its various approaches to practice. Also, identify your own beliefs about how, why, and under what circumstances desirable change by individuals, families, small groups, organizations, and communities is possible and probable.

Background and Context

As explained in Chapter 13, social work is often defined as the activity of helping individuals, families, groups, or communities enhance or restore their capacity for social functioning and for creating societal conditions favorable to these goals. Planned change at all levels is the central focus of social work. Social workers see themselves as assisting clients, families, and communities to make changes that will improve their lives or change the conditions and social policies which impacts their lives.

At the level of the individual, *social functioning* can be viewed as a person's motivation, capacity, and opportunity to meet his or her basic human needs (e.g., food, shelter, health care, education, meaningful work, protection, and self-worth) and carry out his or her social roles (e.g., parent, student, employee, citizen, neighbor). In order to create conditions favorable for effective social functioning, social workers also seek needed changes in social policy, programs, and services.

To accomplish the goals of their profession, social workers assume a wide variety of roles. *Social work practice roles* include those of client advocate, broker of services, case manager, counselor or therapist, group leader or facilitator, community organizer, administrator, supervisor, social planner, evaluator, educator, program developer, researcher, policy analyst, teacher, and trainer. Depending on their practice setting and usual role, social workers are sometimes people changers or sometimes system changers, and often they are both.

Social workers see the connections between people and the social environments of which they are a part. In order to be truly effective, social workers need to be skilled in and committed to interventions that reflect the ways in which people's lives are influenced by societal conditions and social policies. They must believe in clients' abilities to not only address their own needs and goals but also to change and enhance the social environment.

The social worker and client may seek change and formulate interventions at one or more of three levels: micro, mezzo, and macro. The *micro* level of social work practice refers to interventions that focus on personal individual or family concerns such as relationships, communication problems, emotional or psychological problems, and issues related to individual social functioning. The *mezzo* level of social work practice refers to improving social functioning at the level of the neighborhood, the group, or the organization. This may include interventions through the use of support groups, neighborhood development projects, and organizational growth and development. The *macro* level of social work practice refers to interventions aimed at changes in communities, societies, and social policies. These interventions focus on community capacity building, community organization, and large scale social change efforts.

Although these three levels of intervention may have different targets for change, they are all built on the same process of planned change. In addition, social workers often practice at multiple levels simultaneously, recognizing the connections between them.

Social work at all of these levels, whether the client is an individual or a community, typically moves through the *phases of a planned change*. These are:

1. Identifying and defining the problem or concern
2. Gathering data, studying the problem, and identifying strengths
3. Assessing the problem (i.e., deciding what needs to change, what can be changed, how it might be changed, and what resources are available to the client)
4. Establishing goals, objectives, and tasks for change based on client goals and agency guidelines
5. Taking action based on the plan (i.e., intervention)
6. Monitoring of progress and determining if the intervention is achieving the desired outcomes and modifying the plan if necessary and trying again
7. Terminating the intervention once goals and objectives have been reached and evaluating the change process to learn for future practice

This list of phases gives the impression that the change process is quite orderly and linear. In reality, that is seldom the case. Typically, the client and worker move back and forth across these phases several times during the intervention process.

In addition, others involved in the intervention, such as extended family members, may not move through the intervention process at the same pace or with the same goals in mind. This can make the change process more complex and unpredictable, and needs to be taken into account.

Although the use of the problem-solving process is pervasive in social work and in many other professions, it has been criticized for being essentially a negative orientation that results in social workers giving too much attention to what is wrong and too little attention to client strengths and situational assets. When thinking about the concept of a problem and its place in the process of change, it is helpful to recall that dictionaries define the word *problem* as a question raised for inquiry, consideration, or solution and as a question or situation that presents uncertainty, perplexity, or difficulty. The word *problem* is derived from the Greek word *proballein* which means to "throw forward." Thus, a problem is a genuine challenge that pushes us to change how we think or act. Giving attention to client strengths does not require a blindness to client problems. Indeed, successful interventions are built on client strengths while also recognizing real client problems and needs.

When considering the various phases of the problem-solving process, it is helpful to make a distinction between data collection and assessment. *Data collection* refers to the gathering of facts and information about the client and/or the situation targeted for change. *Assessment* refers to the worker's interpretation or explanation of these data in a way that lays a conceptual foundation for a plan of action or intervention. Needless to say, several different meanings can be drawn from the same set of facts. The client may or may not see the situation in the same ways as the social worker, even when viewing the same assessment data. The meaning assigned to data is often shaped by the practice perspectives, theories, and models used by the social worker and his or her agency. Social workers need to be cautious not to overlook or underemphasize the intensely personal meanings that clients attach to their situations. Social workers who do not at least partially understand the situation from their clients' perspectives will be less successful than those who try to build interventions that start where their clients start.

Social workers use a variety of orienting theories and practice frameworks to guide their work. Sheafor and Horejsi (2006, 50) describe an *orienting theory* as a body of knowledge drawn from the social and behavioral sciences such as sociology, anthropology, psychology, economics, and biology. Such theories help explain human behavior and the social environment but do not provide guidance on how to facilitate planned change.

For such guidance, the social worker must look to another type of conceptual framework, which Sheafor and Horejsi (2006, 50) call a practice framework. A *practice framework* is a set of interrelated beliefs and assumptions about how people and social systems change and what a social worker can do to facilitate change at either the micro, mezzo, or macro level. There is no agreed on terminology to describe various practice frameworks. Authors may describe a given framework as either a perspective, an approach, a method, a model, a theory, a paradigm, or a strategy. Sheafor and Horejsi (2006, 51) suggest three categories: practice perspectives, practice theories, and practice models.

A *practice perspective,* like the focusing of a camera, serves to clarify and magnify a particular aspect of the person-in-environment. The general systems perspective and the ecosystems perspective are commonly used in social work for assessing the relationships between people and their environment. The generalist perspective provides a way of looking at practice in ways that broaden the practice roles and consider interventions at various levels (micro, mezzo, and macro) and with various types of clients (individuals, families, groups, organizations, and communities). The feminist and ethnic-sensitive practice perspectives serve to remind the worker that certain client groups face special challenges in our society. Critical theory asks social workers to critique the underlying assumptions of practice, and the constructionist perspective stresses the need to view social problems as socially constructed and not necessarily universally accepted as problems.

A *practice theory* offers an explanation of selected behaviors or circumstances and broad guidelines about how they can be changed. Examples of the micro-level theories include the psychosocial approach, which is based primarily on psychodynamic theory and ego psychology, and the behavioral approach, which is rooted in theories of learning. Examples of macro-level theories include the social planning model, which addresses social problems through the joint efforts of citizens and those possessing influence and power within communities. Social action models address social problems by targeting the underlying causes of such problems, and often require a shift in power in order to be effective.

A *practice model* is essentially a set of principles used to guide certain interventions. However, by definition, these principles are not tied to a particular explanation of behavior. Examples at the micro level include crisis intervention and the task-centered approach. Examples at the mezzo and macro levels include organizational development, community development, social planning, and social action. Most often, a practice model develops out of a demonstration project or experiment rather than, deductively, from a particular theory of behavior.

In addition to the practice frameworks mentioned above, there are many others: the cognitive-behavioral model, the person-centered model, the interactional model, the structural model, the solution-focused model, the family systems theory, the narrative approach, the multicultural model, and various approaches to organizational change and community change.

As a general rule, the practice perspectives, theories, and models used in direct services agencies do not give much attention to the roles and activities that would involve practitioners in efforts to change societal systems and institutional structures. The practice frameworks used in macro-level practice do, of course, have such an emphasis, but they differ in their underlying beliefs about how positive social change can be facilitated by a social work practitioner. Payne (1997) observes that many social workers' viewpoints on system and institutional change fall into three broad categories:

1. The *reflexive–therapeutic view* has as its goal securing the well-being of individuals, families, groups, and communities. This is accomplished by promoting personal growth and self-fulfillment. As people interact more effectively with each other and with existing systems, they gain competence. As a result of this increased personal power they will rise above their problems and disadvantages. Social workers holding this viewpoint do not directly challenge the existing social order.

2. The *socialist–collectivist view* has as a primary goal the creation of a society characterized by cooperation and mutual support. It seeks to challenge oppression and injustice in the existing social order and to empower people, especially those who have been marginalized or disenfranchised, so they will actively participate in creating new systems and institutions. This approach presumes that those in positions of power and authority will need to be confronted and pressured to make the needed changes.

3. The *individualist–reformist view* has as its primary goal the provision of social services to individuals and the gradual improvement of those services. Social workers holding this view may want to see broad social change but they conclude that working for such change is beyond the scope of their job description and ordinary responsibilities. Consequently, they do not seek social or institutional changes and concentrate instead on making incremental changes in the services they provide to clients.

With regard to macro level planned change, Alle-Corliss and Alle-Corliss (1999) outline how social action parallels and yet is distinguished from the problem-solving process that social workers use with individuals, families, groups, or communities. The steps of social action include:

1. *Unfreezing the system* by defining the problem, engaging the community, empowering the forces of change, and building an action organization
2. *Moving to action* that involves understanding the forces creating resistance toward change, working toward reducing the resistance toward change, engaging in action strategies and tactics that often result in conflict and require confrontation
3. *Solidifying change by refreezing it* involves employing political pressure tactics that are intended to change laws and enforce regulations that preserve efforts toward positive change. This stage requires work at the political and policy levels and may involve establishing an agency to operate programs, proposing legislation on behalf of the populations organizing for change, and establishing methods for monitoring and enforcing set policies and procedures.
4. *Terminating the activist's role* is a move that is determined by various factors: Is the community group sufficiently organized with committed members and ample leadership? Have they been successful in accomplishing set goals? Are they sufficiently involved in the political arena and is the power structure responsive to the organization and to its political strength? (234)

Guidance and Direction

Identify the practice frameworks (perspectives, theories, and models) used in your agency. Whether implicit or explicit, these frameworks influence how your agency designs its programs and services and how it works with clients. Determine why these particular practice frameworks are judged most appropriate and most effective for the clients served by your agency. Consider what your agency's choice of practice frameworks reveals about the agency's beliefs and assumptions concerning:

- The causes of personal and social problems
- How clients and client systems change
- Actions that are most likely to facilitate change
- How success is measured
- The importance of identifying client strengths

Your practicum agency will expect you to use the regularly selected forms of intervention used by other social workers, and will train you in these approaches. Do your best to learn the skills required to implement these interventions, remembering that many of these skills can be transferred to another setting even if that organization takes a different approach to intervention.

Over time you will see how interventions, even though they may seem similar for several clients, are customized for each client based on different needs and goals. You will begin to see how your own interventions will be tailored for those reasons as well. As you grow in experience and confidence, your ability to craft appropriate interventions will increase as well.

Because social workers, like all people, are unique with regard to their core values, personality, and style of interaction, individual workers usually find some practice perspectives, theories, and models more attractive than others. We urge

Food for Thought

Are social workers more concerned with maintaining the status quo of the present day, adapting to managed care and privatization practices, buying into the current political and economic agenda, and accepting the fact that there is very little that can be done to deal with what has become known as the "permanent underclass"? Have we accepted the market model approach to social action? Where will social workers function, given the present political climate of devolution, declining resources, managed care, and privatization of social welfare services? (Ray and Nicholas-Wolosuk 2003, 1)

• • •

Reverence toward social workers as experts fabricates a hierarchy of haves and have nots. Proficient experts have the knowledge, foresight, insight, ideas, and action plans which are then bestowed on inept clients who lack insight, ideas, and action plans. Proactive professionals take charge of passive clients. Masterful experts commence action and ineffectual client

systems are acted upon. Interpreted broadly, the expert professionals are the changers and the clients are the chumps! Social workers beware! There are traps in this definition of social workers as experts and clients as passive recipients of service. In fact, there is no successful way out. If clients don't improve, then, of course, social workers are to blame. If clients get better, then social workers get the credit along with the responsibility of being the champion of keeping the clients' lives on track. Ultimately, when expert social workers win, passive clients lose their sense of competence and independence. (Miley et al. 1995, 71)

• • •

Accentuating the problems of clients creates a wave of pessimistic expectations of, and predictions about, the client, the client's environment, and the client's capacity to cope with that environment. Furthermore, these labels have the insidious potential, repeated over time, to alter how individuals see themselves and how others see them. (Saleeby 2006, 4)

you to carefully examine the possible reasons behind your attraction to certain ones and your rejection of others. Usually, one's choice of a practice framework is the result of a combination of factors, including beliefs about the causes of human problems, beliefs about what can be changed and what cannot, beliefs about personal and social responsibility, beliefs about how much people should be involved in defining and assessing their own problems, and beliefs about the role and responsibility of the professional in facilitating change.

Examine your preferences for certain practice frameworks, and decide if they are based mostly on your personal beliefs, values, and attitudes; mostly on effectiveness research and empirical data reported in the professional literature; or mostly on what your field instructor and school faculty have told you about what does and does not work.

Recognize that your practicum experience is limited to one setting and that other agencies and programs may be quite different from the one you know best. There are significant differences between programs, even when they have similar goals and serve the same types of clients. Try to learn how and why other agencies have adopted forms of intervention, practice perspectives, and theories and models that are different from the ones used in your practicum setting.

Social workers are often drawn to certain practice roles, while sometimes preferring to avoid others. For example, some might be attracted to roles related to advocacy and social action because they want to see changes in social structures that can benefit large numbers of people, while others might avoid these same roles because they are uncomfortable with conflict and the use of power and influence. Some might be attracted to the clinician or counselor role because they like intense, face-to-face contact with individual clients and want to make a difference in individual lives, whereas others might be uncomfortable with the discussion of painful personal problems. Still others might either be attracted to or wish to avoid the tasks of budgeting, grant proposal writing, personnel selection, and public relations that are associated with the roles of administration and program planning. Give careful thought to the roles and activities you prefer and ponder the question of why some are more attractive to you than others.

Some of these preferences will be based on your skills, some on your values, some on your previous experiences, and some on your beliefs about what social workers should do. During your practicum, gain experience in as many practice roles as possible in order to understand the nature of these roles and better understand your own abilities. Do not limit yourself to the performance of only a few practice roles. Most likely your career in social work will require that you assume many different practice roles and perform a wide range of tasks and activities. This variety of roles is also one of the most attractive aspects of the social work profession because social workers can move between roles, creatively addressing needs in a variety of ways and at a variety of levels.

Observe how the professionals in your agency go about their work of helping clients and providing services. Identify the practice frameworks, approaches, methods, and techniques used during the various phases of their work with clients. Consider the following questions in your analysis:

Engagement and Relationship Building

- What are the major reasons that clients seek services from your agency?
- Are most clients voluntary or involuntary?
- How does this impact the engagement process?
- How do the experiences of clients or those pressuring clients to seek services impact the engagement process?
- What specific techniques are used to facilitate building an effective helping relationship?
- What approaches are used to make the client feel more at ease and less fearful about entering a professional relationship?
- What approaches are used to address the client's possible questions and concerns about utilizing the services offered by the agency?

Clarification of Client's Concern, Problem, or Request

- What approaches are used to help the client specify, elaborate, and clarify the concerns that brought the client to the agency?
- Are clients actively involved in the process of identifying and defining their problems, concerns, and strengths?

Data Gathering

- What information is routinely gathered about clients and their problems, concerns, and strengths?
- What tools or instruments are used to aid the gathering of this data (e.g., interview schedules, checklists, needs assessment instruments, questionnaires, and observation)?
- What issues of diversity and power need to be addressed in the data gathering process?

Assessment

- How are available data and information organized, combined, and analyzed in order to arrive at a clear picture of the client's situation and a possible plan of action?
- Are clients actively involved in deciding what needs to change and how it might be changed?
- If clients and workers disagree on what needs to change, how is this difference resolved?

Formulation of an Intervention Plan

- When more than one issue is identified, how are they prioritized?
- How are client wishes incorporated into the plan?
- What issues of diversity and power need to be addressed in the plan?
- Is a formal contract developed?
- How is potential resistance addressed?
- How are alternative plans considered?
- Are ethical and legal issues related to the plan addressed?
- Is the plan based on sound theoretical models and perspectives?
- Is the plan based on empirically supported evidence?
- Are the plan's outcomes reasonable and measurable?

Intervention and Monitoring

- What system (e.g., client, family, community) is typically targeted for change by your agency's programs and professional staff? Why?
- What other agencies or organizations often become involved in the client's intervention plan?
- What practice frameworks (perspectives, theories, and models) guide the change process?
- What specific methods, techniques, or procedures are used to facilitate change?
- What specific methods, tools, or instruments are used to monitor whether the intervention is working as planned and expected?

Termination and Evaluation

- In what ways do the agency and its workers determine if their interventions, programs, and services are effective?
- To what extent are clients involved in determining if interventions, programs, and services are effective?
- Does your agency adequately evaluate its interventions, programs, and services?
- What additional forms of evaluation might you suggest?
- Under what conditions are interventions terminated by social workers?
- Under what circumstances do clients terminate their relationships with personnel from your agency (e.g., when legal mandates are lifted, when clients no longer wish to receive services, when their ability to pay for services ends)?
- What specific procedures and techniques are used to bring the professional relationship to a close and terminate the helping process?

Remember that although the process of planned change as outlined previously looks linear and suggests sequential steps in the intervention process, in reality intervention is more circular, with each step of the process being informed by the others and with new information and evolving relationships being incorporated into the intervention over time. Finn and Jacobson (2003) suggest seven core processes that move social workers and clients or participants forward through a mutual process and series of steps resembling waves washing over each other.

1. *Engagement* is the process of relationship building, listening, acknowledging power and position, appreciating difference, and acknowledging the partiality of knowledge.
2. *Teaching/learning* involves collaboration between worker and participant in the process of discovery and assessment, allowing both parties to teach and learn.
3. *Action* is the process of implementing plans, encouraging reflection, awakening possibilities, and paying attention to social justice.

4. *Accompaniment* refers to the partnerships that are used to advance action, and pays attention to power in the helping relationship as well as the worker's commitment to long-term participation.

5. *Evaluation* is the process of examining both process and outcomes of joint efforts, learning from each other and using this knowledge to enhance these efforts.

6. *Critical reflection* leads to learning from the shared experience, interpreting it from individual and collective perspectives, and perhaps reframing initial inquiries.

7. *Celebration* refers to the process of finding joy, honor, and play in the work and with those involved in it.

As you engage in the *assessment* phase of planned change, whether you are assessing a client, a community's capacity to serve its citizens, an organization's ability to provide services, or a social policy's ability to address the needs of a group of people, there are general guidelines that can help you do a thorough and effective assessment. When assessing client situations, ask yourself these questions:

- Am I assessing for strengths as well as problems?
- Am I using effective and appropriate assessment tools?
- Am I involving the client in the assessment?
- Do I remember that assessment is ongoing?
- How can I prioritize the needs to maximize my effectiveness?
- Am I considering the impact of diversity on this intervention, including any personal biases I might have?
- Do I recognize ethical and legal aspects of the assessment?
- What value judgments am I making?
- Am I considering the sociohistorical context of this client?
- What else do I need to know and how can I learn it?

As you design *interventions* from the micro level to the macro level, follow these guidelines for effective interventions. The intervention plan must:

- Address both strengths and needs
- Be built on a comprehensive assessment
- Be feasible and reasonable for both the client and social worker
- Have been mutually constructed by the client and social worker
- Be based on a theory of change that matches the client's situation
- Be within the knowledge and skill base of the social worker
- Allow for modification as needed during the intervention process
- Not be overly intrusive into the client's life
- Have incremental steps
- Minimize possible negative effects on clients
- Be built on evidence based practice principles
- Address issues of diversity
- Include a timeline and termination plan

The profession of social work is rightfully more often being asked to hold itself accountable and to demonstrate its ability to address social issues in effective and efficient ways. Social workers are being asked to use what is commonly called *evidence based practice*, which means that social workers need to base their interventions on some form of empirical evidence whenever possible and engage in proactive program evaluation to determine effectiveness of services provided. Determine whether your agency bases its services on such evidence.

Social Work as Planned Change: A Workbook Activity

This workbook activity asks that you examine the practice frameworks (perspectives, theories, and models) used in your practicum agency. In order to analyze these frameworks, consider these questions.

1. What types of problems, needs, or concerns are typically addressed by your agency?

   _____

   _____

   _____

2. What tools are typically used to assess these problems or concerns?

   _____

   _____

   _____

3. What practice frameworks (perspectives, theories, or models) are typically used to guide assessment and interventions?

   _____

   _____

   _____

4. At what level of practice (micro, mezzo, or macro) are interventions typically implemented?

   _____

   _____

   _____

5. How is a particular practice framework chosen for a specific client?

   _____

   _____

   _____

6. Are the practice frameworks appropriate and relevant for the clients served?

   _____

   _____

   _____

7. When are the practice frameworks effective? Why? When are they ineffective? Why?

_____

_____

_____

8. Are social workers in your agency regularly trained in new intervention approaches?

_____

_____

_____

9. Are interventions tailored to diverse clients (i.e., culture, age, gender)?

_____

_____

10. What evaluation tools does your agency use to evaluate the effectiveness of its interventions?

_____

_____

_____

_____

11. Does your agency adapt its strategies based on the result of its self-evaluation?

_____

_____

_____

12. What recommendations do you have for improved effectiveness in your agency?

_____

_____

_____

Suggested Learning Activities

- Examine the data-gathering and assessment tools and instruments used in your agency.
- Ask social workers or other professionals in your agency to identify the practice frameworks that guide their practice. Ask why those frameworks are preferred over other possibilities.
- Identify the beliefs, values, and assumptions implicit in the frameworks used in your agency.
- Examine the various evaluation tools and instruments used in your agency.
- Ask social workers or other professionals in your agency to describe how they and the agency determine whether they are being effective in their work with clients.

Additional Suggestions and Hints

- In Sheafor and Horejsi (2006), read chapters on practice frameworks and the process of change.
- In the *Encyclopedia of Social Work* (Edwards 1995), read chapters on the various practice frameworks used in your agency and by social work professionals.
- In Payne (2005) and Johnson and Yanca (2004), read descriptions of social work theories and models.

Selected Bibliography

Alle-Corliss, Lupe, and Randy Alle-Corliss. *Advanced Practice in Human Service Agencies: Issues, Trends and Treatment Perspectives.* Belmont, CA: Wadsworth, 1999.

Allen-Meares, Paul, and Charles Garvin. *Handbook of Social Work Direct Practice.* Thousand Oaks, CA: Sage Publications, 2000.

Brill, Naomi, and Joanne Levine. *Working with People: The Helping Process.* 8th ed. Boston: Allyn and Bacon, 2005.

Cournoyer, Barry R. *The Evidence-Based Social Work Skills Book.* Boston: Pearson Education, 2005.

Edwards, Richard L., ed. *Encyclopedia of Social Work.* 19th ed. Washington, DC: NASW Press, 1995.

Finn, Janet L., and Maxine Jacobson. *Just Practice: A Social Justice Approach to Social Work.* Peosta, IA: Eddie Bowers Publishing, 2003.

Hepworth, Dean H., and JoAnn Larsen. *Direct Social Work Practice: Theory and Skills.* Pacific Grove, CA: Brooks/Cole, 2002.

Homan, Mark. *Promoting Community Change: Making It Happen in the Real World.* 3rd ed. Belmont, CA: Brooks/Cole, 2004.

Hull, Grafton. *Understanding Generalist Practice with Families.* Pacific Grove, CA: Brooks/Cole, 2006.

Johnson, Louise C., and Stephen J. Yanca. *Social Work Practice: A Generalist Approach.* Boston: Allyn and Bacon, 2004.

Kerson, Toba Schwaber. *Boundary Spanning: An Ecological Reinterpretation of Social Work Practice in Health and Mental Health Systems.* New York: Columbia University Press, 2002.

Lehmann, Peter, and Nick Coady. *Theoretical Perspectives for Direct Social Work Practice.* New York: Springer, 2000.

Miley, Karla Krogsrud, Michael O'Melia, and Brenda L. DuBois. *Generalist Social Work Practice: An Empowering Approach.* Boston: Allyn and Bacon, 1995.

Miller, William R., Stephen Rollnick, and Kelly Conforti. *Motivational Interviewing: Preparing People for Change.* 2nd ed. New York: Guilford Press, 2002.

Netting, F. Ellen, Peter McKettner, and Steven L. McMurty. *Social Work Macro Practice.* Boston: Allyn and Bacon, 2004.

Payne, Malcolm. *Modern Social Work Theory.* 3rd ed. Chicago: Lyceum, 2005.

Saleeby, Dennis, ed. *The Strengths Perspective in Social Work Practice.* 4th ed. Boston: Allyn and Bacon, 2006.

Schmidt, John J. *Intentional Helping: A Philosophy for Proficient Caring Relationships.* Upper Saddle River, NJ: Merrill Prentice Hall, 2002.

Sheafor, Bradford, and Charles Horejsi. *Techniques and Guidelines for Social Work Practice.* 7th ed. Boston: Allyn and Bacon, 2006.

17

Evaluating Practice

GOALS FOR LEARNING

- To understand the reasons for evaluating student performance during your practicum
- To understand the process of evaluating student performance in your practicum
- To understand the criteria commonly used to evaluate student performance
- To conduct a self-evaluation of performance in order to measure learning and to identify areas for continued learning or remediation

A successful practicum prepares you for competent and responsible practice. This competence, developed over time, is seen when acquired skills and knowledge are compared with student learning goals set early in the practicum. A successful practicum is one that achieves that goal. Ongoing monitoring and frequent evaluations of your performance are necessary to determine whether you are making progress, to document learning, to identify strengths, and to identify areas of performance that may need special attention and remediation. It is important that you become familiar with the procedure and instruments that will be used to evaluate your performance in the practicum, as well as the criteria against which your performance will be measured.

This chapter will provide basic information on the process of student evaluation used by programs of social work education and encourage you to examine and evaluate your own performance so you can make the best possible use of the practicum as a learning opportunity.

Background and Context

Of central importance in a social work practicum is the ongoing evaluation of the student's performance. The social work practicum evaluation focuses on the student's behaviors and actions related to the role and obligations of a professional social worker. The primary question addressed is whether the student's performance is meeting the specified standards expected of the entry-level social work practitioner.

Every program of social work education uses some type of rating scale or evaluation tool to monitor and evaluate student progress. The evaluation process compares the student's performance to standards and criteria established by schools and required by the Council on Social Work Education's Educational Policy and Accreditation Standards, and also to the learning goals, objectives, and activities outlined in the student's learning contract (see Chapter 3).

Evaluations of student performance are of two types: formal and informal. An *informal evaluation* consists of the ongoing feedback and suggestions offered by the field instructor. This type of evaluation takes place on a weekly or even a daily basis. A *formal evaluation* is a detailed review and comparison of the student's performance with evaluation criteria, standards, and learning objectives for the practicum. It occurs at the end of each academic term or more often, depending on school policy or special circumstances.

Formal evaluations are based on a school's specific evaluation criteria and placed in a written report. This report typically consists of the ratings assigned to the various items on the school's evaluation tool and a few paragraphs of narrative that describe special strengths and abilities and/or special problems and deficiencies in performance. The report may also describe how needed learning experiences will be secured or deficiencies corrected prior to the next formal evaluation.

Some practicum programs and field instructors may ask the student to prepare for this evaluation by compiling a portfolio that includes various reports and documents that describe the student's practicum activities and achievements and serves to illustrate his or her level of performance. Students may be asked to evaluate their own performance using the evaluation instrument provided by their university and then compare their self ratings with those of their supervisor.

A variety of agency staff members may be asked to comment on student learning and performance based on their observations of student professional growth. The faculty supervisor may also participate in the formal evaluation. In some cases, other agency staff may be asked to join in the evaluation if they have worked closely with the student and observed the student's performance.

The areas addressed in the practicum evaluation are similar to those addressed in the performance evaluation of the social workers employed by an agency. In order to ensure high-quality performance and reduce their exposure to lawsuits and employee grievances, agencies strive to make their expectations of employees as clear as possible and to use personnel evaluation tools (i.e., rating scales) that are as objective as possible. These same forces have prompted programs of social work education to develop evaluation tools that are as valid and reliable as possible.

However, it must be recognized that it is difficult to develop an evaluation tool that is both clear and specific in its descriptions of standards and criteria, and also flexible enough to accurately and fairly evaluate the practice of social work, which is complex and difficult to observe directly. An evaluation should be objective to the degree possible, but even a well-designed procedure will require judgments by the field instructor, and some of these may be open to charges of subjectivity. For example, ratings of a student's level of cooperation, motivation, adaptability, and use of supervision are difficult to assess except when in an extreme form (i.e., very high or very low motivation). Consequently, there will be times when the field instructor and practicum student disagree on the actual ratings given on a formal evaluation.

An evaluation can be considered fair and relevant when:

- The evaluation criteria, standards, and the agency's preferred practices and outcomes are made known to the student at the beginning of the practicum or at the beginning of the time period to be evaluated.
- It addresses the areas of performance or competency that are truly important to professional social work and carrying out the agency's mission and goals.

- The criteria used to evaluate the student are clear and objective to the degree possible.
- The student's performance is compared to written standards and criteria, rather than to unstated or implied standards.
- The student has been given adequate orientation and training to achieve learning objectives.
- The student has been given ongoing feedback and recognition for professional growth.
- The student has been given ongoing feedback and warnings of unsatisfactory performance prior to the formal evaluation.
- The performance criteria and standards are realistic given the student's level (e.g., first semester versus second semester and BSW versus MSW).
- The evaluation can cite and describe examples of performance that form the basis of the ratings.
- The evaluation gives consideration to extenuating circumstances that may influence the evaluation (e.g., the student had limited opportunity to learn or demonstrate certain skills and the supervisor had limited time to observe the student's performance).
- The evaluation process identifies and records differences in level of performance among students who are different in terms of their motivation, competency, knowledge, and specific skills.
- The evaluation takes into consideration the nature and complexity of the assignments given to the student.
- The evaluation recognizes student growth and good performance as well as student problems or need for continued learning.

An unfair or inaccurate evaluation exists when:

- The student did not understand what was expected of him or her, or did not understand the criteria to be used for evaluation.
- The rules, standards, and criteria used to evaluate the student are changed without the student's knowledge.
- The student receives low ratings without being given a description and explanation of the poor performance that resulted in the low ratings.
- The criteria or standards are unrealistically high or not relevant to the student's performance as a social worker.
- Several students receive essentially the same ratings when there were clear differences in their performances.
- The student was not given ongoing feedback, guidance, and suggestions prior to the evaluation.
- Interpersonal factors such as personality conflicts between student and field instructor influence student performance.
- Student performance has not been observed and evaluations are not based on actual knowledge of student abilities.

Both the field instructor and the student must be alert to certain pitfalls that exist whenever one person attempts to rate another person's performance. These are:

- The *halo effect*—the tendency to rate a person the same on all items based on the observed performance in only a few areas.
- The *attraction of the average*—the tendency to evaluate every student or employee about the same or about average regardless of real differences in their performance.

- The *leniency bias*—the tendency to evaluate all students or employees as outstanding or to assign inflated ratings so as to avoid arguments or conflict or to avoid hurting their feelings.
- The *strictness bias*—the tendency to evaluate and rate all students or employees on the low side because the evaluator has unrealistically high expectations or holds the belief that low ratings will motivate them toward even higher levels of performance.

In some instances the field instructor or the practicum coordinator may conclude that the practicum arrangement is unworkable and unsatisfactory for the student, the field instructor, or both. This may happen when it becomes apparent that the setting cannot meet the student's learning needs or because the student's performance is irresponsible, unethical, or falls far short of expectations. Examples of student behaviors or performance problems that may prompt the field instructor or the school to consider terminating the practicum include the following:

- The student's behavior is harmful to clients, agency staff, or the agency's reputation.
- The student's behavior is irresponsible and unprofessional (e.g., late for work, missing scheduled appointments, unable to spend the required hours in the practicum setting).
- The student is unable to communicate adequately, either verbally or in writing.
- The student is hostile toward supervision and resistant to learning.
- The student displays symptoms of an emotional disturbance that interfere with work (e.g., bizarre behavior, inability to concentrate, aggressiveness, withdrawal).
- The student inappropriately shares personal views, experiences, and problems with clients after being made aware of this unacceptable behavior.
- The student enters into dual relationships with clients (e.g., dates a client, sells a product to a client).

Some behaviors by the student are considered so serious that they may result in the student's immediate dismissal from the practicum. These include:

- Clear and serious violations of the NASW *Code of Ethics*
- Clear and repeated insubordination
- Theft or the clear misuse of agency money, equipment, or property
- Concealing, consuming, or selling drugs on agency premises
- Being intoxicated or under the influence of drugs or alcohol when at work
- Reckless or threatening actions that place clients and staff at risk of serious harm
- Deliberately withholding information from a supervisor or from agency personnel that they need to know in order to properly serve clients and maintain the integrity and reputation of the agency and its programs
- Falsifying agency records and reports
- Soliciting or accepting gifts or favors from clients in exchange for preferential treatment
- Sexual or romantic relationships with clients
- Clear violations of strict agency policy
- Failure to correct or improve inadequate performance
- Inability to deal with the emotional and stressful aspects of practice

Food for Thought

Being told one is below or above expectations can offer a general sense of how one is evaluated, but it does not provide information about what is being done well or how to improve performance. Thus, supervisors should offer, and interns should request, specific suggestions for continued growth. (Baird 2005, 83)

• • •

We are striving to know what we are doing, why and how we are doing it, and what works in particular situations. Use of such an organizational structure as "the evolution of a technique" is an orderly, coherent way to approach this undertaking. (Brill 1998, 139)

• • •

It is essential for interns to understand that the internship experience is fundamentally different from the rest of their academic work. In a typical class, lacking knowledge or skill may mean one's grade is lowered, but otherwise little of any real consequence happens. By comparison, at internships, an intern's lack of knowledge or skill has real consequences and those consequences apply not only to the intern but to the clients, supervisor, and agency with whom the intern works. Because interns need to go beyond the grade mentality and focus instead on learning. . . . When they accept evaluation as an essential part of learning, mistakes, successes, and feedback can be understood for what they really should be—learning opportunities—rather than points added or subtracted from an ultimately meaningless grade book. (Baird 2005, 82)

Guidance and Direction

Throughout your practicum, you will be observed, guided, encouraged, assigned tasks, given feedback, and evaluated. Your field instructor should provide an informal and ongoing critique so that you know how you are doing from week to week. In addition, you will be evaluated in a more formal and systematic manner at the end of each academic term.

When conducting the formal evaluation, your field instructor will most likely use an evaluation tool provided by your school. This tool will rate you on the specific values, attitudes, knowledge, and skills your school defines as important to your professional development. Obtain a copy of this evaluation tool early in your practicum and construct your plan for practicum learning so that you will have opportunities to learn and grow in each of the areas of performance to be evaluated.

You may also be evaluated on the completion of the tasks, projects, and activities you planned at the beginning of your practicum. Review your learning goals for the practicum regularly to determine if you are making satisfactory progress (see Chapter 3).

Your field instructor and your faculty supervisor will want to know how you think the practicum is proceeding, as well as hear any suggestions or questions you might have. He or she may ask you the following:

- Are the tasks and activities that you are performing different from what you were expecting?
- What aspects of your practicum do you consider to be of highest priority? Lowest priority?
- Are the demands on your time reasonable?
- What do you hope to learn and accomplish in the next month? By the time you complete your practicum?

- Do you get enough supervision or too much?
- Is this the right type of social work practice and practicum setting for you?
- What aspects of social work practice in this agency are most appealing, and which are least appealing?
- What new or additional experiences do you want or need?
- How well do you get along with agency staff?
- Which practicum tasks and assignments have you completed most successfully and which have you completed least successfully?
- Have you been able to strike a workable balance between the demands of the practicum, your other academic work, and your personal life and responsibilities?
- Have there been aspects of your practicum that you have had to neglect for lack of time?
- Do you have other comments, complaints, observations, or questions?
- What can be done to improve the learning experience for the next practicum student?

When reviewing and thinking about your performance in the practicum, your field instructor may ask him- or herself questions such as:

- Has this student demonstrated dependability and professionally responsible behavior?
- Can this individual be counted on in a stressful and demanding situation?
- Would I hire this person for a social work job?
- Would I want this person to be a social worker for my mother? My child? For a good friend of mine?
- Would I be willing to write a strong letter of recommendation for this student?
- Would this student be able to handle a social work position in this agency?

Behaviors and personal qualities that impress a field instructor include the following: initiative, dependability, honesty, punctuality, capacity to meet dead-lines, perseverance, ability to handle conflict in interpersonal relations, sensitivity to others, ability to achieve goals and objectives, ability to plan and organize work, clear writing, motivation and willingness to work hard, receptivity to new learning, self-awareness and openness to examining personal values and attitudes, capacity to work under pressure, personal maturity, emotional stability, respect for clients and other students, fairness in decision making, and professionalism.

Behaviors and qualities that cause a field instructor to doubt a student's ability to perform as a social worker include the opposite of the above listed behaviors, especially dishonesty, missing deadlines, disrespect for others, manipulation and efforts to "bend" rules and requirements, attempts to secure special concessions or privileges, not informing supervisors of problems, and the inability to keep personal problems from interfering with professional tasks and activities.

Prepare for a formal evaluation by reviewing your learning agreement and its stated goals and activities, as well as the practicum evaluation tool used by your school. Give careful thought to the question of how well you have managed to carry out your various responsibilities and completed assigned tasks. Prepare a list of your assigned tasks and responsibilities and assemble documentation of your work and accomplishments so it can easily be reviewed by your field instructor. Prior to meeting with your field instructor for the formal evaluation, you may be asked to do a self-evaluation using your school's evaluation tool.

Think of the evaluation as a learning experience that can help you become more self-aware, insightful, and skilled. Become aware of any feelings of inadequacy or any emotional triggers that might be activated during the process of evaluation.

If you know what they are, you are more likely to benefit from supervision and suggestions for improvement than if you lack this level of self-awareness.

Prepare yourself emotionally for the formal evaluation session so that you will be open to hearing feedback about your performance. When receiving feedback on your performance, strive to maintain an openness toward what you are hearing. Although it may be difficult to hear a frank appraisal of your work, avoid being defensive. Consider this feedback carefully and work to improve in the areas noted.

Should you feel uncomfortable receiving feedback on your performance, consider your reaction in light of what clients may feel when you give them feedback on their social functioning or their performance on an intervention plan. Being evaluated will hopefully make you more empathetic and humble, and will remind you of the importance of identifying both strengths and areas for growth.

In addition to constructive criticism, you will receive positive feedback related to areas in which you are doing well. Take note of what your field instructor sees as your skills and gifts. If you want more specific feedback about what you have done well so that you know what your skills or abilities are, ask for it. Review the workbook section of Chapter 1, and determine if the strengths you identified there have been demonstrated in your performance. Build on your strengths because they will form the basis of your professional knowledge and abilities.

Strive to understand what your field instructor observed in your performance that led him or her to draw a particular conclusion concerning your performance. Seek descriptions and examples of your poor performance and ask for specific suggestions on how it can be improved. Request descriptions of performances that were rated higher than most others. Reflect on these descriptions and determine why you perform some tasks and activities better than others.

If you and your field instructor disagree on the adequacy of your performance, prepare factual documentation supporting your point of view. However, if you agree that your performance is deficient, it is best to acknowledge the problem rather than entering into a pointless argument that can only leave you looking dishonest or lacking in self-awareness.

A common problem experienced by social work practicum students in direct services agencies is for the student to have an unusually strong or unexpected emotional reaction to specific client problems or situations. This is usually rooted in the student's own history of personal or family problems. The student should discuss these reactions with his or her field instructor. In some cases it will be necessary for the student to undergo counseling as a way of better understanding these reactions and finding ways to keep them from interfering with social work performance.

It is possible that during your practicum you will discover that you are not well suited to be a social worker, or perhaps you will discover that what you had assumed to be your area of special interest and skill has lost its appeal. Although somewhat painful and upsetting, these are very important discoveries. They may open new doors to exploration and opportunity while closing some that need to be closed. To be happy and content in life you need to make career decisions on the basis of accurate information about your particular strengths and gifts and your particular limitations. You need to understand what you can and cannot do.

Examining Your Performance in the Practicum: A Workbook Activity

Every program of social work education uses some type of evaluation instrument or tool for evaluating student performance in the practicum. Before beginning this workbook activity, carefully examine the instrument that will be used in the evaluation of your performance.

In this activity you are asked to reflect on and evaluate your own performance in relation to eleven broad categories and fifty-five dimensions or specific areas of social work knowledge and skills. These dimensions are fairly typical of those used in various practicum evaluation instruments.* Evaluate your performance in relation to each of the fifty-five statements below.

Category A: Social Work as a Profession

A1. Understands the social work role and purpose as distinct from the role and purpose of other professions.

_____

_____

A2. Demonstrates competence in a variety of social work practice roles (e.g., case manager, advocate, planner, counselor, broker of services).

_____

_____

A3. Understands social work ethics and conducts self in accordance with the NASW *Code of Ethics* and its underlying values (e.g., client self-determination, confidentiality, human dignity, social justice).

_____

_____

A4. Demonstrates competence in the various levels of social work interventions from micro- to macro-level practice (e.g., from direct practice with individuals to social change efforts).

_____

_____

*The author uses the fifty-five items presented here in the program of social work education at The University of Montana. Practicum evaluation items used with permission of Tondy Baumgartner, MSW, Practicum Coordinator at The University of Montana School of Social Work BSW and MSW Program.

A5. Conducts self in a professional manner (e.g., punctual, reliable, efficient, organized, completed assigned tasks, dressed appropriately).

_____

_____

Category B: Organizational Context of Practice

B1. Understands agency's purpose, mission, history, funding, and structure.

_____

_____

B2. Understands and facilitates the flow of work in the agency and follows established agency policies, procedures, and protocol.

_____

_____

B3. Works creatively and collaboratively within agency guidelines.

_____

_____

B4. Understands the relationship of the agency to other human services organizations in the community.

_____

_____

B5. Analyzes tools and instruments used by the agency to evaluate effectiveness and suggests additional evaluation procedures if needed.

_____

_____

Category C: Community Context of Practice

C1. Is aware of various services, programs, and resources in the community that are relevant to the client population served by agency.

_____

_____

C2. Uses those community resources most appropriate for specific clients.

_____

_____

C3. Uses advocacy, when appropriate, to obtain resources needed by clients and empowers clients to advocate for themselves.

_____

_____

C4. Is able to identify gaps in services within the community.

_____

_____

C5. Understands the effect of community factors on clients and services (e.g., rural/urban environment, demographics, funding priorities, attitudes, economics).

_____

_____

Category D: Data Gathering and Assessment

D1. Purposefully and selectively gathers relevant data needed for assessments and interventions.

_____

_____

D2. Sorts, categorizes, and analyzes data in order to understand the nature of client concerns, needs, or problems.

_____

_____

D3. Engages and involves the client in the process of data collection and understanding the meaning and implications of those data.

_____

_____

D4. Addresses the client's strengths, capacity, and opportunity for change.

_____

_____

D5. Identifies the major systems related to the problem or concern being addressed (e.g., social institutions, economic structures, cultural systems).

_____

_____

Category E: Planning and Intervention

E1. Sets priorities and identifies clear and measurable objectives for intervention.

_____

_____

E2. Involves the client in setting goals and choosing interventions and develops a relevant and feasible contract or service agreement.

_____

_____

E3. Understands the various perspectives, theories, and models used to guide interventions.

_____

_____

E4. Is able to determine the most feasible and effective level of intervention (micro, mezzo, or macro).

_____

_____

E5. Selects specific and relevant interventions matched to the client's situation, needs, available resources, and the agency's purpose.

_____

_____

Category F: Termination and Evaluation

F1. Helps clients evaluate movement toward agreed-on goals and objectives.

_____

_____

F2. Terminates helping relationship appropriately and constructively.

_____

_____

F3. Seeks out and uses tools and instruments that can measure client progress and evaluate the effectiveness of an intervention.

_____

_____

F4. Seeks out and uses tools and instruments that can measure and evaluate one's own performance and practice.

_____

_____

F5. Is able to examine and critique one's own performance in an objective and nondefensive manner.

_____

_____

Category G: Understanding Social Problems

G1. Identifies and describes the social problems or conditions that the agency addresses.

_____

_____

G2. Identifies and describes the social problems or conditions faced by clients of the agency.

_____

_____

G3. Understands how social problems develop as a result of the interaction between individuals, social systems, and the larger social environment.

_____

_____

G4. Is aware of the major social problems addressing the community.

_____

_____

G5. Uses an ecosystems perspective and social systems theory to analyze social problems.

_____

_____

Category H: Social Policy and Social Change

H1. Identifies and analyzes social policies affecting clients of the agency.

_____

_____

H2. Recognizes the positive and negative impacts of social policy on clients.

_____

_____

H3. Understands how social policies develop and are modified over time.

_____

_____

H4. Identifies needed changes in social policy.

_____

_____

H5. Is able to participate in social change or social justice efforts.

_____

_____

Category I: Diversity

I1. Is aware of and sensitive to client issues related to diversity (e.g., culture, ethnicity, gender, age, socioeconomic status, disability, sexual orientation).

_____

_____

I2. Treats all people with respect regardless of their behavior, characteristics, and background.

_____

_____

I3. Understands the effects of stereotypes, prejudice, discrimination, and oppression on individuals, families, and communities and on the formation of social policy.

_____

_____

I4. Is effective in communicating with persons of differing backgrounds and life experiences.

_____

_____

I5. Is able to individualize procedures for assessment, planning, intervention, and evaluation for diverse clients.

_____

_____

Category J: Communication Skills

J1. Effectively uses nonverbal communication and verbal helping skills (e.g., empathic responding, active listening, mediating, counseling).

_____

_____

J2. Effectively uses written communication (e.g., correspondence, reports, records).

_____

_____

J3. Is able to engage and work with nonvoluntary, resistant, or hard-to-reach clients.

_____

_____

J4. Recognizes the underlying meaning and significance of clients' concerns and situation.

_____

_____

J5. Handles questions and disagreements with other staff and agency policies and procedures with understanding, tact, and diplomacy.

_____

_____

Category K: Knowledge and Use of Self

K1. Takes the initiative in developing and implementing learning activities.

_____

_____

K2. Uses supervision for guidance, learning, and professional growth.

_____

_____

K3. Understands how personal values, beliefs, and ethics enhance or interfere with social work practice.

_____

_____

K4. Is aware of own biases and deals with them appropriately.

_____

_____

K5. Recognizes personal changes needed in order to function more effectively as a social worker (e.g., habits, personal style, level of knowledge).

_____

_____

Additional notes and comments:

_____

_____

_____

_____

_____

_____

Suggested Learning Activities

- Compare the practicum evaluation instrument used by your school with the evaluation tool used to evaluate the performance of social workers and other professional staff in your agency.
- Evaluate yourself using both your school's evaluation instrument and the sample tools in this chapter.
- Identify fears you may have about being evaluated and discuss them with your supervisor.

Additional Suggestions and Hints

- In Sheafor and Horejsi (2006), read the sections entitled "Developing Self-Awareness" (580-589) and "Worker Performance Evaluation" (501-503).

Selected Bibliography

Baird, Brian N. *The Internship, Practicum, and Field Placement Handbook.* 4th ed. Upper Saddle River, NJ: Pearson Education, 2006.

Collins, Donald, Barbara Thomlison, and Richard Grinnell. *The Social Work Practicum.* Itasca, IL: F. E. Peacock, 1992.

Courneyer, Barry R., and Mary J. Stanley. *The Social Work Portfolio: Planning, Assessing and Documenting Lifelong Learning in a Dynamic Profession.* Pacific Grove, CA: Brooks/Cole, 2002.

Drake, Robert E., Matthew R. Merrens, and David W. Lynde, eds. *Evidence-Based Mental Health Practice: A Textbook.* New York: W. W. Norton, 2005.

National Association of Social Workers. *Code of Ethics.* Washington, DC: NASW Press, 1999.

Rosen, Aaron, and Enola K. Proctor, eds. *Developing Practice Guidelines for Social Work Intervention: Issues, Methods and Research Agenda.* New York: Columbia University Press, 2003.

Rothman, Juliet Cassuto. *The Self-Awareness Workbook for Social Workers.* Boston: Allyn and Bacon, 1999.

Sheafor, Bradford, and Charles Horejsi. *Techniques and Guidelines for Social Work Practice.* 6th ed. Boston: Allyn and Bacon, 2003.

Weinback, Robert. *The Social Worker as Manager.* 4th ed. Boston: Allyn and Bacon, 2003.

18

Merging Self and Profession

GOALS FOR LEARNING

- To clarify your motivation for choosing social work as a career
- To identify important considerations in preparing for a social work career
- To identify factors important to your selection of a particular type of social work practice and practice setting
- To become aware of how the practice of social work might affect your physical and mental health, family, friends, and economic situation
- To develop personal and professional self-awareness

No doubt your family and friends have probably asked you the following questions: What is social work? Why do you want to be a social worker? Why do you need a degree in social work? Will you be able to get a job and earn a living? How will you keep from burning out in a stressful profession such as social work? These are good questions and you should be able to answer them and be comfortable with your answers. It is likely that your responses to these questions will be rooted in your commitment to the welfare of others, to making a significant difference in the world, and to promoting social justice. Hopefully your practicum will serve to cement your decision to pursue social work as a career because you will be able to enhance your knowledge and skills and begin to see how you are suited for this work.

Each of us is a unique individual with a unique personality and set of abilities and interests. In addition, each profession and occupation has a unique set of demands and required skills. For you to be satisfied and effective as a social worker, there must be a good match between you and the profession.

Selecting a career or occupation is one of the most important decisions you will make. That decision will have far-reaching implications for your basic contentment in life, the level of satisfaction you find in work, and your economic situation. A good match between your choice of occupation and your interests, abilities, and values will bring you personal satisfaction, challenge, and stimulation. A mismatch can give rise to general discontent and stress-related health problems.

The practicum provides an invaluable opportunity to examine and test the match between who you really are, your values, beliefs, temperament, abilities, and skills and the demands, requirements, and rewards of social work practice. This chapter is designed to help you examine, once again, that match.

Background and Context

Most social workers feel "called" to the profession of social work because they are committed to and passionate about helping others and they find that the profession's values are compatible with their own. They want to make a positive contribution to their community and world and they see that the practice of social work is a way of doing that. Some also feel drawn to the profession because events and experiences in their lives have opened their eyes to certain problems and to the needs of other people. Others are attracted to social work because they have some of the natural skills and abilities necessary to the profession and see social work education as a formal way of acquiring the ability to make even more impact in social welfare. Most are drawn to social work by virtue of the way they think the world should be, the responsibility they feel toward acting on behalf of others, and the belief that they must become involved in social justice efforts.

Those preparing for a career in social work must be familiar with the types of jobs that are available and the demands of the work. They must have a high level of self-awareness so they can make good choices in relation to the type of job they seek, practice self-care and stress management, and balance personal and professional responsibilities. Social workers must be aware of their unique gifts, their values, and their biases. Such self-awareness is also critical to becoming a professional who is effective in his or her use of self in relating to clients. Social workers must understand how their particular style and manner of interacting is perceived by others, especially clients. Those planning to enter social work must be emotionally healthy, skilled in communication, able to build and maintain relationships, able to manage stress, and willing to continually learn and grow, both personally and professionally.

Choosing a helping profession as one's life's work usually means that you care deeply about those you serve. This commitment to others may take a toll on one's personal life unless the social worker learns to find a healthy balance between work and personal life. It is not possible to make a complete separation between one's personal and professional lives. Our work affects our personal lives and our personal lives affect our work. Sheafor and Horejsi (2006, 17) observe that the social workers' "own beliefs, values, physical and emotional well-being, spirituality, family relationships, friendships, and all other facets of living will both influence and be influenced by the day-to-day experiences of social work practice." Knowing this, it is vital to find a workable balance between one's personal life and one's professional life.

It is important to find this balance because it is easy to allow your concern for clients to overtake you. You may worry about them or take more responsibility for them than is healthy for yourself. It is important to learn to set clear boundaries between your personal and professional selves early in your career because this will help you retain your energy, enthusiasm, and optimism while also preventing discouragement and burnout.

Employers are looking for certain traits when they screen job applicants for social work positions. Knowing what employers seek and value in a social worker will help you to anticipate the requirements for certain jobs and work to develop and demonstrate the ability to meet these requirements. Typically, they are especially interested in seven qualities:

1. Skills related to the job to be performed (as described in the job description)
2. Character traits and prior experiences that reflect creativity, flexibility, and an enthusiasm for solving problems
3. The ability to work cooperatively with others

4. The ability to work creatively and collaboratively within an organizational structure
5. A genuine interest in and an enjoyment of the type of work to be performed
6. Written and verbal communication skills
7. A commitment to professional competence and excellence

In general, there is a close relationship between job satisfaction and one's overall satisfaction with self and life. Those who are satisfied with their jobs tend to have high self-esteem, are able to manage stress, and believe that they have influence and control over the outcome of their work. Other factors also contribute to job satisfaction. Among them are the following:

- *Overall workload*—Most people prefer jobs that are stimulating, challenging, and that keep them busy, but are not overwhelming or exhausting.
- *Variety*—Most people prefer work that provides some variety. Most people do not care for jobs that are highly repetitive.
- *Opportunity*—Most people desire jobs that will provide opportunities for promotion, advancement, ongoing learning, and professional development.
- *Social interaction*—Most people prefer jobs that allow friendly, pleasant, and informal interactions with coworkers.

Guidance and Direction

The practice of social work requires an integration of professional knowledge and ethics with a high level of self-awareness. It is not enough to know "about" people, to have skills, to know theories, or to understand models and techniques. You as a "person" must merge with the you as a "professional." Remember that all the skills and knowledge in the world will not make you an effective social worker. You also need to bring your personal gifts, strengths, creativity, passion, and commitment to the social work profession. It is in the unique blending of your personal qualities and your professional education that you will become a truly skilled and qualified social worker.

Who you are as a person is just as important as what you know or can do. View your practicum as an opportunity to grow both personally and professionally, and to blend your unique personality and professional style with the requirements of your chosen profession. Over time the two parts of you will blend so that you will bring everything that is unique about you to your personal way of being a social worker.

Continually seek opportunities to enhance your professional growth. For example, read books and journals, attend workshops and in-service training, try out new skills and techniques, think critically about intervention strategies, carefully observe the behavior and practice of workers in your agency, and spend time talking with knowledgeable and skilled practitioners. Open yourself to critical self-reflection, asking yourself and trusted colleagues what you can do to continue growing. Open yourself to feedback so that you see yourself as others do. You will certainly see your own growth over time, and this will not only reinforce your choice of social work as a profession, but will also remind you of the importance of self-awareness as a tool for helping others.

Put your thoughts in writing. I suggest keeping a journal during your practicum. Record your ideas and questions about your experiences and observations, list key concepts you are learning, and describe what you are discovering about yourself. Review it often and reflect on your use of self, your biases, your gifts, and how these affect your work.

Food for Thought

Those who work to bring about changes are able to see even in darkest circumstances how improvements are possible if the right kind of effort is made. They can see beyond inconsistencies, human frailty, and fearsome injustice to the goal that beckons them. The constant presence of that goal carries them on and sets them apart from others who do not make a difference. (Armstrong and Wakin 1978, 82–89)

• • •

The moment of commitment cannot be deferred. It must become a lifelong process, one that links our lives to the lives of others, our souls to the souls of others, in a chain of being that reaches both backward and forward, connecting us with all that makes us human. (Loeb 1999, 349)

• • •

You do not have to be absolutely perfect in order to help people. Some of your own most difficult struggles can help you find insights that will later serve your clinical work well. (Baird 2005, 176)

• • •

Self-awareness and critical inquiry go hand in hand. Both encourage contextual awareness—exploring how past and present environments influence what you do, value, and believe and how, in turn, you influence your environments. Critical thinking will help you discover . . . beliefs you have accepted without critical thought which, on reflection, you find problematic.

Critical thinking helps free us from the prisons of unexamined views that limit our vision. It encourages us to examine the perspective within which we reason and the effect of our own cultural experiences in developing them. It can help us identify topics or positions to which we have a strong initial reaction in one direction that prevents critical inquiry. Thinking carefully about problems and possible ways to solve them helps us detect contradictions between what we do and what we say we value. It teaches us to be aware of how our emotions affect our beliefs and actions. (Gambrill 1997, 132–133)

• • •

As I reflect on Jane Addams' impact on our profession, I find myself wondering how we, as practitioners and educators, should build on her legacy. I know that the spirit of Jane Addams is alive in our profession. People who are poor and other populations at risk face the complexities of urban life and still need help. As we wrestle with the problems of life in urban communities, I believe that the essence of Jane Addams' vision of community-based practice is still viable. We must follow her into the community again and renew her spirit. (Johnson 2004, 321)

• • •

Our souls are not hungry for fame, comfort, wealth, or power. Those rewards create almost as many problems as they solve. Our souls are hungry for meaning, for the sense that we have figured out how to live so that our lives matter, so the world will be at least a little bit different for our having passed through it. . . .

If a person lives and dies and no one notices, if the world continues as it was, was that person ever really alive? I am convinced that it is not the fear of death, of our life ending, that haunts our sleep so much as the fear that as far as the world is concerned, we might as well never have lived. (Kussner 1986, 18)

Ask for feedback from coworkers, your field instructor, and clients. Use this information to better understand who you are, what you have to offer, and what you may need to change in order to become a skilled and effective social worker. You are certain to see that you have grown over time, that your questions have become more probing, and your reflections more sophisticated. This will reinforce the fact that you are growing as a professional.

Continue to think about how well your professional and personal lives fit together. Do you have the temperament to be a social worker? Are you able to handle the demands and the stress of the job? What demands of the job make you most uncomfortable? What tasks and activities make you anxious? Do you like to do what social workers do? Can you put your knowledge into practice? What additional knowledge do you need to more effectively enhance your personal skills? Which of the profession's values do you feel most strongly about?

View your practicum as job-related experience. It is relevant preparation for practice and the job market. Do your best and remember that the skills you develop now, combined with favorable evaluations and recommendations from your field instructor, can help you obtain employment in the profession.

Observe how workers in your agency deal with challenges such as high caseloads, potentially modest salaries, unmotivated and difficult clients, seemingly intractable social problems, funding cuts, and the stress of dealing with deeply emotional and painful situations on a daily basis. Begin now to develop stress management skills and habits that will help you avoid excessive job-related stress or burnout. Learn how to set limits, define personal boundaries, make time for your family and yourself, and maintain a positive outlook on clients and the work you do.

Begin now to develop the habit of monitoring your own personal growth. Ask yourself these questions regularly:

- What is my vision for myself as a social worker?
- How can I maintain this vision?
- Am I growing as a person and a professional?
- Do I know myself better than I did last month? Last year?
- Am I satisfied with who I am and what I am doing?
- If I am not satisfied, what can I do about it? What will I do about it?
- How can I continue to grow and change in a positive way?
- Do I continue to see the potential, possibility, and strengths of clients?
- Do I continue to believe in the goals and ethics of the profession?
- Am I optimistic about social change?

Merging Self and Profession: A Workbook Activity

The questions presented below are intended to encourage careful thought about how your choice of social work as a career will enhance and affect your whole being and influence your many other roles and responsibilities.

1. What strongly held values led you to pursue social work as a profession?

   _____

   _____

2. Do you feel a calling to social work? If so, on what is this calling based?

   _____

   _____

3. What is it about a career in social work that you find most positive and attractive? How can you make sure that you retain this view?

   _____

   _____

4. What is it about a career in social work that you find most negative or aversive? How can you minimize or cope with these aspects of social work?

   _____

   _____

5. What impacts, both positive and negative, will your choice of a social work career have on:

   a. Your family

   _____

   _____

   b. Your friendships and social activities

   _____

   _____

   c. Your health and level of stress

   _____

   _____

    d. Your personal interests, recreation, and leisure activities

_____

_____

    e. Your spiritual and religious practices

_____

_____

6. What have you learned about yourself during the practicum that confirms your choice of social work as a profession?

_____

_____

7. What specific self-care activities will you engage in to maintain your energy, passion, optimism, and commitment?

_____

_____

8. After five years of experience and employment as a social worker, what type of work would you like to be doing? After fifteen years? After twenty-five years?

_____

_____

9. What impact do you hope to make as a result of your work?

_____

_____

10. What advice would you give to other social work students who are just beginning their practicum?

_____

_____

Additional notes and comments:

_____

_____

_____

_____

_____

Suggested Learning Activities

- Interview experienced social workers in your agency and in other agencies. Ask about their level of job satisfaction, as well as the pros and cons of a career in social work. If they could do it all over, would they select a social work career?
- Speak with social workers who have obtained advanced degrees (MSW, Ph.D., or DSW) and ask them to help you consider the possibility of further education.
- If you have doubts or questions about whether social work is a good career for you, arrange to take a battery of occupational interest and aptitude tests that may provide you with additional information and insights.

Additional Suggestions and Hints

- In Sheafor and Horejsi (2006), read the sections entitled "Getting a Social Work Job" (582–584).
- Examine the social work–related job openings advertised in local and regional newspapers, public agency bulletins, and in NASW news. (The NASW website is www.socialworkers.org.)
- Read "Taking Heart: Spiritual Exercises for Social Activists" in Macy (1991).

Selected Bibliography

Armstrong, Richard, and Edward Wakin. *You Can Still Change the World.* New York: Harper and Row, 1978.

Baird, Brian. *The Internship, Practicum, and Field Placement Handbook: A Guide for the Helping Professions.* 4th ed. Upper Saddle River, New Jersey: Prentice Hall, 2005.

Gibelman, Margaret. *What Social Workers Do.* 2nd ed. Washington, DC: NASW Press, 1995.

Johnson, Alice K. "Social Work Is Standing on the Legacy of Jane Addams: But Are We Sitting on the Sidelines?" *Social Work* (April 2004): 321.

Loeb, Paul Rogat. *Soul of a Citizen: Living with Conviction in a Cynical Time.* New York: St. Martin's Griffin, 1999.

Macy, Joanna. *World as Lover, World as Self.* Berkeley, CA: Parallax Press, 1991.

Rothman, Juliet Cassuto. *The Self-Awareness Workbook for Social Workers.* Boston: Allyn and Bacon, 1999.

Schon, Donald A., and Aleksandr Romanovich Luria. *The Reflective Practitioner: How Professionals Think in Action.* New York: Basic Books, 1990.

Sheafor, Bradford, and Charles Horejsi. *Techniques and Guidelines for Social Work Practice.* 7th ed. Boston: Allyn and Bacon, 2006.

19

Leadership and Social Justice

Now that your practicum is nearing its completion, you have nearly fulfilled all of the requirements necessary to obtain your degree. You are, no doubt, excited about job possibilities and also seriously thinking about the personal ramifications of entering the world of social work. This is a time of transition. What lies ahead for you? What kind of social worker do you hope to become? Perhaps even more important, what kind of person do you want to become? This chapter invites you to reflect on these questions.

As a social worker, social work educator, and the author of the book you have been reading, I desire three things for you:

1. That you become an effective and ethical social worker
2. That you become a leader within your profession and your community—one committed to the pursuit of social and economic justice
3. That you become the person you want to be and live a life filled with meaning and purpose

In this final chapter, I offer some suggestions on how you might achieve these three ends.

Becoming the Social Worker You Want To Be

It is both exciting and rather daunting to think about being a social worker. There are many problems to be addressed and many clients to be served. Injustices need to be challenged and a number of programs need to be designed or redesigned. There is so much to be done—but so few resources. There is also much more to learn as you move from the academic world of a practicum student to the real world of the professional social worker.

Because you have completed the requirements for a social work degree in a program accredited by the Council on Social Work Education, your professors have concluded that you are ready to begin the practice of social work. Although you may still feel anxious and ill prepared to assume the responsibilities of a social worker, your professors and supervisors believe that you possess the knowledge and basic skills needed to move into a social agency and apply what you have learned. You have been educated in an academic setting, trained in a social agency, and exposed to many social problems and various ways of addressing them. Do not underestimate what you have learned and what you are capable of doing. You are now a professional social worker by virtue of all you have learned and the ways in which you have demonstrated your competence and commitment to ethical practice.

Reflect often on the preamble to the *Code of Ethics* (NASW 1999, 1), which states:

> The primary mission of the social work profession is to enhance human well-being and help meet the basic needs of all people, with particular attention to the needs and empowerment of people who are vulnerable, oppressed, and living in poverty. A historic and defining feature of social work is the profession's focus on individual well-being in a social context and the well-being of society.

This statement describes a profession deeply committed, both by its history and current practice, to creating communities and a society that will nurture the well-being of individuals and families and to making sure that all people have access to the basic resources and opportunities necessary to live with dignity. You have entered a profession that is committed to challenging those systems and institutional structures that do not treat people in a fair and humane manner. If you, as a social worker, do not speak out against and seek to correct a social or economic injustice you are, in effect, giving your tacit approval to the current state of affairs.

View the practice of social work as being much more than the tasks and activities listed in your job description or suggested in your agency's mission statement. Work hard at whatever you are hired to do, but also assume the additional responsibility of becoming an advocate for those who are not able to speak for themselves. Social work, at its unique best, is about going beyond one's job description and acting on a commitment to social justice by weaving together the networks of people and resources that can bring about needed changes at the community, state, and national levels. In fact, a true leader sees what is possible and is not constrained by a job description or limited resources. A leader makes things happen, building on acquired knowledge and skills, combined with the synergy generated by bringing other committed people together.

The preamble to the NASW *Code of Ethics* also reflects the contextual or the person-in-environment perspective that is fundamental to the way social workers view people, assess human problems and concerns, and design interventions. Social workers, whether employed to work at the micro or macro level, must be cognizant of the wider societal context of the lives and problems of their clients and the context of the agencies, programs, and interventions that address these client concerns. For example, a social worker working at the micro level as an advocate for survivors of intimate partner violence should question why such violence occurs and should take macro-level leadership in amending laws to more adequately protect victims and hold perpetrators of violence accountable, while offering everyone involved treatment options that have the potential for improving social functioning. Conversely, social workers attempting to pass legislation protecting the rights of the poor would be well advised to understand the personal plight of those individuals potentially affected negatively by any social policy changes.

The realities and time pressures associated with employment in an agency that has a particular mission and program set in motion a number of forces that tend to narrow a social worker's range of concerns, interests, and vision. You will feel very busy with all of the demands of your job, but it will be important that you find ways to remain involved in social issues beyond the scope of your work responsibilities. Doing so will help to remind you that others care about their work as much as you and can serve as a source of inspiration for you. Strive to maintain a wide range of interests, involvements, and professional activities. Seek out new ideas, even when they are not immediately applicable in your everyday work.

As you enter into the work of a particular agency, you may discover that the agency uses an unfamiliar conceptual framework or rationale to guide its practice activities. As you are exposed to new practice frameworks, remember that each one needs to be examined in terms of its potential to enhance practice effectiveness, its appropriateness for use with particular types of clients in particular settings, its evidence-based research, its stated or implied assumptions about clients and the process of change, and its compatibility with social work values.

Carefully consider why you might prefer one approach to other possibilities. Most likely, you prefer a particular practice framework because it is the one most compatible with your beliefs about human behavior and human problems, and because it instructs you, the professional, to perform those tasks and activities to which you are especially attracted. Although it is natural to pursue your own interests, seek to broaden and deepen your understanding of the various perspectives, theories, and models used in social work practice and carefully examine the assumptions underlying each approach. Strive to understand the strengths and limitations of each one. Be open to gaining insights and guidance from several practice frameworks.

In order to determine whether you are being effective over time, document your work and study the outcomes of your practice, both individually and in concert with other professionals and agencies. Be ready to change your approach if you are not being as effective as you think possible. Needless to say, much of what social workers do and much of what clients experience is difficult to measure, but resist the temptation to use this as an excuse for not making a genuine effort to evaluate your practice. You cannot improve your practice unless you are willing to look at it critically and allow others to offer constructive criticisms.

To the extent possible, build your knowledge base by drawing on findings from empirical and scientific studies, but remember that there are many other sources of useful knowledge. Some are empirical and some are not. Balance the positivist view of knowledge building, which rests on the scientific method of understanding, with contributions from *practice wisdom* (the collective professional experiences and observations of practitioners) and also with the insights derived from study of the humanities, religion, and classic and modern literature. Finally, learn from your clients as you listen to their stories and experiences, and add their wisdom to yours.

As you attempt to understand and use new research findings and theories drawn from the social and behavioral sciences, consider the observation by sociologists that such knowledge is "socially constructed." Our knowledge of a social or psychological phenomenon or a particular human problem is shaped and limited by the context in which it was studied, by our positionality, by the language used to describe it, and is very much tied to our culture, history, economics, and politics. Our knowledge is, at best, incomplete and only temporarily true. The awareness that knowledge is a social construction helps us to put data and conclusions in perspective and better realize that the concepts and theories used in practice, no matter how well-conceived and impressive, are purely human inventions. It is your prerogative and your responsibility to thoughtfully question all findings and claims, regardless of their source.

It is actually the job of critically reflective social workers to deconstruct their knowledge and what is being told to them. This means that you must examine what you know, question how you came to know it, ask yourself how this view might be inaccurate or limited, and become comfortable at times with not knowing. In a similar vein, recognize that the concept of *client* is a human invention or social construction that has arisen out of our cultural views and presumptions about who is in need of help, who is powerless to help him- or herself, and who is qualified to help another person. Always be sensitive to the possibility that agencies, social workers, and other professionals can misuse their power and authority to label a person, family, or group as troubled and in need of certain services or interventions. Remember also that the designation of one person as a client and another as a social worker does not mean that the social worker is more knowledgeable or more insightful than the client. Rather, the opposite could be true. The lines between social worker and client, although useful, are arbitrary and can limit our ability to relate to each other in significant and meaningful ways.

Become involved in those professional organizations that can support your work, challenge you intellectually, and remind you that others are also involved in the struggle to create a just society. Remember that you have a voice in the ongoing development and shaping of the profession, and that social work educators need to hear your observations and suggestions as much as clients need your skills. Voice your opinions about directions you believe the profession should take based on your observations and your projections of future needs. Speak up when you see your profession becoming focused too heavily on one aspect of social work to the detriment of its overall mission.

Remain in the world of ideas and commit to lifelong learning. There are numerous approaches you can take to continue learning and growing, which will not only make you more effective, but will also make you a better, more informed, and capable person. I suggest that you follow these guidelines:

- Continue to read professional literature and attend advanced training sessions.
- Join or form a group of professionals that takes seriously its commitment to continuing education and peer supervision.
- Look globally and internationally for possible solutions to nagging and serious social problems.
- Continue to learn from your clients who experience on a daily basis what you may only observe, read about, or imagine.
- Seek to identify the connections between social conditions and either the social problems or the social benefits resulting from them.
- Stay connected to universities and schools of social work through conferences, by offering guest lectures, and by supervising practicum students.
- Talk on a regular basis to those with whom you fundamentally disagree in order to retain an open mind and clarify your own beliefs and values.
- Find ways to come to know and understand yourself better over time.
- Ask yourself regularly what your vision for the world is and determine what you need to learn to bring yourself closer to your goals.

Recognize your ability to be a catalyst for change. To be a catalyst means that you bring individuals and groups together, contribute your skills and knowledge, and stimulate positive movement or changes that would not have occurred without your intervention. Remember that you are not alone in your efforts to help others. There are many social workers who will support and encourage you in your efforts. Seek them out, offer your support in return, and find avenues of renewal for yourself, both personally and professionally.

Take care of yourself, see the good in the world as well as the problems, celebrate large and small successes, learn to laugh, and cultivate the sources of your passion and strength. Use your family, friends, spiritual beliefs, and core values to guide you, and take pride in your chosen profession.

Becoming a Leader and a Seeker of Social Justice

As a social worker you will encounter many situations of oppression and social and economic injustice. You will also encounter situations in which agency policies, programs, and practices are in need of revision in order to make them fairer and more effective. You will want to change these situations but may quickly discover that bringing about needed and meaningful change is a difficult and slow process. In order to bring about change you must be willing and able to assume the role, tasks, and responsibilities of leadership. Desirable changes do not happen by accident. Rather, they are set in motion by individuals who assert themselves, articulate their beliefs, and step forward to take on the hard work of leading.

Although it may be true that a few leaders are the so-called born leaders, most had to learn the skills of leadership much like they learned any other skill. Aspiring leaders must consciously and continually cultivate the development of those qualities, ways of thinking, attitudes, and interpersonal skills that are associated with effective leadership.

Leadership is much more than having good ideas. It is not enough to know what needs to be done. Leadership is the ability to make things happen and to inspire others to join in the effort. Leaders must have a clear vision of what they want to accomplish. Equally important, they must be able to articulate this vision and explain it in words that the followers understand. The vision must be one that can be translated into action steps and programs that are inspiring but also feasible and realistic.

It is the leader's vision that gives him or her the critically important sense of purpose, direction, and self-confidence to make difficult decisions. This sense of purpose must be evident in all that the leader does. Indecisiveness and the unwillingness to take action when action is clearly necessary can deeply undermine confidence in a leader's ability. It is often said that it is better for a leader to occasionally make a bad decision than to avoid making a critically important decision, so learn to be decisive and bold when necessary as well as thoughtful and well prepared.

Good leaders lead by example. Followers are inspired and motivated by the passion, resolve, courage, hard work, and sacrifices of their leaders. Leaders must model the behaviors they want to see in others. They should not ask others to do what they are unwilling to do themselves.

Leaders must demonstrate respect and genuine concern for the wishes, values, and abilities of those they lead. They must be willing to curtail some of their own preferences and plans in order to avoid moving too far ahead of the followers. Leaders cannot lead unless there are people who choose to follow them.

Effective leaders must maintain open and honest communication with their followers. This communication must keep followers focused on the goal while attending to the concerns, fears, and ambivalence they may have about investing their time, energy, and money in working toward this goal.

Good leaders anticipate possible conflicts and disagreements among their followers. They are proactive in taking steps to prevent or resolve these conflicts before they can distract from goal achievement and splinter the followers into competing factions.

Leaders must be skilled in the art of collaboration and building bridges between individuals and organizations. They must reward others for their cooperation and share the credit for success with others, even those with whom they may disagree. Leaders must be willing to compromise when this is a necessary step toward reaching the sought-after goal.

The exercise of leadership always occurs within a context of competing and conflicting forces. Leaders shape, guide, and redirect those forces, so they move in directions that produce the desired effect and move people toward the desired goal. Because leaders must function within environments and situations that are unpredictable and always changing, they must be willing to take necessary risks and cope with ambiguity and uncertainty.

Effective leaders possess a high level of self-awareness. They understand their own strengths and limitations and constantly examine their own motives and behavior. Many leaders destroy their capacity to lead by allowing feelings of self-importance and a need for recognition to dominate their decisions or by becoming arrogant and overly confident because of past successes.

The capacity to lead is often tied to having a positive reputation within one's organization or community, having prior experience with the issue that has drawn people together, and having a well-developed network of personal and professional contacts. For this reason, an individual who changes jobs frequently or moves from community to community may limit his or her potential for becoming a leader.

In addition to the factors mentioned previously, the following qualities and characteristics are important to the exercise of effective leadership:

- Capacity to think critically and examine personal decisions and actions
- Capacity to speak and write clearly to articulate a vision and purpose in ways people can understand
- Perseverance when faced with difficulties and disappointments
- Ability to delegate responsibility and teach or empower others to perform as well as they can
- Ability to make difficult decisions in situations that are complex and fluid
- Willingness to assume personal responsibility for one's decisions and actions
- Personal flexibility, openness to new ideas, and the ability to work with people with various abilities and with people from diverse backgrounds
- Ability to create a sense of belonging and community among those working toward the same goals
- Ability to make effective use of available time and get things done
- Willingness to assess one's own effectiveness in a nondefensive manner and to adopt approaches that will be more effective

Seek to become what is commonly referred to as a *transformational leader*—someone who understands and embodies the interpersonal and moral aspects of leadership. Through their passion and vision, transformational leaders inspire others through their deeply held beliefs and strong moral values. They are able to get others to join with them because they are enthusiastic and energetic. Their integrity leads others to trust them. Their genuine desire to see others succeed makes others more enthusiastic. This form of leadership, which cares about everyone involved in a common effort, is markedly different from the form of leadership that only pays attention to the tasks at hand. Try to become the sort of leader that balances the work to be done with the professional and personal support of those working together.

Clearly, it is a challenge to be an effective leader in one's agency or one's profession. It is an even more difficult undertaking when the leader's goal is to promote social and economic justice. However, this is at the heart of social work.

At a fundamental level, justice can be defined as fairness in relationships. Although there are several categories or types of justice, matters of social justice and economic justice are of special concern to social workers.

Social justice refers to the basic fairness and moral rightness of the social arrangements and institutional structures that impact the people of a community or society. Although closely related to economic justice, social justice focuses more on how society is organized and whether governmental and corporate policies and powerful groups recognize basic human rights and the dignity and worth of all people.

Economic justice (also called *distributive justice*) can be defined as that dimension of justice having to do with the material or the economic aspects of a community or society. Economic justice denotes the fair apportioning and the distribution of economic resources, opportunities, and burdens. Principles of economic justice relate to fairness in, for example, wages paid for work performed, access to jobs, access to credit, prices charged for essential goods and services, and taxes imposed.

Because social and economic injustices are, by definition, embedded in existing institutional arrangements, many political, economic, and cultural forces are at work maintaining the unjust conditions. Those who seek change will encounter many powerful individuals and groups who will want to maintain the status quo. In order to secure real change, a leader working for social justice must be willing to take substantial risks and make significant personal sacrifices.

Goldenberg (1978, 4–13) identifies several mechanisms (presumptions, beliefs, and deliberate actions) used by those in power to rationalize and perpetuate the oppressive and unjust conditions from which they benefit, directly or indirectly. These include:

- *Containment.*   Efforts to restrict the opportunities and resources available to others in order to retain power and control over them.
- *Expendability.*   A belief that some people and groups are more valuable to society and, therefore, devalued persons can be discarded, displaced, or ignored for the benefit of the society as a whole.
- *Compartmentalization.*   Limiting people's exposure to enriching and empowering ideas, roles, and images in order to lessen their discontent. Creating and maintaining conflict and division among those without power in order to prevent them from developing a sense of shared problems, solidarity, and unity.
- *Personal culpability.*   A belief system that presumes all of the social and economic problems experienced by people are matters of personal choice and moral character. Thus, because these are individual problems, existing systems and structures need not be changed and those with power are excused from trying to improve social and economic conditions for the people of a society.
- *Individual remediation.*   A belief system holding that self-improvement is the only real answer to the existence of social problems. Thus, those who want a better life or who desire political power should first "pull themselves up by their bootstraps." Only after they prove their worth should they expect to participate in the political and economic decisions affecting their lives.

Those who work for justice must be alert to the fact that the belief systems and attitudes that perpetuate social and economic injustice can also be found in the thinking of those who are members of the various helping professions.

Among social workers, one can find a range of attitudes toward and perspectives on the appropriate place of social and political change in social work practice and on how such change is best achieved. Goldenberg (1978, 21–27) describes four of these:

1. The *social technician* identifies with and supports society's dominant values and its institutional structures. A professional with this orientation seeks to help individuals adjust to the existing system and sees little need for changing social systems.
2. The *traditional social reformer* believes that oppressive social systems can be changed over time and works methodically to make those changes. The emphasis is on fact finding as a way of helping those with power understand the problem and decide that it is desirable and reasonable to make changes. The reformer trusts the tools of negotiation and mediation to build bridges between those with power and those without.

3. The *social interventionist* believes that bringing about needed social change will require conflict, consciousness raising, and change from the bottom up. An individual holding to this orientation assumes that those in power will accept change only when their survival and self-interest depend on it.

4. The *social revolutionary* is basically at odds with and rejects existing social institutions and the usual avenues of seeking change. The revolutionary believes that current systems and institutions are corrupt and cannot be salvaged. This individual is not satisfied with small steps or incremental change and believes that radical and revolutionary approaches are necessary to take power away from those who have it.

Alle-Corliss and Alle-Corliss (1999, 233) suggest that social workers can choose from a variety of professional stances as they take social action to effect change. The *social prophet* seeks to promote radical change by not only questioning the status quo, but by envisioning alternative perspectives, attitudes, and policies. The *social visionary* learns from the past and envisions a world in which social problems do not exist. The *social reformer* promotes change by directly confronting those who may be responsible for injustice and by influencing the structure of power through persuasion of actions of power. Whether you are a social prophet, a social visionary, or a social reformer, stay in touch with the values that underscore your views of social action and social justice. Regularly ask yourself how you think the world should be for those who inhabit it. Ask yourself what sorts of social institutions, policies, or programs will support that vision. Think about what sort of community nurtures its individuals and families. Ask what organizations do to help or hinder social functioning. Consider what you can do at each of these levels, sometimes simultaneously, to support individuals, families, and communities. Find others who share your vision, and make sure that your clients' visions for their lives become your visions also.

A good leader remembers the history of the movement in which he or she is involved, as well as the lessons of the past. I recommend that you reflect in a critical and appreciative manner on the evolution of the social work profession and the many significant contributions of social workers to social justice and the building of a social welfare system. Be aware of the contributions of social work in such areas as Social Security, civil rights, child labor laws, Medicaid, unemployment insurance, minimum wage, the peace movement, and many others. Consider the contributions made by those who developed theories of practice, assumed leadership in the academic preparation of professional social workers, and the countless clients whose lives and stories have provided the motivation and inspiration for such service.

Best practices guide the work of leaders. They are the accumulated wisdom of many practitioners, often compiled in written form, describing what social workers consider to be the standards of care and intervention by which we all measure our work. Find best written practices for your chosen field, and remember that your work may define future best practices as you contribute your work and experience to the profession.

While appreciating the progress made by a profession only a century old, look also to the future and the continuing evolution of the social work profession. Claim your history, be proud of it, and become part of the development of new knowledge, improved skills, and deeply felt values.

I urge you to find ways to build a world that will be a better place because you have challenged injustices and held fast to the vision of a world in which opportunity and possibility are the possessions of all.

Becoming the Person You Want To Be

Many social workers say that social work is not what they do, but it is who they are. Their professional lives are guided by their personal beliefs, values, and spirituality, and they believe that being a social worker allows them to live out the beliefs and values they hold dear and feel passionate about. I like that notion because it indicates a compatible merger between person and the profession (see Chapter 18). However, I ask that you always remember that you are now and will always be more than your profession and your job. If your whole identity is tied up in being a social worker, I suggest that you broaden your horizons and life experiences. Narrowness is not a healthy condition.

Any effort to make changes in how we are living our lives must begin with serious reflection on our answer to the question: "Who am I?" This is not a question about the facts of our existence, our accomplishments, or what we list in our resume. Rather, it is a question about the manner of our existence and our basic orientation and attitudes toward life and the people in our life. Who do others—family, friends, and colleagues—say that I am? Do I want to be the person that others experience and perceive me to be?

Food for Thought

Whatever we take on, we should assume that we'll be living with imperfect societies, imperfect human beings, and imperfect solutions, for as far into the future as we can imagine. But this doesn't justify retreat from the admittedly difficult challenges of working for a more humane world. Whatever our approaches to change, and whatever political ambiguities we face, we can't let the apparent limits of our present time prevent us from articulating the very perspective that might open up new possibilities later on. (Loeb 1999, 306)

• • •

Politics is simply social work with power.

—*Barbara Mikulski*

• • •

The struggle for social justice is a social process, not an individual endeavor. People approaching social justice alone, as individuals, will experience a frustration over their limited potential for success. Thorough examination of a complex issue such as social justice necessitates thoughtful reflection with others. The vantage point of any individual, including people in positions of leadership, is restricted. Hence, the ability to promote liberties, opportunities, and rights is as much socially as intellectually derived. (Long et al. 2006, 209)

• • •

We must realize that social injustice and unjust social structures exist only because individuals and groups of individuals deliberately maintain or tolerate them. It is these personal choices, operating through structures, that breed and propagate situations of poverty, oppression, and misery.

—*Pope John Paul II*

• • •

If you think you're not political, guess again. (Reisch 1995, 1)

• • •

As we, as a profession, actively engage in the debate and invite others to participate, we would do well to remember that our ethical responsibility as social workers encompasses both efforts in harmony with the system and in opposition to the system. (Lieberman and Lester 2004, 416)

• • •

The proper measure of social justice in a society is how those without power and influence are treated. We usually treat those having money and power with fairness and respect because we fear the consequences of not doing so or because we hope to get something from them. True justice and genuine compassion is reflected when we treat those who have no power or anything we might want with dignity, fairness, and respect.

—*Charles Horejsi*

Because very ordinary and small choices are so powerful in shaping our lives, strive as Gandhi urges to "become the change you desire to see in others." If you desire others to have more compassion and understanding, strive each day to become more compassionate and more understanding of others. If you desire others to be more generous and more involved in bringing about needed change, strive each day to be more generous with your time and money and involve yourself more deeply in social action and social change. If you desire others to be honest and responsible, strive to be honest and responsible in all of your own choices and actions, both the big ones and the small ones.

Your practicum will soon come to an end, and your professors and field instructors will tell you that you are ready for professional social work practice. You will have earned the designation of a professional social worker by virtue of your academic preparation, your practicum experience, your commitment to the National Association of Social Workers *Code of Ethics,* and your sense of calling to promote social justice. You have all of the tools needed to be a social worker, whether you are working with individual clients or whether your efforts are focused on large-scale social change. Those tools, including your knowledge, your commitment to helping others, and your helping skills, will all come together in a unique way as you become a professional social worker. In fact, you yourself are the tool by which clients will be served and social justice is furthered. Welcome to the proactive, progressive, and visionary profession of social work.

Suggested Learning Activities

- Subscribe to electronic listservs offered by professional organizations and advocacy groups to stay abreast of issues of importance to you, as well as legislative and social justice implications of their work.
- Search out websites that will expand your understanding of social work's responsibility to maintain global standards of practice. For example, read the United Nations Universal Declaration of Human Rights, Resolution 217A, passed by the General Assembly, December 1998.
- Read Pablo Freire's works, which describe the relationship between education and political struggles.

Selected Bibliography

Alle-Corliss, Lupe, and Randy Alle-Corliss. *Advanced Practice in Human Service Agencies.* Boston: Brooks/Cole, 1999.

Bloom, Sandra. *Creating Sanctuary: Toward the Evolution of Sane Societies.* New York: Routledge, 1997.

Chambon, Adrienne, S., Allan Irving, and Laura Epstein, eds. *Reading Foucault for Social Work.* New York: Columbia University Press, 1999.

Finn, Janet L., and Maxine Jacobson. *Just Practice: A Social Justice Approach to Social Work.* Peosta, IA: Eddie Bowers Publishing, 2003.

Freire, Pablo. *Pedagogy of the Oppressed.* New York: Seabury, 1973.

Freire, Pablo. *Pedagogy of the Heart.* New York: Continuum, 1997.

Goldenberg, Ira. *Oppression and Social Intervention.* Chicago: Nelson-Hall, 1978.

Haynes, Karen S., and James S. Mickelson. *Affecting Change: Social Workers in the Political Arena.* 6th ed. Boston: Allyn and Bacon, 2006.

Lieberman, Alice A., and Cheryl B. Lester. *Social Work Practice with a Difference: Stories, Essays, Cases, and Commentaries.* Boston: McGraw Hill, 2004.

Loeb, Paul Rogat. *Soul of a Citizen: Living with Conviction in a Cynical Time.* New York: St. Martin's Griffin, 1999.

Long, Dennis D., Carolyn J. Tice, and John D. Morrison. *Macro Social Work Practice: A Strengths Perspective.* Belmont, CA: Thomson Brooks/Cole, 2006.

MacRaild, Donald M., and Avram Taylor. *Social Theory and Social History.* New York: Palgrave, 2005.

National Association of Social Workers. *Code of Ethics.* Washington, DC: NASW Press, 1999.

Payne, Malcolm. *Modern Social Work Theory.* 3rd ed. Chicago: Lyceum Books, 2005.

Pease, Bob, and Jan Fook, eds. *Transforming Social Work Practice: Postmodern Critical Perspectives.* St. Leonards, NSW, Australia: Allen and Unwin Publishing, 1999.

Reisch, M. "If You Think You're Not Political, Guess Again." *NASW Network* 21.13 (1995): 1.

Specht, Harry, and Mark E. Courtney. *Unfaithful Angels: How Social Work Has Abandoned Its Mission.* New York: Free Press, 1994.

Sample Learning Agreement

The following sample learning agreement used by The University of Montana School of Social Work BSW program presents goals for learning that can be reasonably expected of a typical social work practicum. Spaces are provided for you to devise your own tasks and activities to attain each set of goals, and your own criteria for monitoring progress and evaluating performance. This form can be used to structure the practicum experience and maximize learning. Note that some of the goals may need to be modified to fit the requirements of a particular program of social work education and the unique characteristics of a particular practicum setting.

STUDENT: _____ DATE: _____ AGENCY: _____ AGENCY SUPERVISOR: _____

INSTRUCTIONS: Student learning goals have been outlined in the left-hand column. Students, in consultation with their field instructors, are to select activities that will help them reach these goals. Students are also to describe how their learning and performance will be evaluated. At the end of each academic term, students will be evaluated by the field instructor on their learning and performance.

Learning Goals	Objectives and Activities to Reach Goals	Monitoring/Evaluation Criteria
1. *Social Work as a Profession* • Develop an understanding of generalist social work practice. • Perform a variety of social work roles (e.g., broker, counselor, networker, case manager, educator, advocate, program planner, facilitator, policy analyst, researcher). • Gain experience at various levels of practice (e.g., micro, mezzo, and macro). • Apply the National Association of Social Workers' *Code of Ethics* in a practice setting. 2. *Organizational Context of Practice* • Apply organizational analysis techniques to the practicum agency. • Understand the practicum agency's history, mission, purpose, and function. • Understand the practicum agency's structure and funding. • Understand the practicum agency's methods for evaluating its effectiveness. 3. *Community Context of Practice* • Understand the features of the community that impact clients (e.g., population, unemployment rates, housing costs, attitudes toward diverse populations, available recreation).		

Learning Goals	Objectives and Activities to Reach Goals	Monitoring/Evaluation Criteria
• Identify both the strengths and problems of the community. • Become aware of the range of community resources available and gaps in services. • Utilize a variety of community resources. **4.** *Assessment* • Develop assessment skills for individuals, families, groups, organizations, and communities. • Develop skills in problem and strength identification. • Identify the major social systems involved with the problem or concern being addressed. • Become familiar with the ongoing nature of assessment. **5.** *Planning and Intervention* • Acquire skills in goal setting, identifying measurable objectives, and planning interventions. • Select an appropriate level of intervention for individual client/client system needs (micro to macro). • Develop intervention plans matched to client/client system needs, including client in selection of intervention. • Develop intervention skills based on theoretical understanding of client needs and of interventions selected. **6.** *Termination and Evaluation* • Develop skills in appropriate termination and empowerment of clients.		

Learning Goals	Objectives and Activities to Reach Goals	Monitoring/Evaluation Criteria
• Utilize tools and instruments to evaluate client progress. • Utilize tools and instruments to evaluate own professional performance. • Utilize tools and instruments to evaluate agency effectiveness. 7. *Understanding Social Problems* • Understand one or more social problems from an ecosystems perspective. • Understand the major social problems addressed by the practicum agency (e.g., etiology, incidence, causal factors, impact, consequences, prevention). • Understand how social problems develop as a result of the interaction among individuals, social systems, and the larger social environment. • Identify the major social problems facing the community. 8. *Social Policy and Social Change* • Analyze the development of social policies. • Analyze the effectiveness of social policies. • Assess the impact of social policies on clients. • Participate in social policy and social justice efforts. 9. *Diversity* • Recognize the impact of diversity (e.g., culture, gender, age, disability, class, sexual orientation, religion) on clients.		

Learning Goals	Objectives and Activities to Reach Goals	Monitoring/Evaluation Criteria
• Understand the impact of oppression, discrimination, prejudice, and stereotyping on clients. • Analyze the practicum agency's ability to effectively and sensitively address the needs of diverse clients/client systems. • Communicate effectively and sensitively with members of diverse groups, individualizing interventions for diverse clients. 10. *Communication Skills* • Communicate clearly and effectively in written form. • Communicate clearly and effectively in verbal form with clients, including non-voluntary, or hard-to-reach clients. • Communicate clearly and effectively in verbal form with coworkers and other professionals. • Demonstrate awareness of underlying client concerns. 11. *Knowledge and Use of Self* • Recognize the impact of own personal issues, biases, values, and attitudes on clients and make needed changes. • Establish effective and purposeful relationships with clients and coworkers. • Seek professional growth by taking initiative in designing and implementing own learning activities. • Utilize professional supervision and training for guidance and learning.		

Source: The University of Montana School of Social Work BSW program. Sample learning agreement used with permission of Tondy Baumgartner, MSW, Practicum Coordinator.